The 8th Seal

Its Time Is Now!

The
8th Seal

Its Time Is Now!

Cracking the Code that Solves the
Mystery of *The Book of Revelation*

BY

DON CEROW

IBIS PRESS
Lake Worth, FL

Published in 2017 by Ibis Press
A division of Nicolas-Hays, Inc.
P. O. Box 540206
Lake Worth, FL 33454-0206
www.ibispress.net

Distributed to the trade by
Red Wheel/Weiser, LLC
65 Parker St. • Ste. 7
Newburyport, MA 01950
www.redwheelweiser.com

ISBN 978-0-89254-223-9
EBOOK ISBN 978-0-89254-639-8

Library of Congress Cataloging-in-Publication Data
Available Upon Request

Book design and production by STUDIO 31
www.studio31.com

Jacket photo: EPA / ANSA / Alessandro di Meo

Printed in the United States of America
[MV]

To Yvonne Paglia and Donald Weiser
for paving the way for all of us
Love to you both

Swimming in a Sea of Symbolism

Revelation has been the essential enigma of Christian culture for the last two thousand years, the ultimate mystery whose key has been provided, but whose lock has resisted being opened, until now.

The stories of the Bible have been celebrated in art, literature and music for the last three thousand years. It has become the cornerstone of Christian teachings. In the Bible, there is no chapter whose mystical cup overflows with more symbolism and hidden meaning than the Book of Revelation, a work that clearly provides an encouraging message on its very first page.

> *Happy the man who reads this prophecy,*
> *And happy those that listens to him,*
> *If they treasure all its says*
> *because the Time is close.*
>
> —Rev. 1:3

The question is, what is that message? What does it say, and what must one do to receive the rewards promised in this final chapter, the Bible's rear guard?

Drawing extensively from the Hebrew prophets, the imagery found in Revelation has its roots in the works of those who were to prepare the way for the new Messiah. His birth was foreseen in the stars by those who studied the stars, whether wise man or prophet. Three followed that legendary light to discover where it may lead.

All these centuries later we now follow that star and others in a quest to reawaken the pathways of old.

This is where the journey starts.

Author Contact Information

Website: athenasweb.com
Youtube channel: Don Cerow
Email: athenasweb@gmail.com

Table of Contents

List of Illustrations

List of Tables

Outline of the Structure of the Book of Revelation

The Book of Revelation is a work consisting of twenty-two chapters which may be loosely broken into seven groups.

Rev. 1	Introduction and beginning of the Vision.
Rev. 2 & 3	Letters to the Seven Churches
Rev. 4 & 5	Setting the Celestial Stage
Rev. 6 & 8:1	Opening the Seven Seals
Rev. 7	The Twelve Tribes & White Robes
Rev. 8:2 thru 20	Eighth Seal, 3½ years, 1000 years
Rev. 21 & 22	New Jerusalem and final blessing

Chapter by Chapter Resume of the Book of Revelation

"There came flashes of lightning, peals of thunder and an earthquake, and violent hail."

We are introduced to the 3½ years.

Rev. 12 A new sky picture. The opening words:

"Now a great sign appeared in heaven."

The framework of heaven is set. We meet dragon and beast.

Rev. 13 Continues the relationship between dragon and beast.

Rev. 14 Summons the forces of light to the front of the throne who sing a new hymn. Follow the Lamb. The onset of the conflict as the two forces unleash.

Rev. 15 *"What I saw next, in heaven, was a great and wonderful sign."*

Paves the way for the final seven plagues, affirms power and glory of God.

Rev. 16 Seven angels release the contents of their 'bowls' in sequence.

Rev. 17 The story of the great prostitute. The final line reads,

"The woman you saw is the great city which has authority over all the rulers of the Earth."

Rev. 18 *"Mourn, mourn for this great city."*

Rev. 19 Victory, jubilation in heaven. Heaven opening, evidence of a great battle.

Rev. 20 A heavenly angel with a great chain overpowering the dragon, and his being held for 1000 years, after which time he will briefly return again. The dead are judged.

Rev. 21 *"Then I saw a new heaven and a new earth; the first heaven and the first earth had disappeared now, and there was no longer any sea."*

The New Jerusalem arrives.

Rev. 22 The ban is lifted. The city lives.

"All who want it may have the water of life, and have it free."

Amen.

Foreword

Rarely do we find a book with a universal message for such a widely diverse group of readers. This book's unique contribution to the literature on the Book of Revelation is that it presents an entirely new analysis of the symbolic richness of the biblical text. It resonates with the unmistakable ring of truth. The author presents a scientific analysis of the astronomical data associated with the mythology and symbolism of Revelation in a straightforward and comprehensive manner.

Author Don Cerow is here conducting a magnificent symphony of symbolism, decoding one of the most mysterious religious texts ever written. The Book of Revelation has fascinated, intrigued, and confused people for over two thousand years.

The Eighth Seal sheds light on the religious mysteries of the past, probes the psychological depths of ancient understanding, and offers insight into what we may expect going forward. It explains significant historical events that were triggered by astronomical alignments along with recognizable cultural trends that accompany astrological patterns. It pinpoints the precise astronomical opening of the Age of Aquarius. It warns of the looming dangers of the transition from the Age of Pisces to the Age of Aquarius, while it offers an optimistic and hopeful series of predictions as well.

Don Cerow is both an astronomer and an astrologer. He is also a religious scholar, historian, and mythographer. His spiritual enthusiasm comes through on every page as he seeks to open the mystery of this cryptic holy text. Readers of all religious persuasions will find here a riveting study that explores Revelation through a number of different lenses, while never losing the exotic romance of its rich and mysterious imagery.

We are introduced to an entirely scientific and verifiable astronomical interpretation of Revelation. Revelation is shown to have been written as a historical and cultural commentary on the past, and Cerow explains how its prophesies for the future follow the astronomical and symbolic data as understood by the ancients.

The characteristics of the New Age on which we are currently embarked are described in some detail. It will be a time of both hope and crisis. Familiar institutions and cultural norms will give way to new ideas and revolutionary changes. Such alterations of the old ways of doing things invariably bring disruption, but there is also a sense of excitement as creativity expands to offer new possibilities and models of behavior.

The evolution of the human race is the goal—the purification of the Bride for her marriage with the Divine.

—James Wasserman
(author of *The Temple of Solomon*)

A Stellar Vocabulary

Here is a quick interpretation of some of the vocabulary of the stars, which will greatly facilitate in the comprehension of this work.

The Equator is an imaginary circle around the center of the Earth. The **Terrestrial Equator** divides the Southern and Northern hemispheres. Projected into space it is known as the **Celestial Equator.**

The Ecliptic is the apparent path of the Sun as it "travels around the Earth." The band 8 degrees either side of the Ecliptic is area where most of the planets of our Solar System may be found. The twelve zodiacal constellations most folks are familiar with fall within this zone.

The Vernal Equinox is the intersection of the path of the Sun (the Ecliptic) and the Equator. When the Sun falls on the Equator while traveling north, it is the first day of spring and there are equal amounts of daylight and darkness in the land. The cardinal direction East is measured from this intersection. An orientation is to align oneself with the East, a ritual that, under the time of observational astronomy, had to be recalibrated every year or every few years.

The Autumnal Equinox occurs when the Sun is again on the Earth's Equator, but this time while traveling south.

The Summer and Winter Solstice are when the Sun hits its extreme points of latitude, giving birth to the longest and shortest days of the year.

Precession of the Equinoxes is the annual motion where the cross-hairs of the ecliptic and equator are measured against the backdrop of the stars. The word comes from the Latin praecessio, from praecedere 'go before' or 'precede'. This is a slow motion requiring 72 years to complete one degree of an over 25,000 year cycle.

The Right Ascension Midheaven (or RAMC) is the manner in which astronomers measure the position of the stars in hours, minutes and seconds along the Earth's equator. Zero hours, minutes and seconds, the base line of astronomy, is measured from the position of the Vernal Equinox.

The Cardinal Direction East or **East Point** is measured from the intersection of the ecliptic and equator, from the Vernal Equinox.

Zero degrees of Aries also has its inception from the Vernal Equinox marking, when the Sun aligns with this position, the first day of spring.

These are a few of the many ways that astronomy has interwoven with this important point. Mythologically it also had a persona which was named in various ways. Among these were...

The Throne or **Seat of Power**, illustrated by Isis, who the Egyptians depicted as having a throne on the top of her head, and Hera, who was bound to a throne constructed by her son.

The Alter, used by many cultures to track the motions of heaven, such as the alignments at Stonehenge. Consider it as the most sacred part of an observatory.

The Marriage of the Bride and Groom, the marriage of heaven and Earth, thought to be when the Sun stood precisely on the Vernal Equinox (Spring).

The Marriage of Zeus and Hera is the Union of one of the early depictions of this alignment, as recorded in Greek culture.

The Hieros Gamos, an ancient ritual, performed on the first day of Spring, which depicted the Union of Heaven and Earth, as the King and Queen of a nation would publicly make love to each other, either literally or symbolically, in an attempt to capture the essence of this moment.

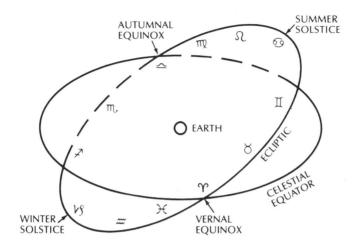

The Intersections between the Ecliptic and the Celestial Equator

The Ram, the symbol of the constellation Aries, but also marked by the sign Aries, whose orientation is marked by the first day of Spring.

The Lamb. Since the Ram marks the first day of Spring, this is the Ram in its infancy, it's inception, it's start, when it is not yet a Ram, but a baby Ram, or Lamb. Mythologically the Lamb marks the beginning of another annual round of Creation, astronomically depicted as Zero degrees of Aries.

The Precession of the Equinoxes (or Ages) advance in reverse order to the progress of the signs through the seasons. Thus, the passage of the Vernal Equinox through the stars of the constellation Aries (the Age of Aries) moved into the stars of the constellation Pisces (the Age of Pisces) over two thousand years ago. The author offers some tantalizing astronomical evidence that we are now poised at the opening of the Age of Aquarius.

What Is the Book of Revelation

The First and the Last

This is the revelation given by God to Jesus Christ so that he could tell his servants about the things which are now to take place, very soon; he sent his angel to make it known to his servant John, /¹ and John has written down everything he saw and swears it is the word of God guaranteed by Jesus Christ.

The Book of Revelation was part of a genre of apocalyptic writing in vogue in Hebrew and Christian circles between 600 BC and AD 200. During these centuries the world was in the midst of huge transformation—a cultural metamorphosis. There was a sense of both fear and excitement; of people spiritually "evolving" through a host of various mystery religions, Christianity among them. Life was being re-cast in various areas; in religion, government, education, astronomy, mathematics and medicine. Each of these branches became immersed in a new sense of wonder, a thirst for discovery. It was against this backdrop that these apocalyptic writings waved their cryptic messages against the blustery winds of change.

Within the apocalyptic tradition Revelation eventually managed to seize the high ground, forming a kind of rear guard for both New Testament and Bible; solemnly warning anyone not to alter a single word of the mysterious messages contained within.

This is my solemn warning to all who hear the prophecies in this book: if anyone adds anything to them, God will add to him every plague mentioned in the book; / if anyone cuts anything out of the prophecies in this book, God will cut off his share of the tree of life and of the holy city which are described in the book.²

---

1 [/] Indicates the original line breaks of scripture.
2 Rev. 22:18–19.

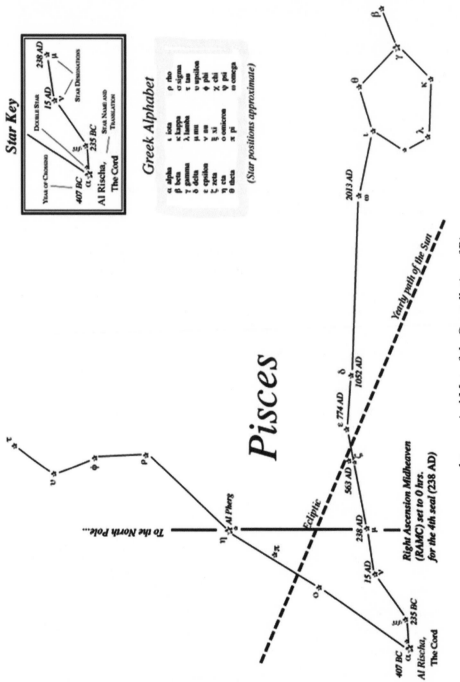

Star Key

407 BC — *Year of Crossing*

DOUBLE STAR

235 BC

238 AD
15 AD — *Star Designations*

α — Al Rischa, The Cord — *Star Name and Translation*

Greek Alphabet

α alpha	ι iota	ρ rho	
β beta	κ kappa	σ sigma	
γ gamma	λ lambda	τ tau	
δ delta	μ mu	υ upsilon	
ε epsilon	ν nu	φ phi	
ζ zeta	ξ xi	χ chi	
η eta	ο omicron	ψ psi	
θ theta	π pi	ω omega	

(Star positions approximate)

Pisces

To the North Pole....

Ecliptic

Yearly path of the Sun

Right Ascension Midheaven (RAMC) set to 0 hrs. for the 4th seal (238 AD)

2013 AD

1052 AD

774 AD

563 AD

238 AD

15 AD

235 BC

407 BC

Al Rischa, The Cord

Al Pherg

Astronomical Map of the Constellation of Pisces

Risky business, this. These are two of the last four lines in Revelation. They were put here to indicate how serious they are. The opening lines of Revelation state that this is a prophecy and it would be wise to listen; the closing lines warn us to follow the story line and not add or cut anything.

Let us now begin to examine what lies in-between.

Orientation

If the spirit of the message being channeled in Revelation is on the mark, today we stand on the precipice of a period of sweeping social and geopolitical transformation. If my understanding of this symbolism is correct, there will be change such as the planet has never known before. If the Bible is to be believed, what is called for is a worldwide shift of unprecedented proportions.

Rev. 16: 17-18 is quite clear.

The end has come. Then there were flashes of lightning and peals of thunder and the most violent earthquake that anyone has ever seen since there have been men on earth.

One would think that as a bellwether, this would be difficult to miss. There is a *Zeitgeist* in the ethers. The stories are everywhere. The planet is warming. The ice caps are melting. *El Nino* and *La Ninya* are giving birth. The sea is polluted. The weather is weird. Too much rain here, not enough there. The forests are disappearing. As I type this, Bonny Doon is experiencing some of its worst fires in decades; distant flames lighting the darkness, devouring windy peaks as seen from our second-story windows. Floods, tsunamis, mudslides and earthquakes; the bears, birds, bats and bees all have their stories. There's a buzz in the breeze. Change is in the air.

Ever since the Harmonic Convergence in 1987, the Mayan calendar with its Winter Solstice of 2012 fanned the flames of public interest, launching waves of speculation about the future. It too spoke of change. December 21, 2012 is when the Mayan calendar system came to an end, suggesting, but not stating, that the whole cycle will begin all over again, but with differences. There's been considerable foreboding accompanying this premonition. Books on the subject proliferate. There was talk of California dropping into the sea in the 1960s. The astrologers and hippies are still singing about Aquarius. At the end of the millennia many focused on the Y2K scare. The media has increasingly been exploring prophecies on the "End Times" from various traditions. They speak of change. For the observant, the signs are there.

But the Mayan tradition that told of 2012 also spoke of another prophecy. There was a long-standing belief among the Maya that Quetzalcoatl would return from the east in a "One Reed" calendar year and take control. "One Reed" was not an annual event that rolled around every year the way January 5th or October 11th does in our calendar. It was part of a 52-year cycle, itself part of an even larger mathematical cycle. Quetzalcóatl's calendar name was One Reed (Ce Acatl). Knowing this led the Aztec sovereign Montezuma II to believe Hernán Cortéz to be an envoy of Quetzalcoatl as Cortez landed from out of the east on the Mexican Gulf coast in 1519, a One Reed year.

Did Montezuma's native empire collapse on the day Cortez landed? No. Did the date of his arrival symbolically mark the beginning of the end of indigenous self-administration in Central America and the new world? Yes.

We might think of 21st of December, 2012 in the same manner. According to Mayan tradition seeds of the new beginning are about to be sown, marked by the ending of a calendar system. Traditionally, myth records that with a new calendar comes a new king, a new reign. It is the end of a style of life, of looking at life, of living life. Civilization has seen these changes before. We have lived through them. Just as change is all about us now, so it was about two thousand years ago, when another wave of change washed the classical world away and left Christian civilization in its wake in Western culture.

It took a century or two to fully blossom.

Fundamental social transformation was underway, reshaping conceptual shorelines as far as the eye could see. Time was being re-cast on the Empire's anvil. Pioneering paths in the form of new laws, social constructs, and methods of healing were appearing. It was an invigorated era. Even the calendar, Time itself, died and was reborn. Julius envisioned a solar wheel while Jesus reset the counter. Creation began again. The classical order was collapsing as the tender new roots of a Christian hierarchy tentatively reached out across a politically receptive landscape.

Apocalyptic writing fueled itself through this time of turmoil. Ezekiel and Daniel are early examples, framed within visions of mysterious supernatural events. The genre speaks of a future, hidden in code, wrapped in symbolism.

The unwritten implication is that by having a map we might better navigate the troubled waters ahead. The Book of Revelation is that map.

Apocalyptic writing foresaw the termination of the earlier era and the birth of a new one. Before the classical tradition fell on its own sword, it had known its fate. Romans had honored the Etruscan ability to interpret the will of the gods, even if they were enemies. Recorded for posterity by Roman authors, Etruscan priests claimed a new world order was at hand. Its stage had already been set.

> But the most striking phenomenon of all was when the sound of a trumpet rang out from a perfectly clear and cloudless sky with a shrill, prolonged and dismal note so loud that people were driven half crazy with terror.
>
> The Etruscan wise men declared that this portent foretold a change over into a new Age and a total revolution in the world…
>
> In each Age the lives and manners of men are different and God has established for each Age a definite span of time that is determined by the circuit of the Great Year. Whenever this circuit comes to an end and another begins some marvelous sign appears either on earth or in heaven so that it becomes at once clear to those who have made a thorough study of the subject that men of a different character and way of life have now come into the world and the gods will be either more or less concerned with this new race than they were with their predecessors. All sorts of changes

occur, they say, as one Age succeeds another and in particular with regard to the art of divination one can observe that there are times when it rises in prestige and its predictions are accurate because clear and unmistakable signs are sent from heaven; and then again in another Age it is not held in much honor, since for the most part its practitioners are relying on mere guesswork and are trying to grasp the future with senses that have become blunt and dim.

This, at all events, was the story told by the wisest men among the Etruscans who were thought to know more than most about such things.[3]

Plutarch lived from AD 46 to 120. Revelation is thought to have been written between AD 68 and 95. The sentiments are current. There was the sense of a new vibration, a new intoxication in the waters. Revelation is a book of prophecy—one destined to fulfill earlier prophecies.

Prophesy deals with mysteries still hidden in the future. What is the greatest mystery of all, if not the future? The Bible is largely a book about prophecy: if you eat of the apple, Noah and the Ark, Moses and Pharaoh, the Promised Land and warnings about Israel's period of captivity.

Revelation is a map, a signpost through the time of darkness, encoded in the trappings of its day. It speaks of a future crafted by a new destiny, a new fate. It is a future that would cut the thread of the past and begin anew, using a new template, a new gestalt, and giving birth to a brave new world.

The Book of Revelation anticipates a new heaven on earth, a new world leader. It was written during a time when imagination and superstition inspired a broad canvas. Rome's iron will had forged a single rule of law upon an unruly and willful Mediterranean world. Then as now, people talked about the changes in markets and ports of call, whispering word of what they had heard to the distant horizons.

---

3 *Fall of the Roman Republic*, Plutarch, pp. 74–75.

Bible Code

Part of the magic of divinity is that it loves to be wrapped in enigma. At the conclusion of his book *Mathesis*, Firmicus Maternus caught the spirit of the muse when he wrote to his friend in the 4th century AD,

> It is for you to remember the sanctity of your oath: guard these books with a pure mind and soul and do not reveal this science to inexperienced ears or sacrilegious minds. The nature of the divine prefers to be hidden in diverse coverings; access to it should not be easy nor its majesty open to all.[4]

This is the spiritual sentiment across the Roman Empire in the 1st century AD. Hide truth in code but in such a way that clues might be spotted by those trained to look for them. Buried firmly beneath the sands of the first century, Revelation is a time capsule programmed to be opened in our day, at "the end" of the epoch. It has a message for us that its composers thought important. It's always been there, and a few have interpreted its encryption over the years. Revelation makes it clear that it is a puzzle meant to be both solved and shared.

In working with this code, we will rely on two classical disciplines to interpret the Biblical imagery: mythology and astrology. They were contemporary themes of Revelation. Hellenistic writings had for centuries described the mythological hierarchy, while astrology continues to maintain its role as an interpreter of archetypes to this day. Both the mythological and astrological traditions were well-established institutions throughout the classical period. Initiates to the mythic mystery religions were let in on secrets—secrets not shared with the general public.

> This is what we would like to accomplish with our book, that it should be open to the religious but denied the profane. In this way we will not pollute the revered theories of the ancients by publishing them for the sacrilegious.[5]

---

4 *Mathesis*. Firmicus Maternus, Noyes Classical Studies, Noyes Press, p. 302.
5 *Mathesis*, Firmicus Maternus, Noyes Classical Studies, p. 302.

Most of the authors of antiquity looked at the divine in a similar manner. It was the sentiment of the time. The same spirit is found in Revelation.

The lords of mythology were masters of their realms. Their "kingdoms" consisted not only of geographic units (although they could be that, too), but also of birds, animals, cities, individuals, qualities and cultures. For instance Jupiter (Zeus) elevated the eagle, was fond of the feminine, held Troy, Priam and his kin near to his heart, and ruled the sky. Lightning, rain and the weather awaited his nod. These are among the "subjects" from the "realm" of Zeus. When we find similar subjects of a particular realm being thematically bundled in the story line, it's like a trail of breadcrumbs, leaving clues of a mythic path for us to follow while rounding up centaurs and chimera along the way.

One important clue was that the New Testament was written in Greek. The Greeks knew the myths better than anybody. It was *their* culture and it was for *them* that the New Testament was originally intended. It was their pride, heritage, and history. Alexander had conquered the known world not long before.

Rome? Greeks schooled Rome. In the eastern empire Hellenistic culture maintained its air of intellectual sophistication as the language of the elite, the lingering ambience of the former ruling class. In the 1st century AD, Revelation was written in Greek. Rome captured Greece militarily, geographically and politically. But Greece triumphed over Rome culturally.

Revelation represents the crescendo of the mythic tradition in the West. It is a multi-cultural effort, describing the next chapter of heaven's mythical path. Same path, new territory. This is a thematic, rather than a linguistic shift. We use the same old mythic vocabulary to read the script. We are simply entering new celestial "territory," with a new personality and vibration. Revelation describes it as a *"new hymn"* in heaven, a new rhythm and chant.

After thousands of years of careful stellar observation, as local gatherings start to lift their voices in joyful hymns, the mythic loom falls silent. Under Rome's keen scrutiny the ancient temples were stripped of their power as places of criminal sanctuary. The roles of the myths are forgotten. In time, even the sciences would start to fall under the control of the Church. The gulf between myths' relationship to the stars (in a scientific sense) begins to widen as the Church assumed and consolidated administrative control.

Greek culture left a rich tapestry of gods and heroes, of travesty and triumph. Although based upon Hebrew tradition, Greek was the language chosen to preserve that tradition, with Greek elements intentionally woven into the fabric.

Revelation is the Bible's final word. What does it have to say?

Revelation and Symbolism

There are various threads being woven into the design of Revelation. There were the newly emerging Christian themes of the mystical love-for and bond-to Jesus. There were the Judaic themes with numerous verses being quoted directly from the Hebrew Bible (Old Testament). There were underlying Zoroastrian themes of duality, of good versus evil. There was the Hellenistic tradition, with its mythology, mathematics, and star lore. There were even numerological elements.

There is need for shrewdness here: if anyone is clever enough he may interpret the number of the beast: it is the number of a man, the number 666.[6]

But while we have in Revelation a multi-spectrum tapestry with cultural contributions from various sources, there is an even older weave that runs through this fabric. The mythological vocabulary used to interpret Revelation is not some separate dialect devoid of contact from external linguistic influences. It is part of an ancient language, an ancient symbolic code born of Heaven and Earth, one that had evolved over generations. The understanding of this symbolic vocabulary, this mythological shorthand, these constellational images was essential

---

6 Rev. 13:18

to anyone attempting to work with time, or as noted for any culture attempting to construct a calendar for its civilization.

To work with time, one must work with the motions of heaven. When working with heaven, there must be stellar maps. These maps, together with their images, became part of a symbolic, image-generated vernacular, just as any discipline soon develops its own nomenclature, to help facilitate communication about the discipline at a deeper level.

Did these cultures each re-invent the wheel in an effort to construct their own calendars, or was essential information shared? The central highways of heaven—the path of the Sun, horizon, Earth's equator, equinoxes, solstices, and northern celestial axis—these are the building blocks of stellar observation. Sacred calendars had to be recalibrated every year keeping the priesthood busy. These astronomers worked carefully to set holidays, to determine the best times to open the gates of Time, the essential purpose of any "holy day." The Divine is not to be kept waiting. Considerable resources were invested in the time, labor and materials needed to undertake such an operation. Their collective observations had the king's ear.

These were the early sky watchers.

How long ago did these observations begin and at what level of sophistication? We don't know, but it might be speculated that we have lost far more than we will recover. Common themes are passed down through time, and we see these themes throughout the Mediterranean world.

The Book of Revelation is using the same vocabulary and the same grammatical style as those who passed before. We have the key to the lock. So how do we navigate our way through this Sea of Symbolism?

CHAPTER ONE

Revelation 1

1:1 *This is the revelation given by God to Jesus Christ so that he could tell his servants about the things which are now to take place very soon; he sent his angel to make it known to his servant John, / and John has written down everything he says and swears it is the word of God guaranteed by Jesus Christ. / Happy the man who reads the prophecy, and happy those who listen to him, if they treasure all that it says, because the Time is close.*

1:4 *From John, to the seven churches of Asia: grace and peace to you from him who is, who was, and who is to come, from the seven spirits in his presence before his throne, / and from Jesus Christ, the faithful witness, the First-born from the dead, the Ruler of the kings of the earth. He loves us and has washed away our sins with his blood, / and made us a line of kings, priests to serve his God and Father; to him, then, be glory and power for ever and ever. Amen. / It is he who is coming on the clouds; everyone will see him, even those who pierced him, and all the races of the earth will mourn over him. This is the truth. Amen. / "I am the Alpha and the Omega," says the Lord God, who is, who was, and who is to come, the Almighty.*

1:9 *My name is John, and through our union in Jesus I am your brother and share your sufferings, your kingdom, and all you endure. I was on the island of Patmos for having preached God's word and witnessed for Jesus; / it was the Lord's day and the Spirit possessed me, and I heard a voice behind me, shouting like a trumpet, / "Write down all that you see in a book, and send it to the seven churches of Ephesus, Smyrna, Pergamum, Thyatira, Sardis, Philadelphia and Laodicea." / I turned around to see who had spoken to me, and when I turned I saw seven golden lampstands / and, surrounded by them, a figure like a Son of man, dressed in a long robe tied at the waist with a golden girdle. / His head and his hair were white as white wool or as snow, his eyes like a* *burning flame, his feet like burnished bronze when it has been refined in a furnace, and his voice like the sound of the ocean. / In his right hand he was holding seven stars, out of his mouth came a sharp sword, double-edged, and his face was like the sun shinning with all its force.*

1:17 *When I saw him, I fell in a dead faint at his feet, but he touched me with his right hand and said, "Do not be afraid; it is I, the First and the Last; I am the Living One; / I was dead and now I am to live for ever and ever, and I hold the keys of Death and the underworld. / Now write down all that you see of present happenings and things that are still to come.*

1:20 *"The secret of the seven stars you have seen in my right hand, and of the seven golden lampstands is this: the seven stars are the angels of the seven churches, and the seven lampstands are the seven churches themselves."*

* * * * *

In the Beginning...

1:1 This is the revelation given by God to Jesus Christ so that he could tell his servants about the things which are now to take place, very soon; he sent his angel to make it known to his servant John, and John has written down everything he saw and swears it is the word of God guaranteed by Jesus Christ.

Happy the man who reads this prophecy,
and happy those that listen to him,
if they treasure all it says,
because the Time is close."

Most scholars agree that the "servant John" is apparently not of the "Matthew, Mark, Luke and John" fame, the authors of the opening books of the New Testament. It is another John, one who had done time on the penal island of Patmos for having "witnessed to Jesus." The information is being passed to John by an angel.

Notice the emphasis on *"the Time is close."* Revelation is here speaking of "stellar" time. The precession of the equinoxes had been observed by indigenous cultures worldwide for thousands of year (See *When the Dragon Wore the Crown.* Our focus in that work involved examining three previous constellations that the Vernal Equinox had passed through, dating back to the 7th millennium BC).

For the Mediterranean world the Vernal Equinox was at the beginning of its passage through the constellation of the Fish as Revelation was being written. What had been seen as approaching for literally thousands of years was now in the home stretch, the final two thousand years (the approximate amount of time (2152 years) it takes for the Vernal Equinox (Spring) to move through one constellation).

1:4 From John, to the seven churches of Asia: grace and peace to you from him who is, who was, and who is to come, from the seven spirits in his presence before his throne, and from Jesus Christ, the faithful witness, the First-born from the dead, the Ruler of the kings of the Earth. He loves us and has washed away our sins with his blood, and made us a line of kings, priests to serve his God and Father; to him, then, be glory and power for ever and ever. Amen. It is he who is coming on the clouds; everyone will see him, even those who pierced him, and all the races of the earth will mourn over him. This is the truth. Amen. "I am the Alpha and the Omega," says the Lord God, who is, who was, and who is to come, the Almighty.

Greetings and salutations. There are many images coming at us all at once, but they basically derive from a framework of heaven. The throne is the Vernal Equinox. The seven spirits in his presence are the seven planetary energies, the seven archetypes. As we will see some think of them as stars or angels.

This theme of *"who is, who was, and who is to come"* is the notion of God's eternal existence. He does now, did then, and always will work this way. We see this refrain repeated in line 8.

We are looking at a stellar framework. The "New Age" has begun, the constellation of the Fish is being honored. Christianity's stars are on the rise, founded on faith, an infant religion newly born. The first four disciples are fishermen. Jesus will make them *"fishers of men."* Jesus Christ is the First born of the dead. Jesus has transcended death and is the first to have done so under this "New Age" covenant, a theme we will pick up again in Revelation 6:9–11. Suffering and standing by one's true beliefs—even through death—is what purifies the soul, one's robes, and makes them white. Or so the early Christians believed.

Astrologers would come to call it the Age of Pisces, whose symbol was the Fish. It was a new "spiritual" kingdom, a new era, what Jesus would refer to as the "Kingdom of God" predicted by the Hebrew prophets. This epoch would sire the Messiah, a new heavenly hymn and a new *"line of kings, priests to serve."*

If we are to believe what is being suggested here by Revelation, Jesus Christ paves the way by being the first born, the first fruit of the vibration to this new celestial pattern. He sets the standard, forms the template, and establishes the role model for others to follow. Christianity's rise as heaven's servant set the stage for the establishment of a line of kings and priests to act as intermediaries for the new religion and epoch, the new covenant with heaven, a new age. We call it the New Testament.

It is he that is coming on the clouds of heaven. This is true because it represents the constellation that can be seen beyond the clouds, aligning with Spring's East Point.

We will return to the theme of the *Alpha* and the *Omega* at the end of Revelation. It will be mentioned twice more in this work for a total of three times. These are the only times *Alpha* and *Omega* are mentioned in the entire Bible, Old or New.

1:9 My name is John, and through our union in Jesus I am your brother and share your sufferings, your kingdom, and all you endure. I was on the island of Patmos for having preached God's word and witnessed for Jesus; it was the Lord's day and the Spirit possessed me, and I heard a voice behind me, shouting like a trumpet, "Write down all that you see in a book, and send it to the seven churches of Ephesus, Smyrna, Pergamum,

*Thyatira, Sardis, Philadelphia and Laodicea." I turned around to see
who had spoken to me, and when I turned I saw seven golden lampstands and, surrounded by them, a figure like a Son of man, dressed in a
long robe tied at the waist with a golden girdle.*

Here John is identifying himself and his experience. He has born
witness to God's word and paid the price for doing so, as had Jesus.
John is a prisoner on Patmos. Suffering and loss are themes of Pisces,
and he is here sharing them with both those on Patmos and the reader.
Later he will share them with the Seven Churches. The administration
(the Roman Empire) is not happy with those who will not sacrifice to
the Emperor, their earthly "Lord and Protector." And here is where—if
he has not already been exposed to the philosophy before—John comes
into contact with magicians and astrologers.

Adela Yarbro Collins, a biblical scholar at Yale Divinity
School, writes:

Early tradition says that John was banished to Patmos by the
Roman authorities. This tradition is credible because banishment
was a common punishment used during the Imperial period for
a number of offenses. Among such offenses were the practices
of magic and astrology. Prophecy was viewed by the Romans
as belonging to the same category, whether Pagan, Jewish, or
Christian. Prophecy with political implications, like that expressed
by John in the book of Revelation, would have been perceived as a
threat to Roman political power and order. Three of the islands in
the *Sporades* were places where political offenders were banished.[1]

With a loud, trumpeting voice, the vision begins. John is possessed
by the Holy Spirit and told to record all he envisions and send it to the
seven churches.

---

1 *Natural History,* Pliny, *4:69–70; Annals,* Tacitus, *4:30, quoted in* Adela Collins,
"Patmos." *Harper's Bible Dictionary.* Paul J. Achtemeier, gen. ed. San Francisco:
Harper & Row, 1985. p. 755.

Rulerships and Exaltations

In order to explain the secret of the churches, a little celestial background is in order. Both the divine composite image at the end of Revelation 1, the mythical man, as well as the letters to the churches are based upon the images contained in the hierarchy of exaltations. Classical authors describe an astrological classification known as "dignitaries." The dictionary defines dignitary as someone considered important because of high rank or office. There are four categories of dignitaries: two are beneficial, two not. The two pairs are known as Rulerships and Exaltations, Detriments and Falls. As one might guess, the former are fortifying while the later are debilitating. Rulerships are what most people know about their sun sign. The following is the list most used in astrology today.

Table of Planetary Rulerships (contemporary)

Sign	Planet
Aries	Mars
Taurus	Venus
Gemini	Mercury
Cancer	Moon
Leo	Sun
Virgo	Mercury
Libra	Venus
Scorpio	Pluto
Sagittarius	Jupiter
Capricorn	Saturn
Aquarius	Uranus
Pisces	Neptune

Naturally, this list includes the outer planets discovered over the last few centuries. The traditional list used in antiquity and the one that strongly influenced Persian, Hellenic and Hindu (still used today) sources was as follows.

Table of Planetary Rulerships (ancient)

Sign	Planet
Aries	Mars
Taurus	Venus
Gemini	Mercury
Cancer	Moon
Leo	Sun
Virgo	Mercury
Libra	Venus
Scorpio	Mars
Sagittarius	Jupiter
Capricorn	Saturn
Aquarius	Saturn
Pisces	Jupiter

Arranged in a Roman manner, the Sun and Moon (luminaries), had dominion over a single sign. Each of the five other visible planets ruled two signs; a day sign (those adjacent to the Sun and Leo), or a night sign (those adjacent to the Moon and Cancer).[2]

Table of Dual Rulerships

Night sign	Planetary Ruler	Day sign
Aquarius	Saturn	Capricorn
Pisces	Jupiter	Sagittarius
Aries	Mars	Scorpio
Taurus	Venus	Libra
Gemini	Mercury	Virgo
Cancer	Moon	
	Sun	Leo

---

2 This is not to be confused with the day (solar) and night (lunar) planetary schemata associated with the Hellenistic doctrine of astrological sect, or *hairesis*. See Robert Hand, *Night and Day. Planetary Sect in Astrology*, Las Vegas: Arhat, 1995, p. 2.

The quality of these dignitaries is invoked in Revelation as part of the angelic personality of the churches. Of the four correlations, Revelation makes extensive use of the exaltations. It is a clue through which we can identify familiar astrological parameters, to help set our orientation, to "ground" our book in ancient stellar wisdom.

It makes sense that the authors of Revelation would seek to use this touchstone, this familiar reference point from which to begin. Exaltations are one of the oldest astrological associations. They can be traced back at least as far as the Mesopotamian sky omens, well before the development and popularization of hand-drawn charts by the Greeks.

The theory of exaltations assumes the highest potential attunement of each of the planetary vibrations. To "exalt" is to hold in high regard, to think or speak highly of. It is to laud, praise, venerate, worship, lionize, idolize, acclaim, esteem, look-up-to, or put-on-a-pedestal. The exaltations identify planetary positions that provide special relationships of symbiosis, spiritual clues tying it to the sign, conferring specific powers upon the holder. Astrologers who look for such clues in a chart understand that not all born to this position necessarily rise to spiritual prominence, but they're on the right track.

Each planetary energy is like two sides of a coin. You can't separate one side from the other. The planetary exaltations in this case (the letters in Revelation to the seven churches) focus on the qualities that are sought to be cultivated. But they also provide warnings about negative characteristics. They are illustrating both sides. "This is how it works when it works, and this is how it works when it doesn't. For those that have ears to hear..."

The tools we are using to open Revelation we know to be contemporary with the literature of the *Pax Romana* of the 1st century AD, This was an extended period of peace within the boundaries of the Empire.

If one accepts the premise that the exaltations manifested the highest potential for individual or nation, it makes perfect sense Revelation would call upon this celestial metaphor as a benchmark from which to establish our bearings. We are working with the celestial superlatives here, the best of the best, in moral terms. It does not matter whether you believe these tenets or not. What is relevant is that *this may be the way the people in the 1st century* AD *saw it*. It was their way of looking at the world. We are here in an attempt to uncover that history, regardless of personal perspectives.

Seen in Christian terms, exaltations are the specially designated areas of responsibility for God's spiritual servants, the angels, and through their examples, the people. This use of "exaltations" as a mythological vehicle to convey a message is about to come up twice in the following verses. The language used in Revelation is not a new dialect cloned simply for the translation of this one book of the New Testament. It is using an already long established symbolic language, the same that has been used to tell the sky story for centuries.

Here is the list of planetary exaltations from classical times. They are presented in their standard Babylonian order of the Secret Places. In the right hand column are their correspndences with the seven cities mentioned in Revelation chapters 2 and 3. We will discuss these attributions in some detail in the next two chapters:

Table of Planetary Exaltations and Cities of Revelation

The Moon is exalted in Taurus	Ephesus
Mercury is exalted in Virgo	Pergamum
Venus is exalted in Pisces	Smyrna
The Sun is exalted in Aries	Thyatira
Mars is exalted in Capricorn	Sardis
Jupiter is exalted in Cancer	Philadelphia
Saturn is exalted in Libra	Laodicea

We pick up from Revelation 1:11. The image that follows is a composite of five of the seven planets in their exaltations. John has been instructed to write everything down and send it to the churches. Next there appears,

a figure like a Son of man, dressed in a long robe tied at the waist with a golden girdle.

This is the image of Aquarius, the constellation and Age that will follow Pisces, speaking to John. He is a figure *"like a Son of man."* Aquarius is depicted as a human. This may not seem so obvious to us now but remember that the "Age" at the beginning of Christianity's birth was the constellation of a Fish, not a Man. Prior to Pisces it had been a Ram, before that, a Bull. From our current vantage point we're already looking back over several thousand years. The Ages deal with extended blocks of time. The skies have not witnessed the Vernal Equinox aligning with a human motif in thousands of years. The "golden girdle" tied at the waist is the path of the Sun (whose metal is gold) passing through the constellation Aquarius. At the time of the writing of Revelation, the Vernal Equinox has yet to pass into Aquarius.

The spirit communicating with John is the constellation that follows Pisces. It's the future that's speaking to him, revealing what will happen in the centuries to come as seen from the 1st century AD.

The following lines are an excellent interpretation of a composite image of several of the planetary exaltations. Backing up just a little so we have the entire thought:

> / and, surrounded by them, a figure like a Son of man, dressed in a long robe tied at the waist with a golden girdle. / His head and his hair were white as white wool or as snow, his eyes like a burning flame, his feet like burnished bronze when it has been refined in a furnace, and his voice like the sound of the ocean. / In his right hand he was holding seven stars, out of his mouth came a sharp sword, double-edged, and his face was like the sun shinning with all its force.

Starting with Mars:

> His head and his hair were white as white wool or as snow,

Mars rules the head astrologically. Capricorn suggests old, cold, or wintertime in the northern hemisphere. Mars in Capricorn is an aging head and hair, depicted as snow. Wool comes from either sheep (Mars) or goats (Capricorn).

his eyes like a burning flame

Astrologically, the luminaries (the Sun and the Moon) were thought to rule the eyes. They are the "lights" of the sky, a burning flame, leaning on the Sun in Aries (a fire sign) for its chief imagery.

his feet like burnished bronze when it has been refined in a furnace and his voice like the sound of the ocean

The next two images derive from the same exalted symbolism, invoking the theme of the upcoming Age. This is Venus in Pisces. Pisces rules the feet, Venus rules copper and bronze. Venus is beauty, Venus is pretty. Highly polished is pretty. The *"refined in a furnace"* deals with the tribulations that are coming. We will discuss this in the opening of the Fifth Seal (Rev. 6:9). Is this his voice in communication or his voice in song? The first would represent Mercury, the second Venus. If Venus is song, then Venus in Pisces is perfect for *"his voice like the sound of the ocean,"* the sign of the ocean. Their voices blend together as one in a new hymn.

In his right hand he was holding seven stars

Our composite image here represents the Supreme Being holding what we will later identify as the *"Scroll,"* an asterism (a grouping of stars smaller than a constellation) that is literally a collection of seven stars. We will see and discuss this same image in Revelation 4 when it is invoked again.

out of his mouth came a sharp sword, double-edged

This is Mercury in Virgo. Mercury rules communications; how we talk, what we think, what we say. Virgo is a critical sign, both articulate and specific. These are cutting words that say some things that are painful or difficult to hear.

and his face was like the sun shining with all its force.

And this is, of course, the Sun in its exaltation in Aries. Aries is the sign (Mars is the planet) that rules the head and face. The Sun is in the face. This series of images ends on a strong note, one of power, leadership and victory. This is the champion, the one who has triumphed (Sun), said what's needed (Mercury) sparing no one's feelings while singing words of wisdom (Venus), and understanding exactly what he was sharing because he'd been there and done that (Mars, Sun). This brief visual sketch has touched upon four of the seven images of exaltation. The Age of Aquarius, the anthropomorphic sign of the stars sharing this wisdom with us, is revealing his best side, his spiritual splendor, his knowledge, and his familiarity with heavenly motion as he passes on prophetic information to John. As we shall see, it's about their past, present and future.

> *1:17 When I saw him, I fell in a dead faint at his feet, but he touched me with his right hand and said, "Do not be afraid; it is I, the First and the Last; I am the Living One; I was dead and now I am to live for ever and ever, and I hold the keys of Death and the underworld. Now write down all that you see of present happenings and things that are still to come. The secret of the seven stars you have seen in my right hand, and of the seven golden lampstands is this: the seven stars are the angels of the seven churches, and the seven lampstands are the seven churches themselves.*

We will discuss The *First and the Last* and the *Alpha* and *Omega* in the final chapters. Line 17 is obvious. John is overwhelmed by the majesty of what he's experiencing. It became too much for him. He fainted. Spirit, here depicted as the Aquarian angel, reassures him, but has a request. Write down the present and the future. Aquarians are interested in the stars, history and chronology. Aquarians gather information for the community and do what they can to share it.

It was believed that both Christianity and the Book of Revelation contained clues to the afterlife. There is One who has passed the test, who now holds the key. The One who has made it is passing down his notes from the future, clues about what is to come.

We are told the secret of the seven stars and the seven golden lamp-stands; one is the spirit of the churches, one is the geographic church itself. The candlestands hold the spirit, this celestial fire. The seven stars are the seven visible planets of the sky; the Sun, Moon, Mercury, Venus, Mars, Jupiter and Saturn.

Revelation is confirming what we have already established. The letters to the churches provide clues to the path ahead.

CHAPTER TWO

Revelation 2

The Church of EPHESUS

2:1 *Write to the angel of the church in Ephesus and say, "Here is the message of the one who holds the seven stars in his right hand and who lives surrounded by the seven golden lampstands: I know all about you: how hard you work and how much you put up with. I know you cannot stand wicked men, and how you tested the impostors who called themselves apostles and proved they were liars. / I know, too, that you have patience, and have suffered for my name without growing tired. / Nevertheless, I have this complaint to make; you have less love now than you used to. / Think where you were before you fell; repent, and do as you used to at first, or else, if you will not repent, I shall come to you and take your lampstand from its place. / It is in your favor, nevertheless, that you loathe as I do what the Nicolatians are doing. / If anyone has ears to hear, let him listen to what the Spirit is saying to the churches: those who prove victorious I will feed from the tree of life set in God's paradise."*

Ephesus was one of the cities of Anatolia, Asia Minor, or what we today call Turkey. It was a lucrative trading center located on the Cayster River until the port later began to silt up, pinching off both navigation and commerce.

The first three letters are to the churches Ephesus, Smyrna and Pergamum, (at that time) all port cities. The remaining four lie further inland on overland trade routes. We are traveling a geographic path from one city to the next, which is the easiest explanation for their order.

The angel of the church in Ephesus is the seat of the Moon in its exaltation in Taurus. In the opening line, the seven stars and lampstands are part of a larger theme we have previously discussed and will come back to again later. Our celestial clues begin with,

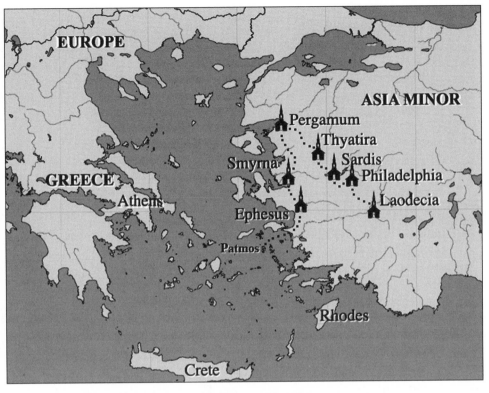

Map of the Seven Churches

I know all about you: how hard you work and how much you put up with.

Taurus is a hard working individual. They strap their shoulders into the yoke or harness and will pull all day long. They do not change their minds or moods readily. They are the farmers and bankers of life.

I know, too, that you have patience, and have suffered for my name without growing tired.

Patience is the flip side of the stubborn Taurean coin. Natives of Taurus can't be pushed from their firmly held beliefs, nor can they be

easily pried from their own particular brand of laziness. Taurus is ruled
by Venus (in other words, by love), but they'll settle for what feels good.
Life is to be enjoyed, whether tasted, smelled, heard, felt or seen. This
moves them.

*Nevertheless, I have this complaint to make; you have less love now than
you used to.*

Because Venus rules Taurus, this is the meter by which all things
are measured, how much you like or love them, shades of Venus. With
the Moon in Taurus, the energy moves in waves, like the tide. The
phases of the Moon ebb and flow. Under very long term cycles even
patience, the forte of Taurus, can begin to wane. Lose linear thinking.
The shortest distance between two points has no business here. You
try pouring water out at point A and see if it moves in a straight line
toward point B. The Moon moves in waves, in cycles, in curves. It is
moods and feelings, adaptable and variable as water, hard as ice, yet
its steam can burn you. Squares, corners, cubicles and compartmental-
ization need not apply. Think damp.

The Nicolatians were the hierarchy of the Church (the new
religion). Jesus didn't want this movement to have a hierarchy. He
wanted everybody to be equals. The Nicolatians come up both in the
letters to Ephesus (line 6) and Pergamum (line 15). They taught that it
was OK for Christians to eat the meat that had been communally sacrificed to the gods, as well as other things generally considered immoral
to the Judaeo-Christian community. Food issues, what you eat, are what
the Moon is about. In the body it rules the jaws, stomach and digestive
system, the parts of the body that deal with processing the food.

The image being conveyed here is one that has a very practical
side that most people tend to misrepresent. When people hear "sacrifice," they often conjure up notions of horrific scenes of blood and
debauchery, but what was generally going on is not really as bad as
people think. Obviously, these were times before refrigeration. Anyone
who works with food knows that it spoils quickly, especially in the heat
of warmer climates or during the summer. The best way to keep that

from happening was to keep the animal alive until you were ready to eat it. If you were part of an agricultural community, then you kept your livestock close by, in fenced in enclosures or nearby fields. If you were more nomadic or part of an army on the move, then your livestock would have to come with you. What the pagans are doing is saying a blessing, a prayer to the gods before eating their food. Because cattle are so large, it was not unusual that a number of folk would be involved in the meal.

The Judaeo-Christian community did not want to eat food that had already been blessed by the pagans. It violated the "me first" notion that Yahweh had established for himself in the early books of the Hebrew Bible. Besides being a spiritual acknowledgement, pagans simply saw sacrifice as a matter of public health and safety.

In Taurus the Moon is in its exaltation. This is "manna of the gods," ritually ordained spiritually blessed food. Our menu is being handed to us. Get it right and the Moon (food, wildcrafting, our environment or the community) will feed you from the Tree of Life (those in tune with the rhythm of the seasons, the planting and sowing of the crops, the agricultural year) set in God's paradise. Fresh food, properly prepared, is a treat that can't be beat in heaven or on earth. Here in the West, food is still the gathering point around which many of our ritual holidays are bonded.

The Moon in Taurus represents many other important virtues not referenced in the Ephesian letter, such as a stable (Taurus) family life (Moon), growth through infancy (Moon-babies), with a secure (Taurus), consistent (Taurus) home (Moon), regular (Taurus) food (Moon), and general emotional (Moon), maternal (Moon) support (Taurus). On the physical (earth) level, the Moon in Taurus can also be a strong, beautiful (Taurus) body, especially for babies and women (Moon).

Many replicas of Artemis of Ephesus have the signs of the zodiac seen clearly running from one shoulder, down across her chest and then up over the other shoulder in a semi-circle. The celestial clues are there, beckoning us to follow where they lead.

Moon City

While interpreting the symbolism from this letter to Ephesus, we've been examining its external casing, what's on the outside, the branches of our metaphorical Tree of Life. If we do a little additional work and dig deeper into the archaeological layers of this Earth sign, a whole new world begins to open up and speak to us.

In the pagan realm, Ephesus was Moon City, known internationally as a religious center. Her temple was easily the most overwhelming sight on the skyline. It was a treasure house, museum and haven for criminals who could find sanctuary at her altar. The temple of Artemis was not only famous; it was one of the seven wonders of the ancient world! Any Greek or Roman schoolboy knew that.

> I have set eyes on the wall of lofty Babylon on which is a road for chariots, and the statue of Zeus by the Alpheus, and the hanging gardens, and the colossus of the Sun, and the huge labor of the high pyramids, and the vast tomb of Mausolus; but when I saw the house of Artemis that mounted to the clouds, those other marvels lost their brilliancy, and I said, 'Lo, apart from Olympus, the Sun never looked on aught so grand.[1]

The Moon was Queen of the town and had been for years. The Moon is woman, mother and matriarch. Taurus is an Earth sign. The angel of the church of Ephesus is the Moon's most exalted earthly manifestation. As Cybele, she was considered "a deification of the Earth Mother." With the Moon in its exaltation in Taurus we have Mother Earth.

In contemporary terms she is the spirit of Mother Nature.

When they realized that he was a Jew, they all started shouting in unison, "Great is Diana of the Ephesians!" and they kept this up for two hours. When the town clerk eventually succeeded in calming the crowd, he said,

---

1 Antipater of Sidon, *Greek Anthology*, IX.58. He was a compiler of the *Seven Wonders of the World*.

"Citizens of Ephesus! Is there anybody alive who does not know that the city of the Ephesians is the guardian of the temple of great Diana and of her statue that fell from heaven?"[2]

Of course the statue fell from heaven. Moonlight falls on us almost every night, unless she pulls a cloud cover over the silver crescent broach she uses to pin her hair. Scholars seem to have a problem with the different "masks" Artemis can wear. The Greek goddess Artemis (and later Roman Diana) was a slender maiden who ran through the woods with her female band on the hunt, her wild hair bounding as she flew. Lunar phases had long been associated with the nocturnal and migrational movements of animals.

Built originally by Croesus, the Artemis of Ephesus has elements of Eastern origins and is clearly derived from Cybele, an "Earth goddess." We know from Acts 19: 23-41 there was a large trade in miniature images of Diana. You came to the temple, said a prayer that is to be offered up to the Goddess, and then left a small token or tribute, in the same way that Catholics will go to church, say a prayer and light a candle. Demetrius is a silversmith who made Artemisian shrines because silver is the metal of the Moon. In this case, it is the spiritual medium of choice. If you stopped by a temple of Apollo, gold would be the choice because it is the metal of the Sun.

The Moon, whether as the Greek goddess Artemis, the Roman Diana, the Hittite Cybele or our own Mother Nature are all simply different masks, different personas of the Moon. Naturally there are differences in the details. Women *are* different. It is not always easy to fit the attributes of a child onto a crone. Yet it is the spirit of the essential energy, the core of the feminine that is being honored in its many guises. Which will she be tonight in your dreams?

Each of these cultural interpretations of the energy of the Moon is part of the divine working through nature. If you understand the link, one finds more similarities than differences. It's a role that requires many parts. The Moon rules women. That the lunar and menstrual cycles correspond is no accident, nor need be explained to the fem-

---

2 Acts 19:34–35

inine gender. They're bonded to the connection. Is the Moon little girls, women or crones?

Yes, yes, and yes. Inside the crone is a little girl, and inside every little girl is a wise woman. As wife and mother, she's everything to everybody anyway. This is why Juno's virginity was periodically restored, and why there can be virgin birth. They are all different facets of "woman," they are all different roles that must be played at different times in life. The archetypes, because they must represent the full circle, the full set of experiences, can develop personality characteristics which can be a little difficult to fit into a single interpretation. At the divine level, this all works perfectly. She is the goddess in three forms.

The Moon is Woman in her many manifestations on Earth. Each of these roles is a separate mask, each a phase of the Moon. In a single lifetime, one may wear them all. The woods come alive with activity as they are bathed in the luminous light of the Moon. The hunt was a chore once employed for the acquisition of food, not fun. The Moon is our Mother, from whose breast we all suck. She continues to nourish us body and soul on a daily basis, no matter how old you are. Ultimately, she watches over the cycles of life and death on both the physical and seasonal levels. The feminine is the vehicle through which life enters the planet, her body the physical gatekeeper for all souls born on Earth.

Or so pagans believed. Because the Moon of Ephesus is not a young huntress of Greek imagination does not make it wrong. It's just one more magnificent manifestation of the Moon. The twenty-eight lunar mansions, daily motions of the Moon through the month, had been known for Ages, their secrets orally passed from generation to generation.

The branches of this new Christian "tree of life" are being grafted onto pagan roots. This angel picked the city that had long ago been dedicated to "Mother Nature."

Think where you were before you fell; repent, and do as you used to at first, or else, if you will not repent, I shall come to you and take your lampstand from its place.

Shake off your tendency to laziness, food and drink for its own sake. Give thanks.

If anyone has ears to hear, let him listen to what the Spirit is saying to the churches...

The Church of SMYRNA

2:8 Write to the angel of the church in Smyrna and say, 'Here is the message of the First and the Last, who was dead and has come to life again: / I know the trials you have had, and how poor you are—though you are rich—and the slanderous accusations that have been made by the people who profess to be Jews but are really members of the synagogue of Satan. / Do not be afraid of the sufferings that are coming to you: I tell you, the devil is going to send some of you to prison to test you, and you must face an ordeal for ten days. Even if you have to die, keep faithful, and I will give you the crown of life for your prize." / If anyone has ears to hear, let him listen to what the Spirit is saying to the churches: for those who prove victorious there is nothing to be afraid of in the second death.

The angel of the church of Smyrna is the exaltation of Venus in Pisces.

This is an especially important moment in the series because it was written at the beginning of the Age of Pisces, the heavenly contract recently born. The themes found in the clues left by the letter to the angel of Symrna reflect some of Christianity's philosophical core, it's spiritual essence. While the Vernal Equinox is passing through the constellation Pisces (from Jesus until now), Venus becomes the "celestially anointed one," the angel most identified with the spirit of Christianity over the past two thousand years.

The essence of Venus in Pisces is peace. Inner, spiritual peace that quiets the tumultuous waters, no matter how they may roar. Venus is rhythm, harmony, balance and beauty; from peace comes satisfaction. Placed in Pisces these qualities pervade the spiritual realm. We draw strength from peace, but it is a quiet strength. It was the strength of

Gandhi, Martin Luther King and John Lennon. It's the Holy Spirit in the form of a dove descending on Jesus. The dove is the bird of Venus, the bird of peace. In the Christian tradition one manner in which Venus in Pisces manifests is as the love of Jesus. It is the source of the spiritual bond with the Catholic nuns. They marry their Savior in order to deepen their love, just as He loved them.

Venus is the Goddess of love and marriage.

The power of Venus in Pisces is faith. Belief in what you can't see, don't know, or find difficult to define. There will continue to be doubt, uncertainty and confusion, but faith lifts us above these and sees us through, even though on this side of the veil we don't always know what the answer will be.

In more mundane terms, Venus in Pisces can be that special song that really lights up your soul, unlocking the key to your inner self like nothing else can. It opens you, turns you on, and lifts you through the clouds every time.

Venus is music.

The celestial shift from Aries to Pisces meant a philosophical shift on the part of civilization. Aries represented the hero, the warrior, the young prince of the classical tradition. The social pillars were crumbling, the old gods were struggling for air. It was giving way to a new vibration, a new tradition, a *"new hymn in heaven."*

Venus is song.

In the material realm, while we are here on Earth, we are all different. We look different, we speak differently, we think differently, colors, genders, geography... We're different. But the deeper we delve into the subconscious, the more alike we become. It's like watching two people asleep. Individual distinctions melt away, layers discarded like so many onionskins—personality, character, habits, idiosyncrasies— leaving only the rhythm of our breathing, rising and falling, quietly at peace.

Venus in Pisces understands that at our core, we are all One. Who else is there?

It is important therefore that we take care of one another because ultimately, we're taking care of ourselves. This is the secret behind the veil. Compassion, empathy and understanding are a few of the special qualities squeezed from Venus in Pisces. It represents love of one another, the same love Jesus had for us. This is the model we need to follow. These are the tools given to us for a lifetime, do with them what we will.

During the Age of Pisces, we turn our attention to those who have lost the most, who have given their very lives in spiritual surrender. Or more precisely, earthly surrender for spiritual triumph.

In the time of Pisces the angel of Pisces receives the heavenly nod.

The opening reference to the *First and the Last* is perfect in this location, and we will encounter it again.

I know the trials you have had...

Pisces is a sign of spiritual triumph born of earthly loss. The image of Jesus on the cross springs to mind. Pisces represents the subconscious, everything below the level of consciousness or awareness. It's what we don't know, can't see, don't understand, and can't find the answer to. It's people who have nothing; slaves, prisoners, in the hospital, asylum, or otherwise outcast. It is the prostitute, beggar and thief. When the spirit of Christianity cast its beacon across the sea of humanity, material riches were not what it was looking for. Self-sacrifice was one of the few spiritual themes that continued to maintain a place of honor throughout the Classical and into Christian morality.

and how poor you are—though you are rich—

Venus deals with our possessions. Venus in Taurus (its rulership) is material possessions (Taurus is an earth sign). Venus in Pisces (its exaltation) deals with spiritual possessions (Pisces is a water sign). In material terms, you are poor. In spiritual terms, you have all the riches of Creation. Smyrna is a good choice of a city as the geographic location, because she has passed through phases of power and influence that over time were seen to ebb.

and the slanderous accusations that have been made by the people who
profess to be Jews but are really members of the synagogue of Satan.

Smyrna was a prosperous city of Asia Minor. Geography blessed
it with advantageous port conditions, ease of defense, and excellent
overland trade routes. It rose to prominence before the Classical Era.
Early on it was one of the finest cities of Asia and was called "the
lovely—the crown of Ionia—the ornament of Asia." The beauty of the
Hellenistic city, clustering on the low ground and rising tier over tier
on the hillside, was frequently praised by the ancients and is celebrated
on coins. In the 1st century AD the view was that this mature lady was
dissolute after a life of ease and opulent living. While still a vital city,
the bloom of her rose was not as fresh as it once was. Alexander's suc-
cessors had rebuilt the city, but that was some three centuries earlier.

With Venus in Pisces, Smyrna was a rich (Venus) key to the seaport
(Pisces), one of the largest in Asia Minor. Venus represents what is
pretty, beautiful or pleasing to the senses. Cosmetics and perfumes
fall within her realm. The name, Smyrna, was taken from the ancient
Greek word for myrrh, an incense which had been the chief export of
the city. Myrrh is referenced in the Hebrew Bible numerous times as
a rare perfume with, like wine, intoxicating qualities (Genesis 37:25,
Exodus 30:23). Before his crucifixion, Jesus is offered wine with myrrh.

Early converts to Christianity were chiefly drawn from the Jewish
faith, those who used the Hebrew Bible. Naturally, this caused jealousy
as traditional Hebrew ranks were depleted, families philosophically
split. Neither did the pagans want to see a new religion in town, as
Homer, the preeminent poet of the classical tradition, had strong
local ties to the area. A new religion would hurt business in trade and
tourism. The early Christians thus had difficulties with Rome and from
the local pagan population in Smyrna. They were being accused and
persecuted on various fronts.

Part of the subconscious realm is the mind's eye, the inner eye or
third eye. It is the portal through which we "see" our dreams, even while
we're asleep. But we also use this eye while awake to paint projections
of others, forming an image of what we think of them. Accusations
attempt to mold these impressions in order to defame or undermine

the intended target. These new Christians were the target of *"slanderous accusations."* On the flip side of our exalted theme coin, they are *not* pretty (Venus) projections (Pisces).

Do not be afraid of the sufferings that are coming to you: I tell you, the devil is going to send some of you to prison to test you, and you must face an ordeal for ten days.

Pisces "lot" in the material realm is suffering. Because of these slanderous accusations, you will be unjustly imprisoned for a period of time. The last two thousand years have been a time of suffering. Look at the record of man's inhumanity to man, century after century. It's called history. Pisces rules prisons, hospitals, and sanctuaries, places where people who are sick, broken, or of a less desirable social distinction are removed from society's view. They are placed in the societal subconscious, where we can't see (be conscious of) them. The ten days is obviously metaphorical for a set length of time.

Even if you have to die, keep faithful, and I will give you the crown of life for your prize.

Spirit is what is behind the scenes and guides us in our terrestrial journey. It is the realm that receives our prayers. There is more than just this life. We are bordering on the themes of Plato's cave here. Base your life on truth and hold onto those sentiments, though death be the choice, and I will give you the crown of life. You will have spiritually passed the test. Eternal life is now yours. This is what you came here for.

for those who prove victorious there is nothing to be afraid of in the second death.

Physical death is what frightens us. It is the ultimate primordial fear. Once re-born to spirit, we are mystically reconnected to all things, times, peoples and places, bar none.

Pisces is symbolized by two Fish. It is a sign of duality. That is the illusion. We consider ourselves to be different from everyone else, when in fact we are all the same. In their sacred union around the sacrament of wine, both Dionysus and Jesus were known as "twice born": Jesus, through the crucifixion and ascension, while Dionysus was saved by Zeus snatching him from his mother's womb (first birth) before she died, and then being born again from the Thunderer's thigh (second birth) after he had taken more time to fully develop.

Wine is twice born, whether of Jesus or Dionysus. It dies first when harvested as the fruit of the grape, only to become the elixir when allowed to properly ferment and mature. It is wine one desires, not grape juice. It is the spiritual kingdom one should seek, not the earthly. To die in service is to gain eternal life. You spiritually succeed. The heavenly crown becomes yours, forever.

The Church of PERGAMUM

2:12 *Write to the angel of the church in Pergamum and say, "Here is the message of the one who has the sharp sword, double edged: / I know where you live, in the place where Satan is enthroned, and that you still hold firmly to my name, and did not disown your faith in me even when my faithful witness, Antipas, was killed in your own town, where Satan lives./*

"Nevertheless, I have one or two complaints to make: some of you are followers of Balaam, who taught Balak to set a trap for the Israelites so that they committed adultery by eating food that had been sacrificed to idols; / and among you, too, there are some as bad who accept what the Nicolaitans teach. / You must repent, or I shall soon come to you and attack these people with the sword out of my mouth. / If anyone has ears to hear, let him listen to what the Spirit is saying to the churches: to those who prove victorious I will give the hidden manna and a white stone—a stone with a new name written on it, known only to the man who receives it."

The angel of the church of Pergamum is Mercury's exaltation in Virgo.

Here is the message of the one who has the sharp sword, double edged:

We have seen this image before, in Rev. 1:16, at the beginning of the vision.

out of his mouth came a sharp sword, double-edged

This is critical judgment, harsh words or a biting tongue. Mercury is communication, and it cuts both ways, hence *"double-edged."* Communication is talking and listening, writing and reading. There is a dualistic quality to Mercury. Two sets of nervous systems, two lungs, two arms, two hands, two people conversing, arguing, laughing, emailing. Communication.

As the fleet footed messenger of the Gods, Mercury is thought, speech and what we call ourselves. It is our name, the verbal ID for which we sit up, turn, stop, go forward, or, by which we are called to supper.

you still hold firmly to my name

Maintain the focus. You mentally (Mercury) still hold to my name (Mercury). In ancient myths, knowing the name of a entity helped to gain control over that entity. The Egyptians tell stories of attempting to find out a god's secret name. Hebrew tradition prohibits the naming of Yahweh, or the writing of the vowels. Names were not always emblazoned on the chest. By knowing the name and holding onto it you have the divine power you need to control its nature.

I have one or two complaints to make

Mercury in Virgo is always making complaints, corrections, adjustments, alterations, critiques and recommendations. Mercury in Virgo is analytical and verbal. They'll tell you if it's not right. No mystery here. Mercury's duality is again being referenced (*"one or two complaints/double edged"*) and confirmed through repetition. We're on the right track.

some of you are followers of Balaam, who taught Balak to set a trap for
the Israelites so that they committed adultery by eating food that had
been sacrificed to idols

Pagans would hold a ritual sacrifice—make a request to a god or
goddess for a good harvest, safe journey, or successful outcome of an
enterprise—then sacrifice an ox or other animal, and eat. Rituals in
the Hebrew tradition around sacrifice may be found in Leviticus. They
were saying a prayer. They were offering a blessing to the divine in the
same way that we do while seated at the table, except that they were
present for the slaughter of the animal.

The best way to keep food fresh was to keep it alive until you
wanted to eat it. It tasted better that way, and of course was better for
you. Everybody did it. After the ritual, the fat, bones and leftovers were
separated and burned as an offering to God (Leviticus) or the Gods
(Homer). It's unhealthy to leave unused body parts around. They draw
flies and disease. The meat was roasted over the fire, eaten and shared
with the community. These rituals were a collective blessing for the
maintenance of life.

But for Jews and Christians, it was the wrong god. This food had
been "contaminated" by the heathens with prayers to pagan gods.
Yahweh had long ago established a tradition of being jealous of the
spiritual attentions of his people and demanded the "first born." If
you're dealing with blessings already offered, you're talking spiritual
leftovers.

In another Mercurial manifestation, they are tricked. Mercury is
the Lord of both thieves and businessmen. Setting traps is one of his
specialties.

and among you, too, there are some as bad who accept what the Nico-
laitans teach.

Teaching is what Mercury is all about. This is the planet of communication, of getting ideas across. Teaching erroneous material is the
worst possible manifestation of the energy. The focus here is still on
Mercury, though the flip side of Mercury.

You must repent, or I shall soon come to you and attack these people with the sword out of my mouth

Now the sword image in the first line of the letter to Pergamum makes sense. It's not just a sword (which suggests Mars, the God of War); it's a sword out of the mouth. Mercury rules communications which emanate from the mouth. Attacking with the sword of his mouth is cutting accusations, sharp words. "What I am about to say may hurt. You may not like it. It's true for the pagans, but it's true for you, too." Repent; say with your mouth and in your own words that you will change.

to those who prove victorious I will give the hidden manna and a white stone—a stone with a new name written on it, known only to the man who receives it.

Notice we're back to the "name" component again. Those who prove victorious are those who have been born to a new life. Stone was an ancient testimonial, meant to record deeds into posterity. The laws of Hammurabi were recorded in stone; the commandments of Moses were recorded in stone; the codes of the Egyptians were recorded in stone. The stone with a new name is an Earth Sign (Virgo) with something written on it (Mercury). According to the ancient texts Mercury rules Virgo; Mercury is exalted in Virgo. Virgo is an Earth Sign. Stone tablets were once a more common way of passing information to the future. If it was really important, it was written "in stone." Stone bears testament to the eternal laws. Stone bears witness to the successful passage. When posterity remembers you by a stone marker (a tombstone), you have honored your people, your place, and your time. You have done well. It is also the testament laid upon the grave in Jewish tradition (at the end of Joshua), a personal memorial to a life well lived.

Now it may seem strange to some that we are conjuring asymmetrical images, disjointed clues, corralling them into a single arena like one great homogenous herd. Names, swords-out-of-mouths, stones of record—strange stuff this! But this is the way the pagans saw it, influenced from above by the gods of heavenly Olympus.

The trick is to have a consistent theme within each framework, from each church. The earthly locations provide us with additional clues. The local history of each helps to "ground" the energy, to give it a personality. The angel of Pergamum has much to teach us about its past, and its future.

Pergamum is Mercury, Mercury is communications. It is messages, notes and anything used to compose them, like pens, pencils and paper. What is the biggest collection of these artifacts you can think of, gathered together in a single location (mythical minions following the cadent beat of a winged caduceus held aloft by a mischievous Mercury)?

Pergamum was known for its vast library of two hundred thousand volumes. It had long ago become famous as a center of learning. This library was removed by Anthony to Egypt and presented to Cleopatra (who absorbed it into the library at Alexandria) in the century before Revelation was written, but its reputation as a city of learning endured. In Pergamum was first discovered the art of making paper, which was called "*pergammena*" or parchment. The discovery was facilitated when the Egyptian trade connection supplying papyrus was interrupted. Necessity dictated a substitute be found. Pergamum invented an answer.

Finally, Virgo is the sign associated with health. Although the lines of scripture do not evoke any of these "health" images, the *Asclepion* at Pergamum was one of the earliest and best-known healing centers in the world at the time. It was a spa that evolved around a holistic approach to healing. This included diet, hot baths, relaxing music, serene settings, classic theater, and divine guidance as suggested by the client's own dreams. Healers were on hand to facilitate much in the same way nurses do today.

Contemporary with the writing of Revelation was one of the giants of the medical world. A thousand years earlier, there had been Asclepius, blasted by a thunderbolt for his presumption in daring to raise a man from the dead. In the 5th century BC there had been Hippocrates of Kos, recognized as the father of modern medicine. But the most significant influence on European medicine until the Renaissance was Galen of Pergamum.

Galen was the cornerstone of Hippocrates' work. After the 9th century AD and the translations of his works into Arabic, Galen became the standard of the medical profession. Because he employed the dietary regimes of Hippocrates, his written work was studied throughout Europe for centuries. His personal contribution was the dissection and recording of mammals, mostly primates. He believed that in the discovery of how these systems worked (nervous, heart, kidneys, etc.) he was uncovering God's divine plan. His Stoic self-discipline would leave volumes, although only a fraction of these have survived. He was the European medical standard-bearer for fourteen centuries. Of the 600 written works mentioned in history, only twenty have been passed on. Most were lost when the library in Alexandria burned.

Between the library and the healing ambience of the spa—the personality of Pergamum with its parchment past was well known to the sophisticated, cosmopolitan community of this Hellenized *polis*. These "clues" would have been much more apparent to those familiar with local traditions and conditions as they existed at the time, in other words, to the local Greek community.

The roots of the pagan tradition, the choice of location and personality of the town selected are all important pieces of the puzzle. Each is part of the door that is being unlocked.

The angel of the church of Pergamum is Mercury's exaltation in Virgo. It is the angel who holds the Rod of Asclepius, the Caduceus of Hermes (Mercury). It is the angel of learning, teaching and healing.

The Church of THYATIRA

2:18 *Write to the angel of the church in Thyatira and say, "Here is the message of the Son of God who has eyes like a burning flame and feet like burnished bronze. / I know all about you and how charitable you are; I know your faith and devotion and how much you put up with, and I know how you are still making progress. / Nevertheless, I have a complaint to make: you are encouraging the woman Jezebel who claims to be a prophetess, and by her teaching she is luring my servants away to commit the adultery of eating food which has been sacrificed to idols. / I have given her time to reform but she is not willing to change her adulterous life. / Now I am consigning her to bed, and all her partners in adultery to troubles that will test them severely, unless they repent of their*

practices; / and I will see that her children die, so that all the churches
realize that it is I who search heart and loins and give each one of you
what your behavior deserves. / But on the rest of you in Thyatira, all of
you who have not accepted this teaching or learned the secrets of Satan,
as they are called, I am not laying any special duty; / but hold firmly on
to what you already have until I come. / To those who prove victorious,
and keep working for me until the end, I will give the authority over the
pagans / which I myself have been given by my Father, to rule them with
an iron scepter and shatter them like earthenware. And I will give him
the Morning Star. / If anyone has ears to hear, let them listen to what the
Spirit is saying to the churches.'"

The angel of the church in Thyatira is the Sun in its exaltation in
Aries. There's a powerful amount of Stoic Fire in this furnace. The Sun
rules Leo, a Fire sign. Aries is a Fire sign. The Sun is our fiery planet,
our local star. The Sun in Aries is the Golden Rule. We will return to
this measure and weigh it when we arrive at the Church of Laodicea.

When the Sun enters Aries each year it's Spring. The Sun is exalted
because this is the time when light triumphs over darkness, together
with all its metaphors and actualities. This is when the battle stands
poised, then inevitably turns to victory, truth and light.

Astrologically, the Sun rules the son, our child. It is us as children;
it is our inner child. It is all God's children.

Here is the message of the Son of God who has eyes like a burning flame
and feet like burnished bronze.

The Son of God is the child of God. He has eyes like a burning
flame because this *is* the power of the Sun. As we saw in the composite individuals, the lights of heaven (the luminaries) were thought
to be the eyes of God. Both Egyptian and Norse myths incorporate
this notion. *"His feet like burnished bronze"* adds seasoning to the over-
riding theme of the Age as it reflects the exaltation of Venus (highly
polished, beautiful) in Pisces (feet). The Sun (heart) and Venus (love)

are the two astrological instruments of affection. A father's love for his children is the underlying bond here.

I know all about you and how charitable you are; I know your faith and devotion and how much you put up with, and I know how you are still making progress.

The Sun is bright, the Sun is bold. The Sun is warm and loving. These are qualities of the heart. Since Aries rules the head, we have not only a victorious champion, but also someone who leads from the heart, who leads with love. Solar energy is very giving. It springs from our core. This makes solar individuals very charitable. They love to give. Their convictions can run deep. The strength of their will keeps them forging ahead.

Nevertheless, I have a complaint to make: you are encouraging the woman Jezebel who claims to be a prophetess, and by her teaching she is luring my servants away to commit the adultery of eating food which has been sacrificed to idols.

Solar energy represents truth, light and consciousness. Together with Helios, Apollo (the Sun) is the Greek god of Truth, wherein no darkness or falsehood could approach. He took over the oracle at Delphi, the place where the ancient world went to seek truth and guidance. Through his powers of divination, Apollo and his priestesses were able to discern the truth of the future. When Mercury lies to Apollo about stealing his cattle, Apollo knows he is lying and takes him to Jupiter for supreme judgment. Jupiter confirms Apollo's suspicions, gets Mercury to tell the truth and return the cattle.

Jezebel claims these same abilities. She is a prophetess, one who is able to discern the future. We have seen the conundrum of *"eating food which has been sacrificed to idols"* twice before in Revelation. Presumably this is the same theme, with one additional nuance.

In the letter to this church, it is *"the adultery"* of eating food etc. that is the problem. Because of its vitality, the Sun also rules pleasure and enjoyment. The problem is, this solar energy likes having fun so much that it overrides moral considerations like marital vows. Adultery can be a whole lot of fun, but it has karmic implications. The entire body of Homer's principle work is based upon infidelity and its ramifications in how it affects the entire generation. What you do comes back to you.

I have given her time to reform but she is not willing to change her adulterous life. Now I am consigning her to bed, and all her partners in adultery to troubles that will test them severely, unless they repent of their practices.

This girl is just having *too* much fun. The Lord is making her sick so she might reflect upon her ways. The Sun deals with will power. It is strong of purpose. The keywords of Leo are "I will." What it is willing and not willing to do is the whole focus of this celestial alignment. Jezebel is not willing. So how do you leverage someone like this into one powerful of continence, unwavering in will? Go right for the heart! You get their attention by hitting them where it hurts, through their children. The Sun rules life itself. The Sun has the ability to take it back again.

and I will see that her children die, so that all the churches realize that it is I who search heart and loins and give each one of you what your behavior deserves.

Do you have ears to hear or eyes to see what is being written here? *"it is I who search heart and loins."*

But on the rest of you in Thyatira, all of you who have not accepted this teaching or learned the secrets of Satan, as they are called, I am not laying any special duty; but hold firmly on to what you already have until I come.

But for those of you who play from the heart and have not been misled, keep on loving one another (in the metaphorical sense) until I come. It is the right thing to do.

To those who prove victorious, and keep working for me until the end, I will give the authority over the pagans

The proper salutation to the Sun is power and victory. The Sun is King. It is the King to whom heavenly authority is given. This is one of many references to "the end." You must wait until the end. The apocalyptic books abound with such langage. You must wait; the time is close.

which I myself have been given by my Father

The Sun represents the authority. At it's best, it is a loving father who sees himself in you. The Sun represents the son, the Sun represents the father. It is the thread of male lineage. But the Sun also rules children, male *and* female. Thyatira was named while Seleucus I Nicator was reconstructing the city circa 300 BC. He was so happy about the news of the birth of his daughter that he named the city after her. Thyatira means "daughter."

to rule them with an iron scepter and shatter them like earthenware

The Sun is exalted in Aries. The Sun in Aries is a martial king, one who has both civil and military control. This is a victorious warlord. The highest expression of the Sun in Aries is a take-charge guy who can get the job done—a successful general for example.

And I will give him the Morning Star.

Say hello to the Sun, donning his auroral cloak at the most dramatic time of the day, in the morning. This is especially so at dawn on the first day of Spring (Aries), when the Sun doubly wins out over darkness, on a daily *and* seasonal sojourn. On your day of victory, you are given the Sunrise as your badge of honor. Yes, Venus has also been called the Morning Star, but Venus pales when compared to the brilliance of the Sun, the true "star" (literally) of our solar system.

Why is Thyatira a solar town? To the Greeks, Alexander was the King of Kings, who established Thyatira after the Persian conquests. We begin by noble decree. In Thyatira, the local Sun God was Tyrimnas. He was the deity to whom the city was dedicated. Games were held there in his honor. The Sun likes games. The Sun likes fun. The emperor was deified and worshipped here, as he should be in any city dedicated to the Sun: the current king or living authority. We would translate it today as a place for prayers for the president in all he undertakes as our leader. Christians and Jews saw it as praying to mortals. In their eyes, spiritual matters should be left to divine, not terrestrial judgment.

This is the Sun in its exaltation in Aries, the martial turf of war. Thyatira was for centuries a frontier (pioneer) fort together with its supporting community. It had an active garrison maintained there first by the Seleucids, then Pergamene, and finally Rome. Its association with legions of the sword would have been obvious and well established during the generation in which Revelation was being written.

The Sun is King, and the King is royalty. The color of royalty in classical times was purple, and the deeper the color, the better. The waters of Thyatira were said to be so well adopted for dyeing that in no place could cloth be so brilliantly or permanently died.

Here's another reference to Thyatira from the Christian perspective.

We went along the river outside the gates as it was the Sabbath and this was a customary place for prayer. We sat down and preached to the women who had come to the meeting. One of these women was called Lydia, a devout woman from the town of Thyatira who was in the purple-dye trade. She listened to us, and the Lord opened her heart...[3]

Thyatira is a loving place. The Lord opens the woman's heart in Thyatira. Sun in Aries; a strong, spontaneous attraction. But the Sun

---

3 Acts 16:13–14.

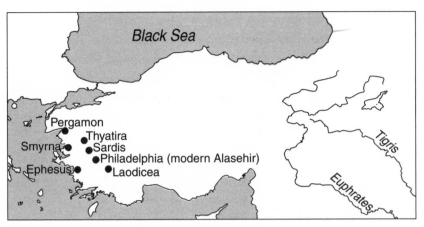

Thyatira is the first of the seven churches to not be a port city

deals with the essence, the heart, the center of our being, our very identity. The pagans warmed themselves by their cultural identity, as did the Jews and the Christians. Each group was proud of their social origins. Being the newcomers on the block, Christian devotees found themselves excluded from local industry and had to establish their own spiritually attuned infrastructure. But their trade network had to be in harmony with the wider community. Yet, pagan Dionysiads could not easily coexist with pious Christian cobblers. A devoted Christian could not in good conscience both practice his craft and live his faith in a barbaric system with their immoral pagan rites.

CHAPTER THREE

Revelation 3

The Church of SARDIS

3:1 *Write to the angel of the church in Sardis and say, "Here is the message of the one who holds the seven spirits of God and the seven stars: I know all about you: how you are reputed to be alive and yet are dead. / Wake up; revive what little you have left: it is dying fast. So far I have failed to notice anything in the way you live that my God could possibly call perfect, / and yet do you remember how eager you were when you first heard the message? Hold on to that. Repent. If you do not wake up, I shall come to you like a thief, without telling you at what hour to expect me. / There are a few in Sardis, it is true, who have kept their robes from being dirtied, and they are fit to come with me, dressed in white. / Those who prove victorious will be dressed, like these, in white robes; I shall not blot their names out of the book of life, but acknowledge their names in the presences of my Father and his angels." / If anyone has ears to hear, let him listen to what the Spirit is saying to the churches.'*

* * * * *

The angel of the church in Sardis is Mars in its exaltation in Capricorn.

Here is the message of the one who holds the seven spirits of God and the seven stars:

Seven spirits of God (once again), the seven visible planetary energies. Seven stars, the *Scroll*. Both of these will be looked at more comprehensively in Revelation 4.

Mars is the planet of physical activity, of personal prowess. He is the champion of the meet, match, game, race, hurtle, marathon or battle. This is male energy at the peak of its youth and power. Theirs is the essential moment, the supreme effort, the personal sacrifice, where everything is put on the line, right here, right now. Aries has a hard time when the supreme effort calls for another supreme effort, and then another, and another. They are better at beginnings (he said diplomatically) than they are at finishing. This is the enthusiasm of youth, squandered by its own immaturity.

I know all about you: how you are reputed to be alive and yet are dead.

All that time at the gym learning to be physically fit does not buy you a ticket to eternal life. You are reputed to be alive and yet are dead.

Mars is the ruler of Aries as we mentioned, but in antiquity Mars was also the Lord of Scorpio. Aries rules Spring and the commencement of life, Scorpio rules the Fall, the spirit of Halloween, and ghosts of the dead, when life is retreating to the root systems as nature prepares for a long winter's nap. Mars rules both Aries and Scorpio. It is both alive and dead.

Wake up; revive what little you have left: it is dying fast.

Mars is the surge of the moment; then it's over. Once a bullet is discharged from the barrel, how long a life expectancy does it have? What about a spring, catapult, or pogo stick? Once the ball has been snapped, how long before the play is done? Such is the speed of Mars, fastest of the gods. It is shooting, thrusting, exploding, surging, rushing and climaxing, all in a narrow window of time. The moment is short.

So far I have failed to notice anything in the way you live that my God could possibly call perfect, and yet do you remember how eager you were when you first heard the message? Hold on to that. Repent.

The energy of Mars, like a coiled spring, is clearly stacked at the beginning. Hold onto the first impulse because that's when you were best, when you were most powerful.

Repent. If you do not wake up, I shall come to you like a thief, without
telling you at what hour to expect me.

What are you doing with your life? The notion of the thief is one
that weaves its way throughout several Biblical locations, such as Joel
and Matthew. The chief notion is of uncertainty, of not knowing when
"the end" is going to come, and therefore to be spiritually ready at all
times. We will come back to the thief when we visit the prophets.

There are a few in Sardis, it is true, who have kept their robes from being
dirtied, and they are fit to come with me, dressed in white.

Sardis is a town known, like Thyatira, for the brilliance of its dyes.
It's not a coincidence that clean, bright (as opposed to dirtied) robes
should be brought here. But in spite of that, the robes are a metaphor.
They are what we today call the aura, seen as the halo in paintings
of spiritually advanced individuals. The covenant with God for this
period (this new Age of Pisces, when Revelation was being written)
embodies loss, suffering and penance as ways of purifying the soul, of
making our robes clean. Those who live by the law keep their "robes"
from becoming dirtied.

Those who prove victorious will be dressed, like these, in white robes; I
shall not blot their names out of the book of life, but acknowledge their
names in the presences of my Father and his angels.

Mars is the God of War; Mars is the champion. "*Those who prove*
victorious…" Mars, like any of the Fire Lords, is a planet of action.
What you do (Mars) is what's important, not what you say (Mercury).
The "book of life" is the spiritual record of all that takes place on Earth.
It is Thoth standing at the Scales of Judgment at the end of life in the
Book of the Dead. It is the Akashic Record. We will come back to this
thread of the "book of life" later in Revelation.

If anyone has ears to hear, let him listen to what the Spirit is saying
to the churches.

The location of the church we are discussing is Sardis. Most of the encoded message in the letter focuses on the planetary energy, Mars, as opposed to telling us about the sign or church.

Mars in Capricorn is youth impressed into public service for professional advancement. These are the guardians of the establishment, the watchdogs of society, those who have been picked by the institutions as role models for the rest of the country, corporation, or other hierarchical model. It is the Eagle Scout or the presidential, senatorial, or congressional nominee. This is controlled (Capricorn) explosions (Mars), concentrated power. Capricorn is a sign of the caste system, status quo, hierarchy, and government.

Once again the geographic location of the church will help us to fill in some of the earth tones. These connections would have been far more apparent to those familiar with the local geography of the time, those who lived there. Due to its military strength Sardis was the capital of the wealthy kingdom of Lydia, the political and cultural center of all Asia Minor from the seventh century BC until the death of Croesus (c. 547 BC). The early Lydian kingdom was a leader as a chief seat of manufacture, an industrial center. One of its more important trades was the dyeing of delicate woolen stuffs (like fine robes and carpets).

The manufacturing edge was thought to be in the stream (Pactolus) that flowed through town. It was said to be imbued with special properties, carrying "golden sands," gold dust from Mt. Tmolus, a steep and lofty spur that was the foundation for an almost impregnable citadel, a fort (Mars) on the mountain (Capricorn). From this vantage point, Sardis was the military authority (Mars), commanding the wide and fertile plain of the Hermus Valley. It was located on an important trade route that ran from the interior to the Aegean ports. It was a commercial (Capricorn) powerhouse (Mars). It remained an important commercial player through Roman and into Eastern Empire times. It stood at the base of Mount Tmolus.

On the hot Anatolia peninsula, the cooler, more rarified air of the highlands produced the best wool in the land, Mars (wool of the Ram) in Capricorn (from the mountains or highlands). We call it cashmere.

Trade and commerce (Capricorn) continued to be sources of

revenue for Sardis. Ruins of its shops have been excavated. As a result of the dyeing industry, support businesses in textiles and jewelry-making did well. The first coins, both gold and silver, were minted here. They bore a depiction of the head (Mars) of the ruler (Capricorn) on the coin.

Because the military establishment and the God of War (Mars) are such an important part of the life of this city, is there any surprise that it would have its own gymnasium and baths, to help keep the soldiers toned and fit, ready for battle? Sardis passed to the Romans in 133 BC. When Revelation is written, it had already been a Roman colony for close to two hundred years.

The Church of PHILADELPHIA

3:7 *Write to the angel of the church in Philadelphia and say, "Here is the message of the holy and faithful one who has the key of David, so that when he opens, nobody can close, and when he closes, nobody can open: / I know all about you; and now I have opened in front of you a door that nobody will be able to close—and I know that though you are not very strong, you have kept my commandments and not disowned my name. / Now I am going to make the synagogue of Satan- those who profess to be Jews, but are liars, because they are no such thing- I will make them come and fall at your feet and admit that you are the people that I love. / Because you have kept my commandment to endure trials, I will keep you safe in the time of trial which is going to come for the whole world, to test the people of the world. / Soon I shall be with you: hold firmly to what you already have, and let nobody take your prize away from you. / Those who prove victorious I will make into pillars in the sanctuary of my God, and they will stay there for ever; I will inscribe on them the name of my God and the name of the city of my God, the new Jerusalem which comes down from my God in heaven, and my own new name as well. / If anyone has ears to hear, let him listen to what the Spirit is saying to the churches."*

The angel of the church in Philadelphia equates to Jupiter in its exaltation in Cancer. The opening reference to *"the holy and faithful one who has the key of David"* comes from Isaiah in the Old Testament.

I place the key of the House of David on his shoulder; should he open, no one shall close, should he close, no one shall open.[1]

Isaiah described a period of Hebrew history just before Jerusalem was attacked and overrun by the Assyrians, when the children of Abraham were pressed into slavery and marched off to Babylon. Because the people had refused to listen to Isaiah, God's prophet (Yahweh Sabaoth in the Hebrew Bible), they were blamed and condemned by God. Rather than observing a day of mourning, as recommended by Isaiah, the people decided to ignore God's word and enjoy a celebration. Rather than humble themselves before God, they were festive.[2]

Isaiah then speaks of two "masters of the palace." Shebna was ignoring God's advice and following his own design. He prepared a tomb carved from the rocks and put his militarily trust in chariots. God removed this servant of the city and appointed in his place Eliakim, who follows the word of the Lord and is found to be pleasing in His Eyes.

I dismiss you (Shebna) from your office,
I remove you from you post,
and the same day I call on my servant
Eliakim son of Hilkiah,
I invest him with your robe,
gird him with your sash,
entrust him with your authority;
and he shall be a father
to the inhabitants of Jerusalem
and to the House of Judah.[3]

---

1 Isaiah 22:22
2 See Isaiah 22:12–14.
3 Isaiah 22:19–23

This master of the palace has a large key, displayed on a sash placed over his shoulder that locks and unlocks the Citadel of David, the inner fortress, the final redoubt of Jerusalem. This key is given to one who listens to and follows the word of the Lord.

He is "holy and faithful." Jupiter is "holy and faithful." He is the spirituality of Creation, religion and piety.

The conditions outlined in this letter to the church in Philadelphia are a microcosm of the conditions being covered in Revelation. We represent a period of time where people have turned away from the commandments, but there's hope for those who represent the spirit of the angel from Philadelphia, that they might be guided under His protection.

The people, in the time of Isaiah and during the period covered by Revelation, have fallen away. With Jupiter in its exaltation in Cancer, towns and communities that work with the spirit of the divine fare better than those who forge their own path. God made man in his own image. It is then up to man to reflect God's Will while here on Earth.

I know all about you; and now I have opened in front of you a door that nobody will be able to close—and I know that though you are not very strong, you have kept my commandments and not disowned my name.

Our "key" so far has been drawn from Bible history. It is a key to the lock on an inner fortress located in Jerusalem. But here we are being offered a metaphorical description of an open door policy that lies in front of us, or did at that point in time. For those who can read the divine heavenly script, God's Word can be followed across time. The door opened in front of you is the map to get through the celestial maze. Once you've tuned into heaven's power and majesty, no one will be able to strip you of it. This information was used to benefit the tribe, clan, or extended family (Cancer), in this case Jerusalem. They have kept God's commandments, and more importantly, continued to follow his advice.

In personal terms, Jupiter is not very strong physically, at least not over the course of years. There can be flurries of activity in their youth when they may be athletic (especially in team sports), but sustained physical endurance is not Jupiter's forte. Spiritual strength, being devout, studying philosophy and wisdom are what this planet is known for. At their most elevated, they are holy, reverent and righteous. As we will later see, it is this spiritual focus our angel from heaven is so pleased with in the Philadelphia letter. In the Hindu class system, Jupiter represents the priestly caste, the keepers of wisdom, those who have been educated in spiritual teachings.

Now I am going to make the synagogue of Satan—those who profess to be Jews, but are liars, because they are no such thing—I will make them come and fall at your feet and admit that you are the people that I love.

Spiritual pride is being evoked here. At its best, it helps to motivate us to do good things for the community, our family, children and the future. At its worst, it can be a smokescreen that hides their true actions behind a veil.

Cancer is the clan, the family, the tribe; all of whom are related. With Jupiter, the planet of expansion, in Cancer, we have the extended family. Most of these early Christians came from Jewish families. Indeed, the translation of Philadelphia, "brotherly love," extends from this notion. This is not so much "sibling" love as it is love for one another within the extended family. It derives from the early Christians calling each other "brother" and "sister" even though there may not have been a blood tie. Pagans were horrified by what they perceived to be these incestuous relations among these Christians (one of many misunderstandings between diverse ethnic groups). When extended families are spiritually united, great favor follows. Blessings from heaven (Jupiter) fall on the clan (Cancer). Another interpretation would be, "Be fruitful" (Cancer) "and multiply" (Jupiter), appropriate to the children of Abraham who were promised to eventually number more than the stars of heaven.

Jupiter rules both Sagittarius and Pisces. Pisces rules the feet. "Holy and faithful" are straight translations of Jupiter in Pisces. Pisces is the sign of faith. This is the Age of Faith, the Kingdom of God. Falling *"at your feet"* is a form of spiritual (Jupiter) surrender (Pisces), of humility and humiliation. The implication here is that the liars are surrendering their spiritual authority to the Christians. The Christians, in their turn, surrender their authority to Jesus, who surrenders his to God. With the shift from Aries to Pisces, from Classical to Christian, the celestial mandate has changed from Fire (trial by fire) to Water (birth by baptism), from Old Testament to New. There was a new energy being born.

It may seem strange to the reader that during the examination of these planetary exaltations we should keep bringing in the qualities of their rulerships, but they help to illustrate the personalities of the planets. It's their nature. This is myth, not math. Language is symbolic; energies blended, instincts awakened, vowels dropped, verbs inferred.

Because you have kept my commandment to endure trials, I will keep you safe in the time of trial which is going to come for the whole world, to test the people of the world.

Jupiter is the sign of spiritual integrity. Good people have kept the commandments and have listened to the message of the Most High. Jupiter is the big picture. Astrology tells us that long distance travel, foreign persons, places, and philosophies all come under the aegis of the sky god. How vast is the sky? Along the horizon is where Earth and Sky meet, be it land or sea. Jupiter rules everything under that great dome. He looks to where it leads. Stellar navigation (Jupiter) for maritime journeys (Pisces) is the way to go; but celestial signals (Jupiter) for long over-land journeys (Sagittarius) also works. Notice the emphasis here on *"the whole world, to test the people of the world."* This is the panoramic view. It carries us beyond the local horizon.

They all lie beneath the same sky. The *"test the people"* is a reference to the time of the end once again. The essence of Revelation is to alert you to the "test," to study and prepare.

Soon I shall be with you: hold firmly to what you already have, and let nobody take your prize away from you.

The time is close. Hang on to your morality. Maintain your wisdom. Heed God's word.

Those who prove victorious I will make into pillars in the sanctuary of my God, and they will stay there for ever; I will inscribe on them the name of my God and the name of the city of my God, the new Jerusalem which comes down from my God in heaven, and my own new name as well.

Both the trials and the New Jerusalem speak of a heavenly changeover yet to come, part of which will be a whole new nomenclature. This is a microcosm of what Revelation is about, the "Time of the End." Not the end of the world *per se*, but the end of this epoch of civilization, just as classical civilization ended.

Jupiter represents the souls who remain true, the spiritual pillars of the new church, yet this church knows no hammer or nail. This is the New Jerusalem *"out of heaven."* It is here that we should look for the stellar foundation stone. The sky is our essence, the Father of all things.

In scientific terms, we all derive from stardust. The "Most High" component of the Almighty are the stars, Vernal Equinox, and North Celestial Pole. I will give these people my blessing.

Notice the new name. Once the divine was called Yahweh; in Revelation it's stylized as a Lamb, yet there's not a single reference to Yahweh in Revelation. The name changes. That's because the sky picture changes and needs a new name from Age to Age. Think of the Vernal Equinox as the crosshairs of heaven, where two lines meet. In the future, blessed by Aquarius, it will have a new name once again. The name for the Almighty has changed before, and will again.

Jupiter is the planet of blessings—the guru, priest or prophet.

which comes down from my God in heaven

They are the very people who translate the wisdom of heaven for us.

So what do the geography and history of Philadelphia tell us? Of the seven cities mentioned in the seven letters, Philadelphia is the least important (*not very strong*). Jupiter in its rulership over Pisces embraces humility, a pious attitude. Those whose strengths are not of this realm fare better in the mystical attitudes of the time, of the then-New Age. The Age of Pisces is the Age of Faith, the Kingdom of God, Christianity's time.

Philadelphia was originally built as a Hellenic outpost. Like the Jews, the Greeks thought themselves the chosen ones, picked by God Almighty (Zeus in this case, the All-Father) to further "His" word, his lifestyle. Both the Greek and Judaic cultures were products of an earlier time. They were born of the previous epoch of Aries. The time of "Go out and conquer as Masters of the World" had come to an end in the Age of Pisces.

Philadelphia was a new city, created by the King Attalos II Philadelphos of Pergamum in the 2nd century BC as an outpost to spread civilization, information and trade throughout the barbaric world. It lay in a valley at the foot of a mountainous plateau in west central Turkey. It was a missionary city, erected as an outpost of Hellenic culture. A commanding highway ran from East to West through Philadelphia, along the length of Anatolia. Another highway ran northwest to southeast linking Pergamum Thyatira, Sardis, Philadelphia and Laodicea, five of the seven cities in the letters to the churches. Philadelphia was at a crossroads where Ionian Greek (Lydian) culture connected with the outside world (Phrygia). It has been postulated that the objective of Attalos was to establish a gateway and Hellenize the Phrygian population, who also spoke the Gallic tongue.

Geographically Philadelphia commanded an important pass through the mountains between the Hermus and Meander valleys. As an outpost, it also held the key to the path (the door) to the east. The hierarchy of Philadelphia had the power to both open and close the doors of trade, commerce and travel as they chose. Astrology tells us Jupiter is a spiritual sign ruling international transportation.

Philadelphia's highway was the Persian Royal Road. Royalty is heaven's missionary on Earth. This is why Zeus (Jupiter) favors Kings. They are ordained by heaven. It is clear that Homer has Zeus protecting Agamemnon from Achilles (through Athena) in the first chapter of the *Iliad*.

Philadelphia was Hellenic culture's window to the world, radiating in the east like the rays of the morning Sun to the hub of mainland Greece. This is what they perceived as a cultural wilderness of savages and heathens. Philadelphia had already earned a "missionary city" association among the Greeks as one of the *Decapolis*—cities known as part of a collective attempt to Hellenize the Mediterranean world. The term *Decapolis* specifically applied to "Ten Cities" (the translation of the word) located in Jordan and referenced by the Roman historian Pliny the Elder. However, as the etymological derivation of the word might suggest, all of these cities were of Hellenistic origin, had the *"polis"* as their design, and were founded to spread Greek culture in the Alexandrian world. It was social engineering being grafted onto the newly conquered realm. There were even two Philadelphias, one in Jordan, and one in modern day Turkey. The one in Jordan is now known as Amman, the capital of the country.

Any of the Decapolis cities were areas where cultures overlapped. It was a rich, cosmopolitan atmosphere, but that also meant there were additional ethnic tensions and misunderstandings. The Hebrew rite of circumcision horrified the Greeks, while Jewish culture thought nakedness and homosexuality was abhorrent to God.

But these were thriving areas of trade with all the benefits of international exchange. In Decapolis cities, local deities began to be called "Zeus" after the Greek god. A few began worshipping these local "Zeus" deities alongside their own *Zeus Olympios*. Since Zeus is the sky god, he is "all people under heaven," especially when they speak foreign tongues and interact with one another. This was one of the reasons Zeus favored both Troy and Crete, as both were multi-lingual cosmopolitan cultures intermingling together as one.

For the Greeks, Hellenizing foreign gods was like dipping each of these unfamiliar entities in a caramel coating of civilized culture! It's still the foreign god but now it has Zeus's blessing. Combining the names provided the familiar link. "Zeus" together with the alien god's name translates as "the foreign holy"—Semitic, Phoenician or Hebrew god—while adorning it in more familiar Hellenistic attire. It also brought a sense of familiarity to the Greek traveler and advanced the Greek tradition of cosmopolitan respect for other people's perspectives.

Jupiter is Lord of Philadelphia. Dionysus was born from the thigh

of Zeus (Greek), Bacchus was born from the thigh of Jupiter (Roman).
While Pisces rules over the feet (*fall at your feet*), Sagittarius rules the
thigh, from whence Dionysus was born.

Philadelphia is wine country. To this day the harvest continues.
Dionysus is Lord of the Grape, the child of Zeus. The flip side of the
coin is that drunkenness continues to be a local social issue in Philadelphia. It would seem Dionysus still holds sway, even today.

Christian translators see the spirit of Philadelphia as representing
the missionary zeal of the church, of spreading it well beyond the territories of the already "civilized" Ionian region. This is in agreement with
the astrological interpretation of the nature of this planet. You take
your spiritual calling, and you carry it far, far away.

One of the more interesting clues regarding Philadelphia and
Jupiter comes not from mythology, astrology, or the Hebrew Bible. It
comes from the modern Turkish name for the town. Remember, this is
the location of the church whose "angel" is in the seat of its exaltation.

The contemporary name is *Ala Shehr*, "The City of God" or "The
Exalted City."

The Church of LAODICEA

3:14 *Write to the angel of the church in Laodicea and say, "Here is the*
message of the Amen, the faithful, the true witness, the ultimate source
of God's creation: / I know all about you: how you are neither cold nor
hot. I wish you were one or the other, / but since you are neither, but only
lukewarm. I will spit you out of my mouth. / You say to yourself, "I am
rich, I have made a fortune, and have everything I want," never real-
izing that you are wretchedly and pitiably poor, and blind and naked,
too. / I warn you, buy from me the gold that has been tested in the fire
to make you really rich, and white robes to clothe you and cover your
shameful nakedness, and eye ointment to put on your eyes so that you are
able to see. / I am the one who reproves and disciplines all those he loves:
so repent in real earnest. / Look, I am standing at the door, knocking. If
one of you hears me calling and opens the door, I will come in to share his
meal, side by side with him. / Those who prove victorious I will allow to
share my throne, just as I was victorious myself and took my place with

my Father on his throne. / If anyone has ears to hear, let him listen to what the Spirit is saying to the churches."

The angel of the Church of Laodicea is Saturn in its exaltation in Libra.

Saturn is the outermost planet visible to the naked eye. In Stoic philosophy, Saturn is the first layer of the planetary energys where the incoming soul picks up its chthonic earthly attributes prior to birth. From there the soul moves through the plane of Jupiter, picking up the jovial qualities it will need from that planet. Mars provides courage and cowardice, and so on. The soul enters our solar system and at each stage gathers the "characteristics" we will be working with in this lifetime. Closest to the Earth and faster than any of the other heavenly bodies, the Moon is the final layer the soul goes through before gaining entry and being "born" (Moon) again. The Moon provides us with our body, the ultimate home and nest for the soul while here on Earth.

At death, the path is reversed. The first thing you do is shed your body (Moon), until you move through the last layer (Saturn), ascend the Milky Way and regain your heavenly perspective. This final layer of "Saturn" being shed is also reflected in the bones left behind in the grave, long after the rest of the body has decomposed. The bones are the final will and testament to a life lived. Terminus. The end.

Saturn is the Lord of Time, calendars, holidays, schedules, structures, walls, Karma, the skin and skeletal system, bones, rules, bosses, hierarchy, government, and the status quo, not necessarily in that order. If Jupiter is the spirit of the law, Saturn is the letter. Saturn is tough, hard, cold, and difficult. It's life's conditions when we reach old age. *Now* try climbing the Matterhorn or swimming the English Channel. Just getting out of a chair can be rough. Gravity gains weight.

Saturn therefore becomes *"the true witness, the ultimate source of God's creation."*

This one goes to your core, to your marrow. It is the most difficult test of all. We are not fully tested until we have lived our life. It is Thoth's recording of deeds in the Underworld before the scales in the Book of the Dead, wherein your heart must weighed against a feather. It is the return journey when all the checks and balances are called in, where we stand at the gates with our ledger being scrutinized by St. Peter. The "Pearly Gates" is actually an image that derives from Rev. 21:21.

But while Saturn is tough, when found in Libra it is fair. This is the sign of the scales, law, balance and justice. When authority (Saturn) is truly motivated by fair play (Libra), you have the essence of social (Libra) responsibility (Saturn). But it is also the internationally recognized standards of measure: be they volume or weight, cup, furlong, rod, or astronomical unit. Everybody works out an agreement and makes it the law.

The fame of Ephesus was established as one of the seven wonders of the ancient world, a seat for Mother Nature. Laodicea had its own Olympian gem.

Saturn in Libra is the Golden Rule, or at least half of it. Strictly speaking, the Golden Rule is the Aries-Libra polarity, taken to its exaltation. It is where we as individuals (Sun in Aries) stand in balance with others (Saturn in Libra). Each of these signs has a piece to play in the Golden Rule.

The Sun in Aries is the Golden Rule because the metal of the Sun is gold, and Aries is the Lord of the Military. Ultimately, this is martial law, the golden rule, the will of the king.

Saturn in Libra is the authority of law, and how we stand in balance (relation) to others, as in, "Do unto others." The Sun in Aries is where it comes home, back to you. "As you would have *others* (Libra) do unto *you* (Aries)." This essential balance is repeated over and over again in antiquity, in variations on a theme.

"Do not to others what would anger you if done to you by others."[4]

"And as ye would that men should do to you, do ye also to them likewise.[5]"

---

4 Isocrates, *Isocrates with an English Translation in Three Volumes,* by George Norlin,   Ph.D, LL.D. Cambridge, MA, Harvard University Press, London, William Heineman Ltd. 1980, p. 57.
5 Luke 6:31.

Do unto others, lest what you do comes back to you. Mud washes back on its own shores; what's good for the goose is good for the gander; play fair, etc. The Lord of Karma is sitting on the scales of justice. Standardized weights, measures, and the rule of law can be good things.

And in the end, the love you take is equal to the love you make.[6]

Saturn in Libra is the Karmic equation.

I know all about you: how you are neither cold nor hot. I wish you were one or the other

Libra is balance. Libra is the scales. On the positive side, Librans are fair-minded and just, smoothing out the situation and applying the most balanced considerations available. But on the flip side, Libra finds it very hard to make up his or her own mind and will defer to another's advice or opinion, and then weigh that into the equation. In learning to walk a balanced path, Libras avoid extremes. We are being shown two different sides of the same coin. Sometimes we need extremes to shake up situations, to make them happen.

but since you are neither, but only lukewarm.

Their decisions can be lukewarm. Not hot, not cold, but in the middle. Balanced.

I will spit you out of my mouth.

This is not worth my time. Your professionally (Saturn) polished, social niceties (Libra) don't work on me. I categorically reject what you're trying to feed me.

You say to yourself, "I am rich, I have made a fortune, and have every-

---

6 Paul 12:15.

thing I want," never realizing that you are wretchedly and pitiably
poor, and blind and naked, too.

Saturn represents the people who have succeeded, who have triumphed in earthly terms. In modern manifestations they are the
CEO's, presidents, and corporate chairs, the talented artists and famous
writers whose names are on everybody's lips. Long ago they might have
become a component of the king's court or town officials. These are the
social role models, the visible examples of worldly success. This is the
reverse of what we saw in Smyrna. There, they had nothing and held
humility in reverence. They were poor and yet rich. In material terms
the Laodicean community has everything they want and are (if we
may judge from the celestial signature) conservative (Saturn) in their
social standards (Libra), "weighing" everybody in the scales, of how
they dress, present, and interact.

Saturn in Libra. Social justice. They are blind because they do not
see their own flaws, naked because they have nothing to hide their
reality from judgment. You don't have to wait for the knock at death's
door to predict the verdict. Everybody sees the flaws. Media feeds on
in the rich and powerful. There is little value being placed on morality
here. Saturn in Libra tends to honor only the letter of the law, and then
seeks ways to surmount it.

I warn you, buy from me the gold that has been tested in the fire to make
you really rich, and white robes to clothe you and cover your shameful
nakedness, and eye ointment to put on your eyes so that you are able to
see.

Saturn is the tester, the Lord of Karma, the Keeper of the Golden
Rule. You will get back as you have given. You will be treated as you
have treated. Your experience, what you have done, is on record, will be
the judge. Time will gavel the verdict. Give more than you took; leave
more than you came in with. In its highest expression, time will grant
you social honors, possibly even carve your name in stone (Saturn).
What must we do in order to wash our robes clean? Actually, it's not
all that difficult as Isaiah explains.

Take your wrongdoing out of my sight,
cease to do evil.
Learn to do good.
Search for justice,
help the oppressed,
be just to the orphan,
plead for the widow.[7]

I am the one who reproves and disciplines all those he loves: so repent in
real earnest.

Two wonderful tough-love virtues; reproof and discipline. Saturn.
Repent in real earnest works, too. You have to mean this one. At your
core.

all those he loves

Libra is ruled by Venus. Ultimately, love is the source of this discipline. Saturn in Libra wants to be fair with everyone, wants everyone to
be measured by the same standards. On a professional level, one could
think of it as civil service. On a mechanical level, this is the office of
weights and standards (Libra). This is the realm of the Scales.

Look, I am standing at the door, knocking. If one of you hears me calling
and opens the door, I will come in to share his meal, side by side with
him.

All of the Air signs (Gemini, Libra and Aquarius) deal with communication, the transmission of information. In Gemini, it is individual expressive abilities, a quick mind learning to be developed. In
Libra, the social graces and fair play are entertained. In Aquarius the
emphasis blossoms to the collective. What's best for the people, the
network, the community? We're making rational, intelligent decisions
here.

---

7 Isaiah 1:16–18. For more from Isaiah, see also verses 1:19–20.

But if you won't open the door, the whole communicational network shuts down. There must be talking and listening, writing and reading, sending and receiving. Whether you're dealing with the individual, interpersonal or collective levels, it all boils down to a one-on-one interaction. If you are willing to be open, I will come in and share with you what there is. Saturn can be very status oriented. It will often not open the door to an unworthy passerby.

Those who prove victorious I will allow to share my throne, just as I was victorious myself and took my place with my Father on his throne.

Saturn is the seat of judgment. Saturn is the seat of power. It is the collective established power of the corporation, nation, or state. It is the government. Saturn is the Lord of Empire and he rules from his throne. If we focus on the positive attributes of this combination, it is not blind or naked power, it is heavenly sanction, ordained from above. If you successfully pass the Saturnian tests of time, patience, responsibility, and loyalty, God in heaven will grant you authority over others. From throne to throne, helping to shape the rule of law and social justice.

What does the location of Laodicea tell us? With Saturn as our "angel" here, one would expect a commercially viable town, and Laodicea qualifies. Located on an important crossroads, the banking and money exchange industry was strong. Known for its "raven-black" wool and its thriving agricultural base, it had a strong garment industry (third city of the Seven Seals) for textile manufacture and sale. Saturn's color is black; his relationship to the Earth and farming strong. Both Saturn (Latin) and Cronos (Greek) were known for their agricultural associations mythologically. Interestingly, Laodicea was also a source for the eye salves and Phrygian powders used in eye treatment referenced in the lines of scripture.

The persona of the city derives from the name. Laodice was the queen of a Hellenistic Seleucid king in the 3rd century BC. In coming to power the king had inherited a nasty war with Ptolemaic Egypt.

In settling into the harness he took care of routine business, founded and named this city for her, but things didn't turn out as planned. As time went by, the new king made a new peace with Egypt. Unfortunately for Laodice, the settlement commanded a royal marriage to help connect the two dynastic families, thereby paving the way for future international understanding. The king had to divorce Laodice in order to marry Berenice.

Saturn in Libra. The city of hard, difficult, broken corporate marriage. The marriage with Laodice was repudiated and she was exiled to Ephesus. Her ex-husband married Berenice and was compensated with a full dowry.

Saturn in Libra. A five-star marriage with all the trimmings, state-sanctioned. After using her feminine wiles to work her way back into favor with the royal court, Laodice poisoned both the king and Bernice and arranged to have their children murdered. She then proclaimed her own son to be king, the royal line having been successfully pruned. This was in 246 BC, more than three hundred years before the writing of the Book of Revelation. The Greek community knew the history of their town. They knew her story. Saturn in Libra. Tough love indeed.

There's a final note. A few short miles from Laodicea the hot calcium waters of modern Pammukale pour up through the earth. Someone in Laodicea long ago thought it would be a good idea for the town to bring the healing hot waters to the city as an added tourist attraction. The only problem was that it was discovered that after the time it took for the water to cover the four miles to reach the town, it was lukewarm and had to be re-heated. The final results were less than impressive. Aside from the temperature though, these were calcium waters. Calcium is what's in your bones. Saturn rules the bones. In Biblical terms, the following lines seem to sum up Saturn in Libra nicely. Saturn in Libra—the one who disciplines and reproves, the angel of social responsibility, structure, the spirit of the angel of the church of Laodicea.

CHAPTER FOUR

Revelation 4

The Throne of Power

4:1 *Then, in my vision, I saw a door open in heaven and heard the same voice speaking to me, the voice like a trumpet, saying, "Come up here: I will show you what is to come in the future." / With that, the Spirit possessed me and I saw a throne standing in heaven, and the One who was sitting on the throne, / and the Person sitting there looked like a diamond and a ruby. There was a rainbow encircling the throne, and this looked like an emerald. / Around the throne in a circle were twenty-four thrones, and on them I saw twenty-four elders sitting, dressed in white robes with golden crowns on their heads. / Flashes of lightning were coming from the throne, and the sound of peals of thunder, and in front of the throne there were seven flaming lamps burning, the seven Spirits of God. / Between the throne and myself was a sea that seemed to be made of glass, like crystal. In the center, grouped around the throne itself, were four animals with many eyes, in front and behind. / The first animal was like a lion, the second like a bull, the third animal had a human face, and the fourth animal was like a flying eagle. / Each of the four animals had six wings and had eyes all the way around as well as inside; and day and night they never stopped singing:*

> *"Holy, Holy, Holy*
> *is the Lord God, the Almighty;*
> *he was, he is and he is to come."*

4:9 *Every time the animals glorified and honored and gave thanks to the One sitting on the throne, who lives for ever and ever, / the twenty-four elders prostrated themselves before him to worship the One who lives for ever and ever, and threw down their crowns in front of the throne, saying, / "You are our Lord and our God, you are worthy of glory* *and honor and power, because you made all the universe and it was only by your will that everything was made and exists."*

* * * * *

In Revelation 4, heaven's framework continues to be established. The introduction was made to the composite figure, "a figure like a Son of man, dressed in a long robe," in Revelation 1:13–16. As we mentioned, his form is derived from "sketches" of the planets in their exaltations, the highest spiritual manifestation of the planetary vibrations according to astrological tradition.

Then, letters to each of the seven churches are drawn up with secretly encoded messages using mythic clues revealing the pagan personalities of the cities. That was Revelation 2 and 3.

Revelation 4 and 5 complete the foundation.

"Then, in my vision, I saw a door open in heaven"

We are now looking up to the skies.

and heard the same voice speaking to me, the voice like a trumpet, saying, "Come up here: I will show you what is to come in the future."

There is continuity here. The "inner voice" that has been speaking to us in Rev. 1 is the same. This is where the path of the future lies. It is the backbone of astrology, the spirit of prophecy. This fanfare is about to announce many important players among the heavenly host. It's coming through loud and clear and here is what it has to say. You must look to the stars to determine the future. This is the "path" our vision is guiding us to. It is not the only path and many threads are being interwoven here; but it was one of the most important, established, and oldest traditions on the African, Asian or European continents. Looking to the stars for answers about the future is well within the interpretive mainstream during this period. Revelation is sweeping us up to the skies for a peek.

With that, the Spirit possessed me and I saw a throne standing in
heaven, and the One who was sitting on the throne,

In the spirit of understanding, we look to heaven and we see the
seat of power and the One who is sitting on it at this time. Looking
back at Rev. 1:13.

a figure like a Son of man dressed in a long robe tied at the waist with
a golden girdle.

It is the *"same voice"* that we now hear. The *"Son of man"* is one of
the key images of Aquarius, usually depicted as a kneeling individual,
urn on shoulder, pouring forth a stream of celestial waters. It is the
future that is speaking. We're not there yet, but there are things it can
teach us from the future. This is still the 1st century AD. In the 1st
century AD the Vernal Equinox has just left the constellation Aries
and recently entered Pisces. It will not enter the *"Son of man"* (the constellation Aquarius) for about another two thousand years. The future
knows what happened in the past. *Their* future is describing *our* present.
The *"voice"* is telling us the story.

The Vernal Equinox is the great timekeeper of the stars. In the
West, Spring (aka East Point,) is what most often seems to step forth
as the hero of the mythic tradition. Together with the Vernal Equinox,
these ancient stargazers also looked to the Autumnal Equinox and
Solstices, a perspective on which the Hindu mythic tradition focuses.
These seasonal ingresses were the second great secret of the initiates.

The first was *"Know Thyself."*

The Vernal Equinox is the seat of power, symbolized by a throne.
But it seems that this throne "moves" across the skies over time. Or
you could think of it as the "throne" holding still, and the stars moving
into, onto, and off the throne over time. Each is a matter of perspective.
The "Image," the "Picture," the "One" who is seated upon the throne
changes over the course of time, depending on who (or what) part of
the skies it happens to be passing through at the moment. When a new

"slice" of heaven comes into focus, it brings with it a new name, a new epoch.

The *Vernal Equinox* is also related to *zero degrees of Aries*, the *first point of Aries*, the *East Point*. It is zero hours and zero minutes of Right Ascension, and these are just the astronomical names for it. It is ALWAYS our "orientation." It aligns us with the "East," our Orient. It provides our frame of reference for time, space, and navigation. Astrologically, this is linked to the *Ascendant*, where the ecliptic cuts the plane of the horizon as it rises. In astrology, the Ascendant rules the head and face, what you look like. What is on your Ascendant when you were born is said to be one of the chief determinates of your physical appearance.

This is standard astrological interpretation, the "A" of our ABCs.

In the pagan tradition, this mythic image becomes translated as the "face" of the sky, the "face" of heaven, the "Face of God." What is on the Celestial Ascendant, the Vernal Equinox, is what the face of God "looks like" at any given time in history. It changes very, very slowly, requiring approximately 25,824 years per cycle. That breaks down into 2,152 years (the "two thousand years" we keep referring to) for the Vernal Equinox to move through one sign of the zodiac, assuming a steady rate of progress. As one looks to the skies, this is the divine picture. This is what each of these civilizations saw above their homes, and what it meant in very practical terms for their relationship to the world around them. In the sky they saw the face of God looking down on them from above.

This is what peoples of the indigenous world believed as they pondered fate. As above, so below. What happens in the heavens affects what happens here on earth. But it goes far, far beyond the rain and the snow, the sunrise and the sunset, the months and the years. Myths record how the divine beings played across this earthen stage, supported by the Earth's broad bosom. The Book of Revelation describes a celestial hierarchy and predicts how the "angels" play their part for this next chapter. It was the next step on the mythic trail—a snapshot of the sky nailed to the Cross of Time. It is where the myths met Christianity, fused, and were captured in the capsule of both the New

Testament and Revelation. It was a time when Spring began to slowly swim through a school of Fish.

The composite figure in Revelation 1, "like a Son of man," is the future speaking to us. It can see how the pattern plays out across the skies, and then is supplying us with the best answers prophecy can offer. At the end of this period, things will change. From Rev. 10:7;

> *The time of waiting is over; at the time when the seventh angel is heard sounding his trumpet, God's secret intention will be fulfilled, just as he announced in the Good News told to his servants the prophets.*

Indeed, the "secret intention" has not yet been revealed. It is all part of "God's plan." The end of Pisces and the beginning of Aquarius was to be the ultimate message of the Book of Revelation, providing us with a sense of what would happen, and when. References to "the end" generally relate to "the end" of the Age of Pisces.

If we look to the Spring stars to see where we are now, we can also look back to see where we've been. It takes many years to move even a small distance in precessional terms between these "star gates." But you can also look ahead to see what is "prophesied" for the future, what is about to happen, and wonder about it as people have across the centuries. Employing the tools of stellar observation, we are getting ready to read the future from the vantage point of the 1st century AD. That is what the Book of Revelation does. Chapters 4 and 5 are the final stage of the "set-up." In Revelation 6 we actually begin to use the stellar map, the sky itself, to mark our changing prophecies across time.

The Vernal Equinox is the fusion point. But, again, the picture keeps changing as the Vernal Equinox slowly slides through the stars of heaven. The map is a star map, the one spot everyone can see, but few people do. It's been there "all the time." Written in the stars. Yet it's all simple applied astronomy.

> *and the Person sitting there looked like a diamond and a ruby. There was a rainbow encircling the throne, and this looked like an emerald.*

The zero Aries point is reflective of the diamond. It remains a standard among precious stones; it's hardness being set at "10" by definition. There is nothing harder in the gem realm. It has superlative physical qualities and makes an excellent abrasive, holding its polish and luster well. Diamonds can only be scratched by other diamonds. The etymological root of the name reveals its true nature. The Greek translation of diamond means "invincible" or "untamed." Each of these qualities smartly describes the personality of the noble, courageous, self-assured Aries.

The ruby underscores Aries martial side through the red-headed planetary Lord Mars (Greek Ares). The "rainbow" encircling the throne is the path of the planets as they ride around the Vernal Equinox and Earth each year. We might assume that it is a rainbow of seven colors that was intended, a band of color for each of the seven planets to "ride" upon. Mars, for instance, would have the red carpet, Venus the green, etc. The standard astrological colors associations to the seven planets are the following:

Table of Planetary Colors

Sun	sunlight, gold or orange
Moon	silver, pearl, pale, shaded or shadow
Mercury	yellow
Venus	green, brown
Mars	red
Jupiter	blue or purple
Saturn	black

As we have seen evoked in the angel of Smyrna, Venus is in its exaltation in Pisces. Of the seven planetary lords during the Age of Pisces, Venus is to be especially honored. What is the message of Venus in Pisces? Even though we can't see it (Pisces), God loves us (Venus). Or, if you prefer, Jesus loves us. The rainbow looked like an emerald.

All the children of the rainbow receive God's Love. We are all God's children. That's part of the beauty of Venus in Pisces. We don't (as a rule) realize (Pisces-subconscious) how much we are loved by those who have preceded us in the spirit realm, all those who have gone before.

Our revelatory list includes three of the four precious stones, diamonds, rubies and emeralds, leaving out only sapphires. It's time we took a closer look at "*the throne*."

Deus Ex Machina

If we are successfully interpreting heaven's imagery, the throne is the seat of power, from whence all authority flows.

From here we must digress in order to explain a very important mythic structure, one fundamental to the comprehension of the throne.

If the Vernal Equinox is as powerful as those in the pagan world imagined, it's not surprising it would garner many names or have many images associated with it. Within Revelation we come across a number of motifs which all relate back to this point of power, what Revelation is about to introduce as the "*Throne of Heaven*."

At first glance, one might imagine that the Throne of Heaven is a part of the province of Zeus or Jupiter, the Sky. But, in fact, the Throne of Heaven is the *union* of the King and Queen of Heaven, of Heaven and Earth. It is the point when the eternal masculine and feminine merge, giving birth to the New Year and all that goes with it. We are stepping back into time, when many of the old agrarian calendars celebrated New Year in Spring, not January. The calendars of many mideastern cultures still commence in Spring. The Vernal Equinox, our seasonal marker, is the marriage of Heaven and Earth. It is when day and night are equal, a point that bursts into flames when ignited by the timely arrival of the Sun.

Jupiter is the Sky, the All-Father. His realm includes the eagle, thunderbolt, and rain. He commands Olympus, that mythic land far above us, where no snow ever falls. Those hallowed halls are out there beyond the atmosphere.

Juno is the Queen of Heaven. She is the earth-based, temple-oriented feminine, celestially characterized as the Earth—and her belt, the equator, an imaginary band that runs around the bulging belly of Mother Earth. The terrestrial equator projected into space is the celestial equator. Here Mother Earth's belly crosses the ecliptic. It is the place where they make love. When these two lines cross, the union of Heaven and Earth occurs.

In astronomical terms, it's called the Vernal Equinox and is, by definition 0 hours, 0 minutes and 0 seconds of Right Ascension. It marks the start of Spring.

Jupiter's realm is symbolized as the path of the ecliptic, the path of the Sun, the Sky. Juno's realm is symbolized as the path of the equator, the belt of Mother Earth.

Sparked by the Sun, they are fused by the equinoxes, days of celebration when the Sun rides his chariot along the equatorial road from sunup to sundown. Life stands in balance as the seasons are renewed. Myth tells us the seasons reared Juno. Here on Earth we look at it as though it may have been the other way around.

Who was the child of the union between Jupiter and Juno, between Zeus and Hera? They had only one mythical male heir—the Roman Mars, the Greek Ares. Astrologically he is the ruler of Aries, the Ascendant, head and face, what you look like, the 1st house, and Vernal Equinox. This was the mythic map, a slice of sacred time.

When Christianity swept away the pagan king and queen of the skies, the Vernal Equinox simply becomes the "marriage." In this case, Jesus was the bridegroom and life on earth was the bride—this is the union of Heaven and Earth. Life is born to its moment and plays across the World Stage. We all watch. History records the final tally. Time is now, for the last two thousand years, measured by the annual birth of Jesus as part of the New Year.

Mythic clues involving the sacred marriage can be found throughout ancient cultures. The Greeks called it *Hieros gamos*, the "holy wedding" or "coupling." It was conducted in the Spring and involved participants who felt they had profound religious experiences or ecstasy through sexual intercourse. Participants assumed characteristics of the deities, sometimes channeling the deity themselves, and sought fertility for the animals, land, people and *polis*.

Looking to the earlier Chaldaean period, marriage between two deities was enacted in a symbolic ceremony (*hasadu*) in which the cult statues were brought together. A ceremonial bed was provided so the statues could "marry." Marduk and Sarpanitu are but one example and are part of New Year ceremonies; others are Nabu and Tasmetu, Samas and Aya, and Anu and Antu. This is not a new concept.

While these ancient ceremonies occurred every year, they were especially important when the New Year—an alignment observed by watching the heavens—left one asterism or constellation and moved into a new one, or when the Right Ascension aligned with a specific star.

The whole point of astrological advice, of heavenly advice, is to provide the "when." The ritual (Time) provided the framework of "when" to reflect Heaven's will on Earth. The Vernal Equinox is a hot spot, the power point, the Author of Creation as the Lord of Spring and new beginnings.

The "marriage" was to be consummated. It was to be grounded on Earth. That was the whole point. These rituals were not simply symbolic.

Working with the heavens observationally can be difficult, as there are few fixed frames of reference. With the development of spherical trigonometry we have learned how to figure out the skies using a mathematical framework. The ecliptic pole, the axis around which the heavens spin, is itself pirouetting through space. It is not a "visual" frame of reference, it is a mathematical one. Observation evolved before calculation, and a system of observation developed before a system of calculation.

The Earth provides a steady frame of reference. The rising and setting of the stars and planets can be measured against the horizon. Natural horizons were first employed, using the desert, mountains, islands or sea, but artificial horizons followed later. The pole star, when there is one, is a result of the Earth's rotational motion, not the sky's. The pole star provides a fixed frame of *observational* reference. Stone columns provide fixed frames of reference; temples, steeples and may-poles all provide fixed frames of reference. They are all rooted in the earth.

This is the Queen's realm, the realm of the Earth and the feminine. Mythologically the throne is associated with Isis and Hera. Isis wears a throne on her head as a symbol of power, while Hera was known as the Goddess of the Throne. Her son, Hephaestus (Roman Vulcan), had crafted a beautiful chair for her as a gift. Once she sat in it, she could not get up. Yet, just as both parents are involved in conception, it is the woman who must carry the child to term. So the celestial union involves both, but is framed by the Earth. It is formed by the feminine.

The union of the Vernal Equinox moves steadily against the backdrop of the sky, year by year. As a new constellation mounts the throne, as a new asterism mounts the throne, a new "vibration" seizes power and heralds the awaited dawn. But each new dawn gives way to the next, and the next. These "myths" are not merely limited to the classical realm. Isaiah also sings of the Creator husband in the Old Testament:

> *For your Creator is your husband,*
> *Yahweh Sabaoth is his name,*
> *the Holy One of Israel is your redeemer,*
> *he is called God of the whole world.*[1]

In this case the divine is mirrored by heaven above (and specifically the Vernal Equinox) while the feminine is represented by one of her mortal offspring. Divine marriage, *a la* Judaism. Time marches on.

All of this brings up a very important technical point for astrologers. The astrology of today is born of mathematics and computers. These systems are based upon the ecliptic, the yearly path of the Sun. These "alignments" that we keep speaking of are not the "aspects of longitude" that astrologers work with in reading charts, these are the parallels of declination. Parallels of declination are observational in nature, not mathematical. Astronomers maintain this tradition by calling the union of the two lines (ecliptic and equator) 0 hours, 0 minutes, and 0 seconds, but then the clock begins to track along the equatorial, not the ecliptical belt.

This is the older, observational system. This is the tradition that

---

1 Isaiah 54:5.

myth is attempting to preserve in its story line. This was the offspring of the Queen of the Feminine, Hera. The mathematical is not right; the observational system is not wrong. They are each two different ways of looking at the picture. However, to interpret the "code" of the Book of Revelation, we need to look at the older traditional form.

Working with this design, we have a parade of New Year's Creation myths going as far back as people can remember. Western civilization tends to view Creation differently than the pagans do. Judaic tradition believes that Creation began with Adam and Eve. In AD 2000, this was 5760 lunar years earlier or in 3760 BC. Using his Biblical computations, Archbishop Ussher thought Creation started in the year 4004 BC. Scientists speculate that Creation began with the Big Bang some 13.73 billion years ago. Each of these notions defines a particular "moment" for the beginning of Creation.

Pagan nations felt that Creation didn't start from a particular point in time, but rather that it began again each year, as part of a new cycle. New Year's is when they collectively celebrated this birth together. History was seen as a tapestry of eastern stars, specific life dramas threaded together, one after the other. They rise, mount the throne, have their moment and move on, like the old bearded man with the sickle giving way to the baby with the numerical sash on New Year's Eve.

Framed against the heavenly throne, we have seen birds, bulls, and rams led to the altar. What's important is to stand in right relation to God, successfully interpreting the Divine Will, which is ever eternal, but also ever changing.

The point, in the pagan perspective, is not so much to honor any one of these *previous* images, as to honor the *current* position in the time/space continuum. What is vital is where the Spring-marker stands now—and to be able to successfully *interpret* what that means to correctly stand in right relation in *this* day and time. The gods of the past were appropriate to their time, but they're over. The religions of the past were appropriate to their time, but they're history. The essential question is, what does heaven have to say now? It's for this reason that Moses was so critical of the Golden Calf during the Age of Aries. That time had passed.

The message derived from years of observation is that we must "eat" whatever Heaven serves us, through each of these "Ages," and that we must do it with reverence, appreciation, and while giving thanks. Civilization learns specific lessons during each Age. It's akin to teaching children different abilities in each grade. This is the "spiritual food" that must be digested, the food of *"this"* time. We each eat and drink of the body and blood of God, of Life. Each is part of a long line offering heaven's Will for mortals. We might consume the manna of our time. It's the communion of the moment.

The ecliptic and celestial equator are the astronomical markers used to identify the "throne" across time. It has been interpreted as the "throne," "chair," "marriage," "power," "altar," "union of Heaven and Earth" or simply "union." It has been called the names of each of the various stellar images that have occupied its seat.

The Right Ascension Midheaven, the RAMC is our familiar Ram. Naturally, this image of Vernal Equinox "married" to the first point of Aries was perfectly appropriate while it moved through that constellation. But in mythic and astrological terms it wasn't correct following the 1st century AD. It was then the time of the Fish, the sign of Jonah.

The Greeks greatly enhanced the study of modern spherical trigonometry, but with the birth of celestial mathematics, the observational tradition began to fail. The temples were neglected. The baton of stellar evolution passed to the Romans, who renamed the gods and left it at that. The incoming Christian administration was not interested in a discipline that evoked a chorus of pagan gods. In the West, astronomy suffered as a result. Astronomical development passed to the Arabs and the Hindus. At the end of the Age of Aries, people were conditioned to using the sign of the Ram as the celestial starting point. They had been doing so for many centuries.

To this day, the first day of Spring starts with *"zero degrees of Aries,"* by definition. Yet the Springtime point is clearly in the constellation of the Fish. There is a temporal imbalance here. We haven't updated our software. With the loss of a mythological helmsman at the rudder, the Ram drifted in time as the last official marker of a new Spring, even though star patterns continued to shift and had long since passed this constellation by. This is the difference between constellation and sign.

Two thousand years ago the "East Stars" were in the constellation Aries, and the image correctly initiated Spring. But as Spring passed through Aries to Pisces, the constellaton Aries NO LONGER marked the start.

In using the "Lamb" as a metaphorical image (as we have seen, there were many to choose from), Revelation is guilty of the same "crime" the Hebrews of the Exodus were committing when they donated all their jewelry to the making of a "Golden Calf" during the time of the Ram! Moses was outraged and smashed the tablets. He had been up in the high places reading the skies, away from the people for an extended period of time. When he returned, he was not happy.

Across the Sea of Time the arthritic grip of tradition held onto this dated image—that of Ram as Spring's marker. We've "hardwired it" to the Vernal Equinox, even though a watery world was for centuries the rightful heir. The Vernal Equinox has not so much clung to the Ram, as there has been no new mythic scribe to paint the new picture, at least not in the West. We have preserved a system of stale symbolic "metrics" whose time ran out two thousand years ago. We have forgotten how to look for a "sign," yet it's as simple as the marriage of two-crossed lines; ecliptic and equator. "X" marks the spot.

As the Vernal Equinox moves across heaven, it should jettison these older, outdated images. What was once the greatest point of power for Creation has moved on. We have a new orientation (literally, a new "East Point"), a new focus, a new Spring. Twins gave way to Bull. Bull gave way to Ram. The Ram gives way to the Fish. And, of course, the Fish gives way to the Man. Creation. New. Every year. It's a far cry from Archbishop Ussher's 4004 BC.

Revelation marked the inception of a New Age and a new era—the Age of Pisces; but it looked ahead to the future, to the Age following the Age of Pisces, the start of yet another New Age—the Age of Aquarius, the coming of the "Sign of Man." This conceptual overlap of New Ages, one just commencing (1st century AD) and prophecies of another in the future (21st century AD), was to cause much confusion. Even the disciples had a hard time understanding the notion, as evidenced by their question recorded in the book of Matthew.

And when he was sitting on the Mount of Olives the disciples came and asked him privately, "Tell us, when is this going to happen, and what will be the sign of your coming and of the end of the world?[2]

First of all, where was Jesus sitting? He was sitting on the Mount of Olives. The olive is Athena's "fruit." Athena is the Goddess of Wisdom. Jesus was sitting in a grove of wisdom. He was getting ready to tell them something important, something "wise." Notice that the disciples asked about *"the end of the world."* But the response was as follows; he described the conditions that will transpire before circumstances unfold and then answers with,

All this is only the beginning of the birth pangs.

They asked about the end of the world, he replied with images of labor pains. They don't fully understand. It's not the end of the world; it's the end of a period of time, a way of doing things. A new epoch had come onto the planet, and in the West it largely manifested as the cohesion of Christianity in its various forms. The disciples asked about "the end of the world," but in the centuries just past, civilization had just experienced another "end of the world," the end of the Age of Aries. Yet life went on. The disciples are being schooled by the teacher.

Returning to our lines of Revelation,

Around the throne in a circle were twenty-four thrones, and on them I saw twenty-four elders sitting, dressed in white robes with golden crowns on their heads.

Notice that there is more than one throne. There are other "points" of power or symbols of authority. They are not as strong or as powerful as the main throne, but they each have their say, in their time. Here, they admit to the common unity shared by all.

In ancient astrological thinking, each of the 24 hours had a planet

---

2 Matthew 24:3.

ruling over it, rulership designated by a regular sequence. The planet that ruled over the Sunrise hour became the ruler over that day of the week. Sunrise marked the birth of the day and was "defined" as 6 AM. The planetary hour that ruled sunrise claimed that day as his "prize." It was part of His or Her realm.

The sequence of planets is based upon the relative speed of the planet through the sky. Sunrise (6 AM) was when the day was born. The Moon ruled Sunrise on Monday, therefore the Moon ruled Monday. This sequence of the planets is listed in the table below. Starting with Saturn, the outermost visible planet, next comes Jupiter, Mars and then the Sun, Venus, Mercury and the Moon. The nomenclature for the planetary rulers of the days of the week is more easily seen in the Romance languages. Monday is, of course, Moon day, while Mardi (Tuesday) is Mars, Mercredi (Wednesday) Mercury, Jeudi (Thursday) Jupiter, and Vendredi (Friday) Venus. Saturday and Sunday are obvious.

Around the throne are the 24 lords, part of and subservient to the greater authority, but each with his own sphere of influence. Because they are dressed in white robes, they have gone through the purification process. The gold crowns on their heads naturally describe their power and authority.

Flashes of lightning were coming from the throne, and the sound of peals of thunder, and in front of the throne there were seven flaming lamps burning, the seven Spirits of God.

The Vernal Equinox is a source of thunder and lightning. These are the calling cards of the Sky God. When stars cross the Vernal Equinox, sparks fly. When the Vernal Equinox aligns with significant celestial triggers, discharges of power are released—either literally as bolts of lightning, or as life-events that suddenly "rain down" on the mortals here on Earth below. The seven flaming lamps are the seven visible planets, grouping the Sun and Moon in with the other five visible moving celestial bodies. These are the seven Spirits of God.

And this is why the Sun is not what is being "circled" here in astronomical terms as the center of our solar system. This is the heavenly perspective as seen from the geocentric bosom of Mother Earth, with our feet planted squarely on the ground, not from some academically removed location for the sake of mathematical formulas. The myths describe what they saw "circling" above them in the sky. It was an

Sunrise Table / Days of the Week

	Mon	Tues	Wed	Thurs	Fri	Sat	Sun
Midnight	Saturn	Sun	Moon	Mars	Merc	Jupiter	Venus
1 AM	Jupiter	Venus	Saturn	Sun	Moon	Mars	Merc
2 AM	Mars	Merc	Jupiter	Venus	Saturn	Sun	Moon
3 AM	Sun	Moon	Mars	Merc	Jupiter	Venus	Saturn
4 AM	Venus	Saturn	Sun	Moon	Mars	Merc	Jupiter
5 AM	Merc	Jupiter	Venus	Saturn	Sun	Moon	Mars
Sunrise:	Moon	Mars	Mercury	Jupiter	Venus	Saturn	Sun
7 AM	Saturn	Sun	Moon	Mars	Merc	Jupiter	Venus
8 AM	Jupiter	Venus	Saturn	Sun	Moon	Mars	Merc
9 AM	Mars	Merc	Jupiter	Venus	Saturn	Sun	Moon
10 AM	Sun	Moon	Mars	Merc	Jupiter	Venus	Saturn
11 AM	Venus	Saturn	Sun	Moon	Mars	Merc	Jupiter
Noon	Merc	Jupiter	Venus	Saturn	Sun	Moon	Mars
1 PM	Moon	Mars	Merc	Jupiter	Venus	Saturn	Sun
2 PM	Saturn	Sun	Moon	Mars	Merc	Jupiter	Venus
3 PM	Jupiter	Venus	Saturn	Sun	Moon	Mars	Merc
4 PM	Mars	Merc	Jupiter	Venus	Saturn	Sun	Moon
5 PM	Sun	Moon	Mars	Merc	Jupiter	Venus	Saturn
6 PM	Venus	Saturn	Sun	Moon	Mars	Merc	Jupiter
7 PM	Merc	Jupiter	Venus	Saturn	Sun	Moon	Mars
8 PM	Moon	Mars	Merc	Jupiter	Venus	Saturn	Sun
9 PM	Saturn	Sun	Moon	Mars	Merc	Jupiter	Venus
10 PM	Jupiter	Venus	Saturn	Sun	Moon	Mars	Merc
11 PM	Mars	Merc	Jupiter	Venus	Saturn	Sun	Moon

observational system. These positions "focus" on the Vernal Equinox, a metaphorical, social, and spiritual "center" derived through both observation and mathematics. All Spring, all Creation, all Time is subservient to this "center."

The seven Spirits of God are "*in front of*" the throne.

Between the throne and myself was a sea that seemed to be made of glass, like crystal.

The throne seems to be "suspended" in something as we gaze through its translucent surface to the planets and stars above. A sea through which mythical beings appear to "swim." Here that essence is being described for us. It "*seemed to be made of glass, like crystal.*"

In the center, grouped around the throne itself, were four animals with many eyes, in front and behind. The first animal was like a lion, the second like a bull, the third animal had a human face, and the fourth animal was like a flying eagle.

Together with the rainbow, the twenty-four thrones and the seven Spirits in front of the throne, we now have other stars being described. These lines leap out at any student of astrology.

Lion, bull, human and eagle; Leo, Taurus, Aquarius and Scorpio, the four fixed signs of the zodiac, in correct sequential order, starting with Leo and moving "backwards" (precessional and daily order, not seasonal). Notice Aquarius is here being depicted as "*an animal*" with "*a human face.*" This is a mythological device for putting him on the same "level" (animal) as the others, while at the same time distinguishing it from the others.

Each of the four animals had six wings and had eyes all the way around as well as inside; and day and night they never stopped singing:

"Holy, Holy, Holy
is the Lord God, the Almighty;
he was, he is and he is to come."

In order to understand what these four "fixed" constellations are singing, it is first important to understand the nature of fixed energy. The six wings and incantation come from Isaiah 6: 2–3,

> *Above him stood seraphs, each one with six wings; two to cover its face, two to cover its feet and two for flying; and they were shouting these words to each other:*

> *"Holy, holy, holy is Yahweh Sabaoth,*
> *His glory fills the whole earth.*

The "feet" are a euphemism for the sexual organs. Also, note that the Old Testament team is shouting, while the Revelation team is singing. That's an apt shift from raw nature of Aries to the gentle spirit of Pisces.

The Celestial Qualities

The qualities of astrology are divided into three; cardinal, fixed and mutable signs. Each of the twelve signs of the zodiac is allocated one of the following qualities.

Cardinal Signs initiate activities. These are the start of the seasons, Aries (Spring), Cancer (Summer), Libra (Autumn) and Capricorn (Winter). When the Sun (our timekeeper) enters any of these four signs, it marks a new cycle of seasonal activity.

The **Fixed Signs** (Taurus, Leo, Scorpio, Aquarius) mark the middle month of each season. This is the heart of Spring, Summer, Fall and Winter where conditions have stabilized into picture post-cards—beautiful flowers in Spring, hot days and fun in the Sun in summer, gathering the harvest of Fall, or husbanding provisions for the long cold months of Winter. In life these signs deal with the absolutes: always, never and forever. Durability and permanence are important components of their worldview.

The **Mutable Signs** (Gemini, Virgo, Sagittarius, Pisces) mark the final month of each of the seasons. These are times of adaptation and transition. In a positive context they are flexible and adaptable, rolling with life's fluctuations. On the flip side they vacillate and are often reluctant to set out on bold new initiatives. (Sagittarius is better at this than the others. As the mutable Fire sign of the group, it has more spark, more daring.) Nevertheless, these are the explorers and the information seekers, often worldly wise in their ways.

What the Fixed Signs, (Leo, Taurus, Aquarius and Scorpio) have done is to hymn their praises to the glory of the Lord of Eternity. "This is the way it always has been, is now, and forever will be." These are the eternal truths, and the four signs that deal with permanence and longevity come together in their celestial choir to help us remember. Even though the four fixed signs are lords, even though the 24 elders are lords, they are subservient to the over-riding power, the Supreme Power. They are collectively getting down on a metaphorical knee and acknowledging celestial supremacy to the throne and the One sitting there. It all emanates from this source, or so Rev. 4 would seem to suggest.

Now, let's put them all together.

Come up to the skies, and I will show you what is to come in the future. We are being shown the stars. There was a rainbow around the throne, the path followed by the stars and planets, the twenty four elders are the hours of the day, and the Seven Spirits, the seven planets themselves which have been named for the days of the week. The four fixed signs represent the four seasons, which together equal a year.

The 24 hours of the day (24 thrones), seven days of the week (Seven Spirits), and the four seasons of the year (four animals) are not more powerful than the throne—the Vernal Equinox, or Spring and its position in the heavens at any given time. He (the Lord), She (Hera, Juno or Isis with the throne on her head) or It (the Lamb), is more powerful than any of the others (who threw down their crowns and paid homage to the one sitting on the throne).

because you *made all the universe and it was only by your will that everything was made and exists.*

We are here establishing the celestial hierarchy in mythic form. This is the Creator in all His Power and Glory, which is even more powerful than the planetary combinations astrologers are so fond of. Or so says Rev. 4.

Blessings to All from the Most High.

CHAPTER FIVE

Revelation 5

The Lamb takes the Scroll

5:1 *I saw that in the right hand of the One sitting on the throne there was a scroll that had writing on back and front and was sealed with seven seals. / Then I saw a powerful angel who called with a loud voice, "Is there anything worthy to open the scroll and break the seven seals of it?" / But there was no one, in heaven or on earth or under the earth, who was able to open the scroll and read it. I wept bitterly because there was nobody fit to open the scroll and read it, / but one of the elders said to me, "There is no need to cry: the Lion of the tribe of Judah, the Root of David, has triumphed, and he will open the scroll and the seven seals of it." Then I saw, standing between the throne with its four animals and the circle of the elders, a Lamb that seemed to have been sacrificed; it had seven horns, and it had seven eyes, which are the seven Spirits God has sent out all over the world. / The Lamb came forward to take the scroll from the right hand of the One sitting on the throne, / and when he took it, the four animals prostrated themselves before him and with them the twenty-four elders; each one of them was holding a harp and had a golden bowl full of incense made of the prayers of the saints. / They sang a new hymn:*

> *"You are worthy to take the scroll*
> *and break the seals of it,*
> *because you were sacrificed, and with your blood*
> *you bought men for God*
> *of every race, language, people and nation*
> *and made them a line of kings and priests,*
> *to serve our God and to rule the world."*

5:11 *In my vision, I heard the sound of an immense number of angels gathered around the throne and the animals and the elders; there were* *ten thousand times ten thousand of them and thousands upon thousands, / shouting, "The Lamb that was sacrificed is worthy to be given power, riches, wisdom, strength, honor, glory and blessing." / Then I heard all the living things in creation—everything that lives in the air, and on the ground, and under the ground, and in the sea, crying, "To the One who is sitting on the throne and to the Lamb, be all praise, honor, glory and power, for ever and ever." / And the four animals said, "Amen"; and the elders prostrated themselves to worship.*

* * * * *

With Rev. 4 setting the stage, all of the characters take their appointed places. Here, the One sitting on the throne (the Vernal Equinox) is holding a Scroll in His Hand.

The stars of heaven are linked together in various patterns. At the largest level, we group stars in constellations, for instance, the Lion, Crab and Swan, etc. But there are other groups, like the Beehive in Cancer. These are called "clusters," a smaller (size is relative) grouping of stars in a bundle. In-between clusters and constellations, there is another grouping called "asterisms." For instance: within the constellation of the Bull (Taurus), there are several stellar images. There is the Pleiades, a star cluster in the shoulder of the charging bull, and the Hyades, the "V" or white triangle in the head of the Bull. The head of Medusa in the hand of the constellation Perseus is another asterism. They are part of the bigger picture.

In the first century AD the Vernal Equinox was moving through the *asterism* known to the Chinese as *Wae Ping*, "a rolled screen." This is our "Scroll" in Revelation. It is the same image being described by two different languages.

Here's what the dictionary says about a scroll:

scroll |skrōl|, noun
• a roll of parchment or paper for writing or painting on.
• an ancient book or document on such a roll.
• an ornamental design or carving resembling a partly unrolled

scroll of parchment, e.g., on a capital column or at the end of a
stringed instrument.

 • Art & Heraldry a depiction of a narrow ribbon bearing a
motto or inscription.

Chinese rolled screen = Western scroll.

The God of Heaven is holding a Scroll in his hand. From 407 BC
to AD 1052 the seven stars of the Scroll were in the hand, or under the
influence of, "the power," as seen in the sky picture. One by one, Spring
was passing over these stars.

> *I saw that in the right hand of the One sitting on the throne there was
> a scroll that had writing on back and front and was sealed with seven
> seals.*

There are seven stars that represent the Seven Seals. As Spring
passes over each of these, the "seal" is opened, and we, all those living
and watching the choreography play out, look to these times as the
celestial script unfolds here on Earth.

The "*writing on back and front*" describes where they stand in time.
Notice that it starts with "back," rather than "front and back." This
is intentional. Stars have come, stars have gone. *Alpha Piscium*, the
brightest star in the constellation Pisces, aligned with Spring in 407
BC. The second star, *xi Piscium*, aligned with Spring in 235 BC while the
most recent star to have crossed the cardinal direction East at the time
of the writing of Revelation was the third star in the series *nu Piscium*
in AD 15.

Why would the authors of Revelation make "predictions" about
events already past? There are several reasons. One of which is because
they are giving us the *entire* stellar picture. It's difficult enough
attempting to decipher a sky story, never mind having to jump right in
the middle of the symbolism. The "*writing on back and front*" is telling
us some of the "seals" (stars) have already gone by, "*back*" first (those

gone by) and *"front"* (those yet to happen). This follows the correct chronological order for all the seals.

The stars placed in the right hand of the one seated on the throne are on the left side of the Vernal Equinox as seen from Earth. We are being asked to look back to the direction from which they came, to stars that have already aligned. These stars were written about before the author of Revelation put pen to parchment—centuries before.

> *Then I saw a powerful angel who called with a loud voice, "Is there anything worthy to open the scroll and break the seven seals of it?"*

Can anybody or anything open it?

> *But there was no one, in heaven or on earth or under the earth, who was able to open the scroll and read it. I wept bitterly because there was nobody fit to open the scroll and read it,*

There is no one to open it.

> *but one of the elders said to me, "There is no need to cry: the Lion of the tribe of Judah, the Root of David, has triumphed, and he will open the scroll and the seven seals of it."*

There is hope. David, the King (Lion) of Judah has triumphed. This is the key, the tool, the way to open the Scroll and the Seven Seals (stars). He, or his administration, figured out the sky, the Vernal Equinox and how to translate it in tangible terms.

> *Then I saw, standing between the throne with its four animals and the circle of the elders, a Lamb that seemed to have been sacrificed; it had seven horns, and it had seven eyes, which are the seven Spirits God has sent out all over the world.*

We're back to the mythical framework of heaven. The four animals are the four fixed signs of the zodiac. The *Lamb that seemed to have been sacrificed* is both Jesus and the Spring position of the Vernal Equinox, at least while Revelation is being written. Zero degrees of Aries is the sign of the Ram at its beginning, in its infancy, when it first starts. Mythologically it is symbolized as the Ram in infancy, the Lamb. Code for Zero Aries. Spring!

The Lamb joins a long line of stellar images that have been on the seat of the "throne." He is now being honored as "divine." The Lamb IS Spring, the cardinal direction East, the Sun at Sunrise on the first day of Spring, when it sits on the equator and triumphs over darkness. *The Lamb* has the power to open the seals, to astronomically align with the stars, to trigger their influences. Even the astronomical marker draws from this image of the Ram. It is the Right Ascension Midheaven, or the RAMC, at zero degrees, zero minutes and zero seconds. It is the "Lamb" as it is being born.

This has been the pagan model all along. What is different is that there was a New Age and a new religion being born called Christianity, the outline of a Fish. The seven horns and the seven eyes are identified for us. They are *the seven Spirits God has sent out all over the world*, the planets or "wanderers" of heaven which impact all peoples in all places at all times. It is seven sets of eyes watching what each of us do.

This is the picture being described in heaven, and its secret message is left there for those who know how to follow such clues.

> *The Lamb came forward to take the scroll from the right hand of the One sitting on the throne*

The Lamb is now the image that takes the Scroll from the hand of the One sitting on the "throne." They are becoming One. This is Spring's celestial marker.

> *and when he took it, the four animals prostrated themselves before him and with them the twenty-four elders; each one of them was holding a harp and had a golden bowl full of incense made of the prayers of the saints.*

The Lamb is now assuming the position of power, and all the other lords of Creation are getting ready to acknowledge this higher power. The final clause sets the stage:

They sang a new hymn:

"You are worthy to take the scroll
and break the seals of it,
because you were sacrificed, and with your blood
you bought men for God
of every race, language, people and nation
and made them a line of kings and priests,
to serve our God and to rule the world."

There is indeed a new hymn in heaven. There is a new covenant. What this new hymn is saying is that the Lamb (Spring) offered up its life to the people of the world and molded a new generation of kings and priests (the Christian hierarchical community) to serve God and rule the world.

In my vision, I heard the sound of an immense number of angels gathered around the throne and the animals and the elders; there were ten thousand times ten thousand of them and thousands upon thousands,

Pisces has been a time of misunderstanding, loss, suffering and persecution. These are the themes that Pisces needs so that faith can be exercised and tested. The number of people who have stood up for truth and died in its defense are the immense number of souls gathered around the throne watching the show on Earth. There were ten thousand times ten thousand of them and thousands upon thousands. We will hear from these victorious souls again in Rev. 6: 9.

shouting, "The Lamb that was sacrificed is worthy to be given power, riches, wisdom, strength, honor, glory and blessing."

What are all these voices shouting? The Lamb now has the power. Spring has the power. The power to do what? The power to open the seals.

And the four animals said, "Amen"; and the elders prostrated themselves to worship."

It has been done. Everyone of consequence agrees.

CHAPTER SIX

Revelation 6

The Lamb Opens the Seals

6:1 *Then I saw the Lamb break one of the seven seals, and I heard one of the four animals shout in a voice like thunder, "Come." / Immediately a white horse appeared, and the rider on it was holding a bow; he was given the victor's crown and he went away, to go from victory to victory.*

6:3 *When he broke the second seal, I heard the second animal shout, "Come." / And out came another horse, bright red, and its rider was given this duty: to take away peace from the earth and set people killing each other. He was given a huge sword.*

6:5 *When he broke the third seal, I heard the third animal shout, "Come," Immediately a black horse appeared, and its rider was holding a pair of scales; / and I seemed to hear a voice shout from among the four animals and say, "A ration of corn for a day's wages, and three rations of barley for a day's wages, but do not tamper with the oil or the wine."*

6:7 *When he broke the fourth seal, I heard the voice of the fourth animal shout, "Come."*

6:8 *Immediately another horse appeared, deathly pale, and its rider was called Plague, and Hades followed at his heels. They were given authority over a quarter of the earth, to kill by the sword, by famine, by plague and wild beasts.*

6:9 *When he broke the fifth seal, I saw underneath the altar the souls of all the people who had been killed on account of the word of God, for witnessing to it. They shouted aloud, / "Holy, faithful Master, how much longer will you wait before you pass sentence and take vengeance for our death on the inhabitants of the earth?" / Each of them was given a white* *robe, and they were told to be patient a little longer, until the roll was complete and their fellow servants and brothers had been killed just as they had been.*

6:12 *In my vision, when he broke the sixth seal, there was a violent earthquake and the sun went as black as coarse sackcloth; the moon turned red as blood all over, / and the stars of the sky fell on to the earth like figs dropping from a fig tree when a high wind shakes it; / the sky disappeared like a scroll rolling up and all the mountains and islands were shaken from their places. / Then all the earthly rulers, the governors and the commanders, the rich people and the men of the influence, the whole population, slaves and citizens, took to the mountains to hide in caves and among the rocks. They said to the mountains and the rocks, "Fall on us and hide us away from the One who sits on the throne and from the anger of the Lamb. For the Great Day of his anger has come, and who can survive it?"*

* * * * *

We have now reached a critical point in this book. We now shift from standard astrological framework, our literary foundation so far, into application. Rev. 1 was the introduction and composite mythic figure saying hello to us from the future. Rev. 2 and 3 establish the seven spirits before the throne of god as the planetary energies, rooted in the cities culturally appropriate to their forebears, written in Greek for a mainly Greek audience. With Rev. 4 and 5 we are introduced to the throne of heaven, together with the hourly, daily and yearly seasonal entities. So far, it's all been generic. Six of the Seven Seals are opened in Rev. 6. Now we lay these stellar maps across the skies in real time.

The First Seal

6:1 Then I saw the Lamb break one of the seven seals, and I heard one of the four animals shout in a voice like thunder, "Come."

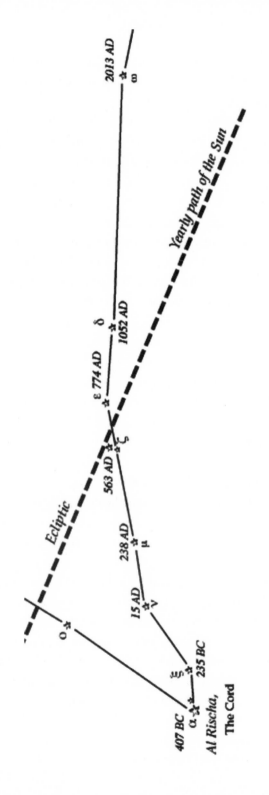

The Scroll

This is what we've been waiting for. The Lamb (Vernal Equinox) aligns with the first of the seven stars, and one of the four animals calls forth the power of the first Star Gate.

The year is 407 BC. *Al Rischa* (the Cord, *Alpha Piscium*), aligns with Spring. The star was given this name because from here extend the cords leading to the two fish of the constellation Pisces. *Al Rischa* is the stellar knot where the two cords are tied together.

The mythic and stellar records suggest that this should be the beginning of the New Age, several centuries prior to the birth of the Messiah, another marker for the start of the Age of Pisces. Pisces is a sign of the people, but it is not a sign of the people in the same way Aquarius is. Aquarius people means everybody, high, low, in, out, mainstream, non-mainstream. Pisces people represents those people left on the fringes of society; the poor, the lost, the humble and the ailing. These are the people that are being referenced by Pisces: the mobs and the "riff-raff," those bereft of social distinction.

In 410 BC one layer between patrician and commoner was being dissolved, a legal wall beginning to crumble. For the first time in history (according to Livy), the people's (plebeian) candidates were given office, given a vote.

... the important thing was that a beginning had been made... the time had come for the commons to have their share of real power.[1]

In 406 BC, at the start of a war with Veii, the Roman Senate...

... issued a decree for the payment of soldiers on service out of public funds. Hitherto every man had served at his own expense.

The joy at this innovation was unprecedented. Men mobbed the Senate House, wrung the hands of members as they came out, called them Fathers indeed, in every sense of the word, and declared that thence forward not a man, while any strength remained, would spare his body or blood in defence of so munificent a country.[2]

---

1 *The Early History of Rome*, Livy, Penguin Classics, pp. 329–330.
2 *The Early History of Rome*, Livy, Penguin Classics, pp. 335–336.

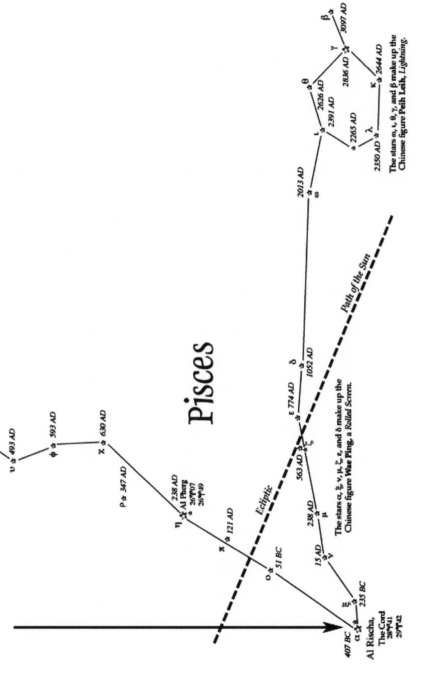

Pisces

τ 643 AD

υ 493 AD

φ 593 AD

χ 630 AD

ρ 347 AD

η 238 AD
Al Pherg
26°♈07
26°♈49

π 121 AD

o 51 BC

Ecliptic

ξ 235 BC

α Al Rischa,
The Cord
28°♈41
29°♈42
407 BC

ν 15 AD

μ 238 AD

ζ 563 AD

The stars α, ξ, ν, μ, ζ, ε, and δ make up the
Chinese figure Wae Ping, a Rolled Screen.

ε 774 AD

δ 1052 AD

Path of the Sun

ω 2013 AD

ι 2391 AD

θ 2626 AD

β 3097 AD

γ 2836 AD

κ 2644 AD

λ 2265 AD

2350 AD

The stars ω, ι, θ, γ, and β make up the
Chinese figure Peih Leih, Lightning.

The First Seal

In 403 BC, another dimension was added to the annals of war.

> The Roman commanders, in the belief that a siege offered better
> prospects of success than a direct assault, took the hitherto unprec-
> edented step of beginning the construction of winter quarters,
> intending to continue hostilities throughout the year ...
>   So this was the reason that the soldiers had been granted
> pay... The liberty of the commons had been sold; the young men,
> having been permanently removed and banished from the City and
> from the state, were no longer free, even in winter and the stormy
> seasons, to see to their homes and their affairs.
>   ... whilst the Roman soldiers were enduring toil and danger,
> overwhelmed with snows and frosts, in tents, not even laying aside
> their weapons in the winter time, a season of respite from all wars
> both by land and by sea.[3]

The war referred to is Rome's ten-year long struggle with Veii, pre-
miere city of the Etruscan federation to Rome's immediate north. It
marks the end of a four hundred year period of back and forth civil war
between the two cities.

> This struggle between Rome and Veii marked the first definite step
> in Rome's career of world conquest... It was remembered in Roman
> traditions as turning point in the military history of the city.[4]

And this is precisely what the lines of Revelation seem to reflect.

> *Immediately a white horse appeared, and the rider on it was holding*
> *a bow; he was given the victor's crown and he went away, to go from*
> *victory to victory.*

With the conquest of Veii, Rome doubled her territory and seized

---

3 *The Early History of Rome, Book V, II.*, Livy, Penguin Classics, pp. 5–7.
4 *A History of Rome: Early Wars of the Republic*, H. H. Scullard, pp. 72–74.

upon a vast amount of spoils. Rome had forever changed the rules of warfare. Commoners had been given a share of legislative power, were voted pay to serve, but in return were bound to the army all year long. A new era was indeed at hand, the willing enslavement of the landless class to do the state's bidding, what would later become the "riches" of the Church. This was also the first time Rome officially acknowledges Greek culture. Prior to the final assault, Camillus offered a prayer to Apollo, wherein one tenth of the spoils would be donated to a successful Roman victory. Although the triumph was recorded, Camillus allowed his oath to lapse until the Roman Senate stepped in and voted the pact honored.

With the breaking of the First Seal, Revelation records it is a white horse that emerges. In the triumph after Veii, white horses were indeed part of the center stage celebration.

> The return of Camillus drew greater crowds than had ever been seen on such an occasion in the past, people of all ranks in society pouring through the city gates to meet him; and the official celebration of his Triumph left in its splendor all previous ones in the shade. Riding into Rome in a chariot drawn by white horses he was the cynosure of every eye and indeed in doing so he was felt to be guilty of a certain anti-republican arrogance, and even of impiety. Might there not be sin, people wondered, in giving a man those dazzling steeds and thus making him equal with Jupiter or the God of the Sun? It was this disquieting thought that rendered the celebration, for all its magnificence, not wholly acceptable.[5]

The First Seal has been opened. It is the dawn of a new era. We have a pivotal war, marking the beginning of legendary Roman ascendancy. We have the Romans believing their own history reached a turning point at this time. We have white horses.

We have our Star Gate.

---

5 *The Early History of Rome*, Livy, Penguin Classics, p. 23.

The Second Seal

6:3 When he broke the second seal, I heard the second animal shout, "Come."

The Second Seal is broken; Spring aligns with the second star, *xi Piscium*, in 235 BC.

Hannibal Barca was born in Carthage in 247 BC. He was taken to Spain (Iberia) in 237 BC when he was nine or ten years old. Here is what Livy had to say about his youth.

> Moreover, high passions were at work throughout, and mutual hatred was hardly less sharp a weapon than the sword; on the Roman side there was rage at the unprovoked attack by a previously beaten enemy; on the Carthaginian, bitter resentment at what was felt to be the grasping and tyrannical attitude of their conquerors. The intensity of the feeling is illustrated by an anecdote of Hannibal's boyhood; his father Hamilcar, after the campaign in Africa, was about to carry his troops over to Spain, when Hannibal, then about nine years old, begged, with all the childish arts he could muster, to be allowed to accompany him; whereupon Hamilcar, who was preparing to offer sacrifice for a successful outcome, led the boy to the altar and made him solemnly swear, with his hand upon the sacred victim, that as soon as he was old enough he would be the enemy of the Roman people.[6]

Given our current chronology, these would have been some of the events of Hannibal's youth. We can only imagine how these events may have psychologically influenced him.

The Romans believed that Hannibal's father forced his son to promise eternal hatred against the Romans. This may be an

---

6 *The War with Hannibal,* Book XXI, Livy, Penguin Classics, p. 23.

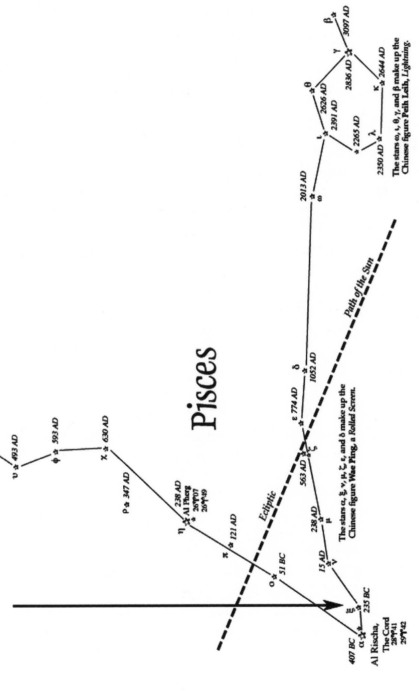

Pisces

τ ☆ 643 AD
υ ☆ 493 AD
φ ☆ 593 AD
χ ☆ 630 AD
ρ ☆ 347 AD
η ☆ 238 AD
Al Phorg
26♈07
26♈49
π ☆ 121 AD
ο ☆ 51 BC

Ecliptic

ε ☆ 774 AD
δ ☆ 1052 AD
ζ ☆ 563 AD
μ ☆ 238 AD
ν ☆ 15 AD
ξ ☆ 235 BC
α ☆ 407 BC
Al Rischa,
The Cord
28♈41
29♈42

Path of the Sun

ω ☆ 2013 AD
ι ☆ 2391 AD
θ ☆ 2626 AD
λ ☆ 2265 AD
κ ☆ 2644 AD
γ ☆ 2836 AD
β ☆ 3097 AD
☆ 2350 AD

The stars α, ξ, ν, μ, ζ, ε, and δ make up the
Chinese figure Wae Ping, a Rolled Screen.

The stars ω, ι, θ, γ, and β make up the
Chinese figure Peih Leih, Lightning.

The Second Seal

invention, but there may be some truth in the story: the Carthaginians had good reasons to hate their enemies.[7]

Hannibal was six years old when Carthage lost the war to Rome, a twenty-three-year long conflict. Returning African mercenaries who had fought for the Carthagians during the war demanded pay, and turned on the city when it was not forthcoming. At the end of this second war Hannibal was ten years old. Some of the losing mercenary soldiers fled to Sardinia while Carthage pursued them. Rome declared war on Carthage and stripped them of both Corsica and Sardinia, having already taken Sicily as spoils of the first Punic War. Weakened by the loss of the first Punic War and the winning of the second mercenary war, Carthage had no choice but to surrender again to Rome. She was forced to pay an additional war tribute.

The seizure of the islands and increased indemnity fostered resentment and revenge among the hawks of the Carthaginian Senate. It was after this war that Hamilcar decided to move his troops to Spain, outside of the sphere of Roman influence. At the age of ten Hannibal accompanied his father to Spain and saw the new colony grow under his father's guiding hand. Hamilcar died in 219 during a native skirmish while Hannibal was only eighteen.

Livy says that Hannibal was "about nine" when he made the vow against Rome on the altar. I suggest he was twelve, either when he made the vow or deemed himself old enough to become Rome's enemy. This would have been in 235 BC, two years after having first journeyed to Spain.

Following the oath, the legend is better known; of his early victories in Spain, his dramatic move through the Pyrenees with approximately 50,000 men, the crossing of the Alps with his equipment and elephants, and his arrival in Italy with but half that number. In two short months he carried Italy north of the Po River. And in three major military actions in three years—outnumbered and on foreign soil—he

7 *The War with Hannibal*, Book XXI, Livy, Penguin Classics, p. 23.

defeated the Romans decisively, collectively eliminating approximately 100,000 of their men.

After seventeen years of conflict every Latin schoolboy would come to know the tale of "*Hannibal ad portam*," Hannibal at the gates.

And out came another horse, bright red, and its rider was given this duty: to take away peace from the earth and set people killing each other. He was given a huge sword.

Was Hannibal a part of some divine plan, as seen in the heavens? Livy records a dream Hannibal was said to have had as he was preparing to lead his army into Italy.

From Gades Hannibal returned to the army's quarters in New Carthage, and then proceeded by way of Etovissa to the river Ebro and the coast. There, it is reported, a youth of divine aspect was seen by him in his sleep, who said, "that he was sent by Jupiter as the guide of Hannibal into Italy, and that he should, therefore, follow him, nor in any direction turn his eyes away from him." At first he followed in terror, looking no where, either around or behind: afterwards, through the curiosity of the human mind, when he resolved in his mind what that could be on which he was forbidden to look back, he could not restrain his eyes; then he beheld behind him a serpent of wonderful size moving along with an immense destruction of trees and bushes, and after it a cloud following with thunderings from the skies; and that then inquiring "what was that great commotion, and what the cause of the prodigy," he heard in reply: "That it was the devastation of Italy: that he should continue to advance forward, nor inquire further, but suffer the fates to remain in obscurity.[8]

Hannibal's dream would seem to suggest a force greater than himself was behind the prodigy.

---

8 Livy- *The History of Rome*, Chapter XXI paragraph xxii.

The Third Seal

6:5 When he broke the third seal, I heard the third animal shout,
"Come," Immediately a black horse appeared, and its rider was holding
a pair of scales

Our next Star Gate is AD 15. *Nu Piscium* now aligns with the cardinal direction and heralds yet another new dawn.

This is the Third Seal in our series. Note that the tenor of the message has changed. The first star spoke of a bow and victory, the second of a sword and war. This one suggests a dark justice (scales on a black horse) about to be meted out.

The Roman world pivoted on a new axis through these years. Having finished an extended period of civil war, Augustus finally brought peace by steamrolling the opposition. In order to ensure a peaceful transition of power, Augustus, the Father of the Roman Empire, had "groomed" several choices to be his heir, one of whom was Tiberius. After a long period of falling into and out of favor with the administration, in AD 13 Augustus promoted Tiberius so that the two shared equal power. In AD 14 Augustus died, leaving Tiberius sole ruler of the Empire. But Tiberius had no desire to be Emperor, had nursed periods of seclusion and self-imposed isolation, suffered through an enduring grief over the death of his son, and was unstable.

In AD 15 Tiberius appointed Sejanus the Praetorian Prefect, head of the city police, to help him run the Empire. Sejanus did so until Tiberius had him executed in AD 31. As the *Pax Romana* of the first and second centuries unfolded, our focus suggests the apple was rotten at the core. For seventeen years after his appointment, Tiberius would come to rely on Sejanus as a trusted advisor. "My partner," he called him. While Tiberius wanted nothing to do with the daily operations of the state, Sejanus was his front man. Sejanus read and manipulated Tiberius's dark moods, and bidied his time, assuming he would have a chance to succeed him to the throne.

The fears which Sejanus nurtured in Tiberius ran amok once the formers' duplicity was uncovered. After the prefect's execution, Tiberius's withdrawal from Rome was complete. Tiberius was utterly par-

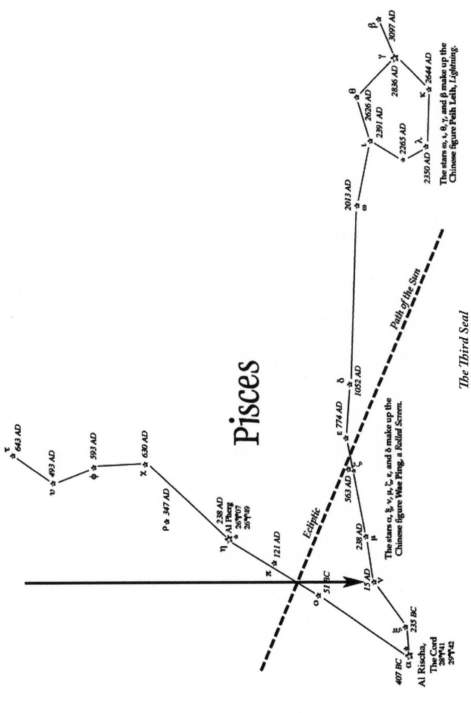

Pisces

τ 643 AD
υ 493 AD
φ 593 AD
χ 630 AD
ρ 347 AD
η 238 AD
Al Pherg
26♈07
26♈49
π 121 AD
ο 51 BC
ε 774 AD
δ 1052 AD
ζ 563 AD
μ 238 AD
ν 15 AD
ξ 235 BC
α 407 BC
Al Rischa,
The Cord
28♈41
29♈42

Ecliptic

Path of the Sun

ω 2013 AD
ι 2391 AD
θ 2626 AD
γ 2836 AD
β 3097 AD
κ 2644 AD
λ 2265 AD
2350 AD

The stars ω, ι, θ, γ, and β make up the
Chinese figure Peih Leih, Lightning.

The stars α, ξ, ν, μ, ζ, ε, and δ make up the
Chinese figure Wae Ping, a Rolled Screen.

The Third Seal

anoid. He murdered hundreds. While some historians may laud the time of the *Pax Romana*, the following was playing out currently.

> Soon Tiberius broke out in every sort of cruelty and never lacked for victims: these were, first, his mother's friends and less intimate acquaintances; then those of Agrippina, Nero and Drusus; finally, those of Sejanus. With Sejanus out of the way his savageries increased; which proved that Sejanus had not, as some thought, been inciting him to commit them, but merely providing the opportunities that he demanded...
>
> A detailed list of Tiberius's barbarities would take a long time to compile; I shall content myself with a few samples. Not a day, however holy, passed without an execution; he even desecrated New Year's Day. Many of his men victims were accused and punished with their children—some actually by their children—and the relatives forbidden to go into mourning. Special awards were voted to the informers who had denounced them and, in certain circumstances, to the witnesses too. An informer's word was always believed. Every crime became a capital one, even the utterance of a few careless words. A poet found himself accused of slander—he had written a tragedy which presented King Agamemnon in a bad light—and a historian had made the mistake of describing Caesar's assassins, Brutus and Cassius, as "the last of the Romans." Both these authors were executed without delay, and their works—though once publicly read before Augustus, and accorded general praise—were called in and destroyed.[9]

Augustus and Tiberius were the emperors of Rome during the life and ministry of Jesus.

The tone of our message in Revelation has indeed shifted. This is a black horse, it's rider carries the scales, not a bow or a sword. Compared to the first two riders, this is not war. It is the distribution of justice under a dark cloud of fear and corruption. It was a time of utter

---

9 *The Twelve Caesars,* Suetonius, Penguin Classics, pp. 139–140.

depravity, decadence and degeneracy, unchecked by any moral constraints.

> *... and I seemed to hear a voice shout from among the four animals and say, "A ration of corn for a day's wages, and three rations of barley for a day's wages, but do not tamper with the oil or the wine."*

A proper set of weights and measures is used in the fair allotment of grains. The price of food was often used to help manipulate public opinion, and during these times became a political football. These were hard economic times for the workingman.

> Levies of grain, indirect taxation, and the other revenues belonging to the State were managed by associations of Roman knights ... The public suffered, it is true, from oppressive food prices.[10]

Indeed, Tiberius was personally associated with these political issues. He had been called upon in his early career before he became emperor to come up with a solution.

> Tiberius's civil career began with his defence, against various charges, of the Jewish King Archelaus, (and he was asked to...) reorganize the defective grain supply ...[11]

At the time of the writing of Revelation between AD 60 and 95, these events were still fresh in the collective memory. The Julio-Claudian dynasty was not known for its morality, although Claudius fared better than expected. Here is what Tacitus had to say about the early emperors of Rome.

> ... the histories of Tiberius, Gaius, Claudius, and Nero, while they

---

10 *The Annals*, IV:30, Tacitus, Penguin Classics, p. 160.
11 *The Twelve Caesars*, Suetonius, Penguin Classics, p. 114.

were in power, were falsified through terror, and after their death
were written under the irritation of a recent hatred.[12]

The generation prior to Revelation's authorship had been witness
to the events described under the Third Seal. The author (or authors)
had to be careful about what he inferred about the royal family as we
have just seen. Freedom of speech was not in their constitution. The
first three seals are armchair prophecies, composed with all of the
advantages of hindsight.

Again, we note that the authors of Revelation were writing in the
first three Seals about events that had already taken place. They were
showing us the entire cosmic pattern, the entire asterism, the whole
picture. All seven stars (seals) were being written about, because they
were part of the overall celestial "dynasty" to which the Roman world
was being subject. Rather than starting from the middle, the author
or authors included these three events so that they might reveal the
workings of all seven. They were demonstrating how the system works.

Each of these "stars" corresponded to important shifts in Roman
history. From here on Revelation will be addressing a series of seals
that had not yet been opened: the fourth, fifth, sixth, and seventh—
events that lay in the future.

This is where a prophet's skill will be revealed if he or she can successfully interpret events in the future, rather than simply chronicling
periods that were already history.

We are following the path of the Vernal Equinox across the constellations, weaving eastern stars into our tapestry of time. Throughout
the previous two thousand years, the Ram and Lamb marked Spring
as it moved through these stars. Here's another mythical manifestation
from a different quarter. The Romans also used the "Lamb" as a symbol
for the Vernal Equinox. It was a cornerstone of time for them also.

Tiberius moved this important "ritual" to the day of his accession.

By a Senatorial decree the festival of Parilia, which commemo-
rated the birth of Rome and had always taken place at the Spring

12 *Annals*, 1.1.

Equinox, was transferred to the day of his accession, as though Rome had now been born again.[13]

Rome had been born again, through Tiberius. He was its leader, father and protector. But it is a dark star, and these seeds sow a somber prototype.

The *Parilia* was a ceremony initiated by country sheepherders. At the first sight of light on the appointed day the shepherd would spiritually purify his sheep. He would first jump through the fire dragging his sheep after him. After various additional offerings, the shepherd turned to the East and said a prayer four times. The end of the ceremony came when the shepherd again jumped through the flames three times.

These are the Springtime energies: sheep, fire, turning to the east and more fire. It was one of many spiritual channels of its day.

Seutonius links this ceremony to the Vernal Equinox and Rome's birthday. Ovid sets it as April 21st, remembering back to a time when the Vernal Equinox would have first entered the stars at the rear of the Ram. Each is correct; they are simply measuring two different ends of the constellational Ram, marked by two different eras. Myth was no stranger to the Ram's use as a Springtime marker.

This is the same mythic model the Book of Revelation is using. It's part of a larger and far older celestial language.

The Fourth Seal

6:7 When he broke the fourth seal, I heard the voice of the fourth animal shout, "Come."

> *Immediately another horse appeared, deathly pale, and its rider was called Plague, and Hades followed at his heels. They were given authority over a quarter of the earth, to kill by the sword, by famine, by plague and wild beasts.*

It was now AD 238. *Mu Piscium* had just aligned with the Vernal

---

13 *The Twelve Caesars*, Suetonius, Penguin Classics, p. 157.

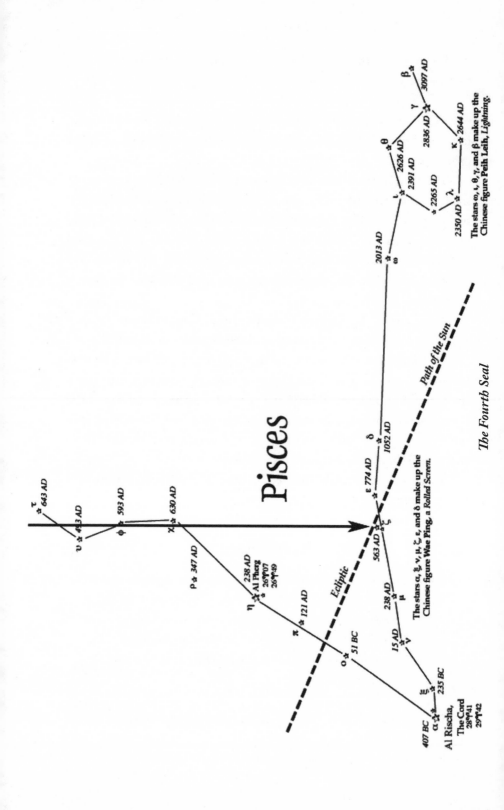

τ
643 AD

υ 463 AD

φ 593 AD

χ 630 AD

ρ 347 AD

η 238 AD
Al Pherg
26♈07
26♈49

 π 121 AD

ο 51 BC

ξ 235 BC

α 407 BC
Al Rischa,
The Cord
28♈41
29♈42

ν 15 AD

μ 238 AD

The stars α, ξ, ν, μ, ζ, ε, and δ make up the
Chinese figure Wae Ping, a Rolled Screen.

ζ 563 AD

ε 774 AD

δ 1052 AD

ω 2013 AD

ι 2391 AD

θ 2626 AD

γ 2836 AD

κ 2644 AD

λ 2265 AD

2350 AD

β 3097 AD

The stars ω, ι, θ, γ, and β make up the
Chinese figure Peih Leih, Lightning.

Pisces

Ecliptic

Path of the Sun

The Fourth Seal

Equinox. This date focuses upon what is called the "*Crisis of the Third Century,*" a period that lasted about fifty years during the middle of the century. The imagery of the Fourth Seal re-invokes the power of the first two: of bows, swords, and people killing each other. This is the first of the seals to reside in the future as seen from the first century AD. It is the first true "prophecy" for the seals of Revelation.

On the historical, social, economic and personal levels, this dark star inflicted a deep wound on Rome. This period has been described as a watershed between the classical and early medieval worlds. The wars, mutiny and chaos which defined these years forever tarnished the sense of confidence in the safety of Roman roads—essential for transporting goods of commerce and manufacture from one end of the empire to the other.

The sea had long united ports of call, but it was Roman roads that carried the produce of these ports inland in greater bulk, uniting the geography of the empire in a common trade.

Along these roads passed an ever-increasing traffic, not only of troops and officials, but of traders, merchandize and even tourists. An interchange of goods between the various provinces rapidly developed, which soon reached a scale unprecedented in previous history and not repeated until a few centuries ago. Metals mined in the uplands of Western Europe, hides, fleeces, and livestock from the pastoral districts of Britain, Spain, and the shores of the Black Sea, wine and oil from Provence and Aquitaine, timber, pitch and wax from South Russia and northern Anatolia, dried fruits from Syria, marble from the Aegean coasts, and—most important of all—grain from the corn-growing districts of North Africa, Egypt, and the Danube valley for the needs of the great cities; all these commodities, under the influence of a highly organized system of transport and marketing, moved freely from one corner of the Empire to the other.[14]

So what happened to so disrupt business?

14 *The Birth of the Middle Ages*, H. St. L. B. Moss, Oxford University Press, London, New York, p. 1.

The fifty years (AD 235–285) that followed the death of Severus Alexander constitute a dark Age in a double sense. They were a period of disaster and of crisis for the Roman Empire, and the record which they left of themselves is scanty and broken.[15]

Under the influence of his mother, Severus Alexander had been raised to be a munificent emperor. He had been tutored by a team of scholars and carefully groomed to be regent. After 13 years of rule and an unsuccessful military campaign, he was murdered by his troops.

The man picked to be his successor could not have been more the opposite of Severus. Maximinus Thrax was the first of the "barracks emperors." He had never been a senator before "wearing the purple" and, indeed, had never even set foot in Rome. A battle-hardened soldier who worked his way up through the ranks, he was enormous, said to stand eight and a half feet tall. Maximinus Thrax was convinced that the throne could not be held except through cruelty and fear. He practiced what he preached. The Senate begrudgingly bequeathed the title of emperor on him (after he had been so voted by the army), but later reconsidered and offered it to Gordian I and his son Gordian II of Africa.

Having learned of the Senate's duplicity, Maximinus immediately set out with his army and marched for Rome. The Senate had many reasons to fear Maximinus.

But by this time the Romans could bear his [Maximinus] barbarities no longer—the way in which he called up informers and incited accusers, invented false offences, killed innocent men, condemned all whoever came to trial, reduced the richest men to utter poverty and never sought money anywhere save in some other's ruin, put many generals and many men of consular rank to death for no offence, carried others about in waggons without food and drink, and kept others in confinement, in short neglected nothing which he thought might prove effectual for cruelty—and, unable to

---

15 *A History of Rome: Early Wars of the Republic,* H. H. Scullard, Bedford/St. Martin's, p. 507.

suffer these things longer, they rose against him in revolt. And not only the Romans, but, because he had been savage to the soldiers also, the armies which were in Africa rose in sudden and powerful rebellion and hailed the aged and venerable Gordian who was pro-consul there, as emperor.[16]

The year was AD 238. Before it was over there were no less than six imperial claimants to the throne. Only one would survive.

As the year opened, Maximinus was in charge. The next two emperorers, as mentioned, were a father and son team, Gordian I and Gordian II. They were appointed by the Senate, but both were to die after a joint reign of only three weeks. Two more emperors were then appointed in Rome to deal with the impending attack from Maximinus. Balbinus and Pupienus were doomed from the start. Popular riots, military discontent, and even an enormous fire in June, 238 consumed the capital. Notoriously suspicious of each other, these two were seized by the Praetorian Guard one day as they argued. They were stripped and dragged through the streets, tortured and murdered.

The cruelty of Maximinus to his army proved his undoing; his starving troops turned on him. Both he and his son Maximus were killed, and the heads delivered to Rome on pikes. Having survived Maximinus, the newly-appointed emperor was Gordian III. Grandson and son of Gordian I and Gordian II, his appointment was a nod to the people—who were rioting in the streets in Rome because their opinion had not been solicited. For fifty years after the death of Severus some twenty to twenty five different individuals claimed the title Caesar. Not one of them died a natural death.

Some were killed in battle, others were murdered by their own sup-porters, and at least one died of the plague. The period ends with the Roman Empire at its nadir, and a Roman emperor dying in slavery among the Persians.[17]

---

16 *Historia Augusta*, edited by Thomas A. Dorey, p. 343.
17 *Chronicle of the Roman Emperors: The Reign-By-Reign Record of the Rulers of Imperial Rome*, Chris Scarre, Thames and Hudson, pp. 166–167.

With politics in turmoil and the military with its hands full, is it any surprise that runaway inflation would also have its day? The Severan emperors had enlarged the army by a quarter and doubled the base pay. The quickest way to raise money is to devalue what you already have, adulterating silver coins with less valuable metals. By the time of Diocletian (AD 284-305), the coinage of the Roman Empire had nearly collapsed. Currency had almost no value and trade increasingly turned to barter. This fundamental shift impacted nearly every aspect of Roman life. Taken together with the constant attacks from across the frontier, Rome was faced with what some have called a perfect storm. The Roman trade network was never able to fully recover.

From across the Rhine, Danube, and Euphrates Rivers poured waves of attacks from outlanders, the barbarian hordes. Politically, socially, militarily, and economically Rome was knocked on her heels.

> Whether these attacks on different fronts were concerted or not—the lack of strict synchronism between them makes it appear improbable that there should have been any understanding between the invaders—the Roman defences were everywhere caught at a disadvantage. Nature too intervened: for nearly twenty years from the time of Gallas (253–268 AD), a plague raged in different parts of the Empire. By 262 it reached Italy and Africa … The plague is alleged to have carried off 5000 victims a day in Rome.[18]

The unleashing of the Fourth Seal invokes Plague. Here's another account of its impact.

> Another plague occurred during the reigns of Decius (249–251 AD) and Gallus (251–253 AD). This pestilence broke out in Egypt in 251, and from there infected the entire empire. Its mortality rate severely depleted the ranks of the army, and caused massive labor

18 *A History of Rome: Early Wars of the Republic,* H. H. Scullard, Bedford/St. Martin's, p. 516.

shortages. The plague was still raging in 270, when it caused the death of the emperor Claudius Gothicus (268–270).[19]

Even at the end of this temporal window, there was a plague of note. The opening of the Fourth Seal occurred in AD 238. The Fifth Seal was opened 325 years later in AD 563, In 541 and 542, shortly before the opening of the Fifth Seal, the world was ravaged by perhaps the most noteworthy plague in history, called the Justinian Plague. The onset of this plague occurred during the reign of Emperor Justinian, who had spent much of his reign attempting to reconstruct the old Roman Empire. Although Justinian caught and personally recovered from the plague, it depleted the population of the East Roman Empire at the critical time when his armies had retaken Italy and might have credibly reformed a Western Roman Empire.

The most widely known plague to us is, of course, the Bubonic Plague of the 14th century. However, the 6th century Justinian Plague was nearly worldwide in its scope and would return for each generation throughout the Mediterranean until about 750.

Is this what the lines of Revelation mean? The rider is Plague, and Death follows at his heels. When is it done? Does it happen as it is going by? What does it mean to "follow at his heels"?

Modern scholars believe that the plague killed up to 5,000 people per day in Constantinople at the peak of the pandemic. It ultimately killed perhaps 40% of the city's inhabitants. The initial plague went on to destroy up to a quarter of the human population of the eastern Mediterranean. New, frequent waves of the plague continued to strike throughout the 6th, 7th and 8th centuries AD, often more localized and less virulent. It is estimated that the Plague of Justinian killed as many as 100 million people across the world.[20]

---

19 Christine A. Smith, *Plague in the Ancient World: A Study from Thucydides to Justinian.*
20 *The History of Bubonic Plague*, Rebecca A. Bishop, Graduate School of Biomedical Sciences, University of Texas Health Science Center at Houston.

If you think that this was a common occurrence in the ancient world, here's the report following the 8th century. Major epidemic diseases would not appear in Europe again until the Black Death of the 14th century, more than 600 years later. Let's compare these lines once more.

The initial plague went on to destroy up to a quarter of the human population of the eastern Mediterranean.[21]

They were given authority over a quarter of the earth, to kill by the sword, by famine, by plague and wild beasts.

The Fifth Seal

6:9 When he broke the fifth seal, I saw underneath the altar the souls of all the people who had been killed on account of the word of God, for witnessing to it. They shouted aloud ...

It is AD 563. *Zeta Piscium* has aligned with the Vernal Equinox, our new eastern star. Of the Seven Seals, this one lies closest to the path of the ecliptic.

The souls under the altar who have been killed for witnessing to the word of God are the same multitudes referenced in Rev. 5: 11. The underlying message here seems to be that if you stand your ground, if you have faith through death, you pass the test. It is evident, both from the nature of the seals we are opening and from the above lines, that the souls under the altar feel as though they may have been unjustly killed. There is a call for vengeance at a spiritual level. Yet having gone through this experience entitles the owner to the coveted white robe, the spiritually cleansed aura or soul.

The message here is that through suffering, persecution and humility the soul is purified. This is inherently the message of Christianity. Through complete surrender we lose the world but regain our souls.

---

21 Rebecca A. Bishop.

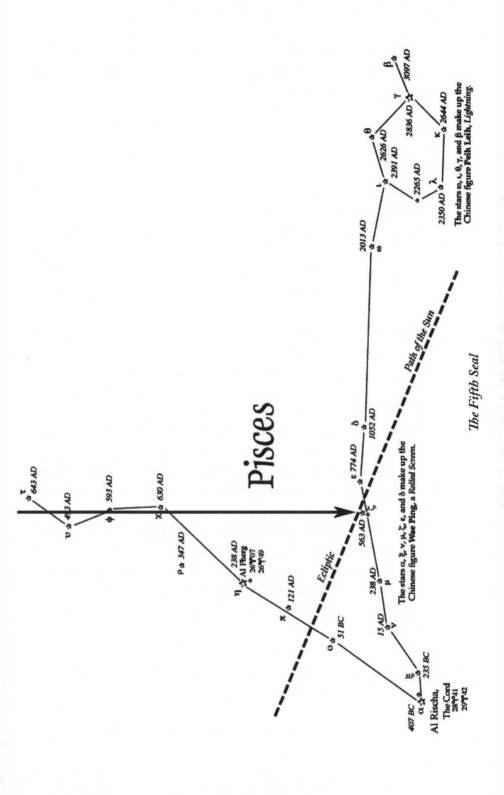

Pisces

The Fifth Seal

The stars ω, ι, θ, γ, and β make up the Chinese figure Peih Leih, Lightning.

The stars α, ξ, ν, μ, ζ, ε, and δ make up the Chinese figure Wae Ping, a Rolled Screen.

Path of the Sun

Ecliptic

τ 643 AD
υ 463 AD
φ 593 AD
χ 630 AD
ρ 347 AD
η Al Pherg 238 AD 26°♈07′ 26°♈59′
π 121 AD
o 51 BC
ξ 235 BC
α Al Riscia, The Cord 407 BC 28°♈41′ 29°♈42′
ν 15 AD
μ 238 AD
ζ 563 AD
ε 774 AD
δ 1052 AD
ω 2013 AD
ι 2391 AD
θ 2626 AD
γ 2836 AD
β 3097 AD
κ 2644 AD
λ 2265 AD
2350 AD

This is also the signature of Pisces, the constellation of which all of these "seals" are a part. There is a continuous theme at work here, a common thread running throughout our stellar tapestry.

Holy, faithful Master, how much longer will you wait before you pass sentence and take vengeance for our death on the inhabitants of the earth?

If the First Seal is where we began, and if we are correct about the pattern, *zeta Piscium*, the Fifth Seal suggests we are through some 40% of our Revelatory journey in AD 563.

Each of them was given a white robe, and they were told to be patient a little longer, until the roll was complete and their fellow servants and brothers had been killed just as they had been.

It is clear that we are talking to the dead here. Furthermore, it is also clear that a spiritual path is being outlined. This is what you must do to qualify for... what? The goal or reward of such endeavors is not spelled out, only that this is what must be done. It does, however, begin to lay the groundwork for the notion of reincarnation.

Justinian reigned in Constantinople as the Eastern Roman Emperor, whose suzereignty included the eastern half of what had once been the Roman Empire. He had spent his lifetime attempting to bring back into the fold territories that had been peeled away from the earlier empire by repeated barbarian invasions.

In Italy much of Justinian's time had been spent battling the Ostrogoths. His long campaign, together with the plague of 541, depleted much of the Eastern Empire's resources. When the Lombards appeared in northern Italy in 568 just three years after Justinian's death, the Eastern Roman Empire was in no shape to stop them. The Lombards were a Germanic people who would rule large parts of the Italian Peninsula from 568 to 774.

In 568 a new Germanic people, the Lombards, appeared at the

eastern gateways of Italy, coming from Pannonia and Moricum. Their number were about equal to those of the Ostrogoths, but they were considerably cruder, had no links with the East Roman Empire, and looked on Italy as a land to be conquered... The clergy and population of many places fled before the Lombard invasion to inaccessible coastal areas, where they could count on the protection of the Byzantines, who still controlled the seas...

It is certain, however, that the class of the Roman "possessores" (land owners) was broken up and practically destroyed.

Whereas the Goths and other barbarians had respected the Roman political and administrative framework, the Lombards did away with it completely in favour of their own customs. The only institutions to be saved were the churches.[22]

The Fifth Seal would have been "opened" in 563. Alboin was the king of the Lombards, a post he inherited from his father Audoin, who died in either 563 or 565 (I have seen dates for both). Justinian, the driving force behind the Eastern Empire passed away in 565. We do know that there had been contact between the Eastern Roman Empire and the Lombards prior to these dates. The two powers formed an alliance in an effort to expel the Gepids in 546. Following this successful foray, the Lombards turned their eye on northern Italy.

Meeting with little opposition, for the country had been ravaged by war and plague, they occupied the great plain between the Alps and the Apennines, ever since called Lombardy. It was a thorough conquest. They made no pretense of alliance with the empire, as the Ostrogoths had done, nor did they leave the conquered Italians in possession of their estates. The continuity of Roman civilization, which had survived so many invasions, was at last broken ...[23]

22 1986 *Encyclopedia Britannica*, v. 22, p. 186–188.
23 *A Survey of European Civilization, Pt. 1*, Wallace Klippert Ferguson, p. 143–144.

The Sixth Seal

6:12 In my vision, when he broke the sixth seal, there was a violent earthquake and the sun went as black as coarse sackcloth; the moon turned red as blood all over,

The Sixth Seal is being opened. The year is 774. The star is *Epsilon Piscium.*

The USGS website only lists six earthquakes between the 9th through the 16th centuries, none before that. This is the 8th century. According to Seutonius we know that Tiberius came to the aid of Philadelphia after an earthquake in AD 27, while Amos tells us that his prophecies were made two years before the earthquake in 756 BC under the kingship of Uzziah, but literary allusions fall far short of a complete earthquake log. Whether the above lines of Revelation are metaphorical or literal, it would seem that events were severely shaken up. These were not good omens.

and the stars of the sky fell on to the earth like figs dropping from a fig tree when a high wind shakes it;

The framework of Revelation—if we are interrupting the imagery correctly—is based upon celestial design. If the stars are described as falling to the earth, then the whole system is being shaken at its core; it is collapsing. The "tenor" of this star is opening with some of the same power as our earlier seals. There is great change afoot.

the sky disappeared like a scroll rolling up and all the mountains and islands were shaken from their places.

This is the sixth of our seven stars of "The Scroll" or *Wae Ping*, the Rolled Screen. We are coming to the end of the series. More properly, this *"scroll rolling up"* should be placed with the Seventh Seal, the last of the series, but not much is said about the Seventh Seal, as we will see.

Once again, it is apparent that the system is being shaken. We're

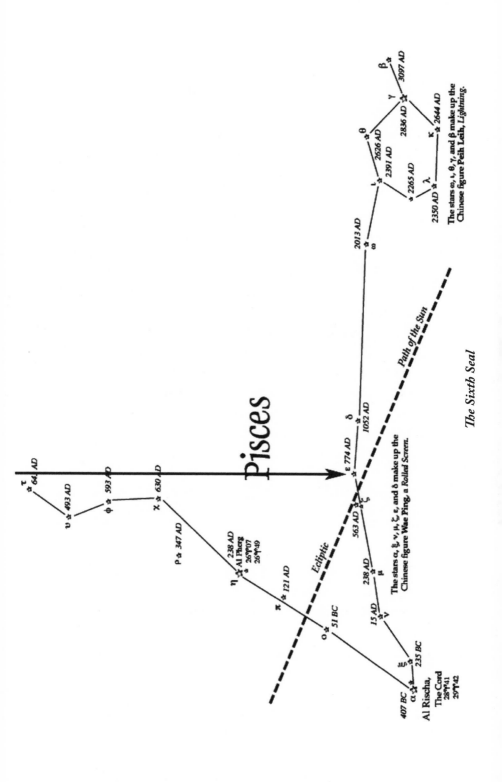

τ ☆ 64 AD

υ ☆ 493 AD

φ ☆ 593 AD

χ ☆ 630 AD

ρ ☆ 347 AD

η ☆ 238 AD
Al Pherg
26♈07
26♈49

π ☆ 121 AD

o ☆ 51 BC

ξ ☆ 235 BC

ν ☆ 15 AD

μ ☆ 238 AD

α ☆ 407 BC
Al Rischa,
The Cord
28♈41
29♈42

Pisces

Ecliptic

ε 774 AD ☆

δ ☆ 1052 AD

ζ ☆ 563 AD

Path of the Sun

ω ☆ 2013 AD

ι ☆ 2391 AD

θ ☆ 2626 AD

λ ☆ 2265 AD

κ ☆ 2644 AD

γ ☆ 2836 AD

β ☆ 3097 AD

☆ 2350 AD

The stars ω, ι, θ, γ, and β make up the Chinese figure Peih Leih, *Lightning*.

The stars α, ξ, ν, μ, ζ, ε, and δ make up the Chinese figure Wae Ping, a *Rolled Screen*.

The Sixth Seal

repeating the theme of the earlier clause. Now, having examined the heavenly framework (*"the stars of the sky fell... the sky rolled up..."*), we turn to how this affects things here on Earth.

> *Then all the earthly rulers, the governors and the commanders, the rich people and the men of the influence, the whole population, slaves and citizens, took to the mountains to hide in caves and among the rocks. They said to the mountains and the rocks, "Fall on us and hide us away from the One who sits on the throne and from the anger of the Lamb. For the Great Day of his anger has come, and who can survive it?"*

People of all social classes, the whole population, will be impacted by the changes. It is clear that class and social distinction are no refuge from the external danger. People are seeking to hide.

What is important in these lines is that "the One who sits on the throne" and the "Lamb" are being identified together, as they should be. The Lamb at this time is ON the throne. He is IN the seat of power. Celestially, the influences are being triggered in the same manner contemporary astrologers feel that planetary alignments stir events here on Earth—alignments such as the Full Moon, Mercury going retrograde, or the Saturn return.

The Sixth Seal ends the period of Lombard domination in Italy, the focus of the Fifth Seal. In 771 Charlemagne became the sole Frankish king. In 772 he undertook a war to convert the remaining organized pagans of Europe—the Saxons—to Christianity. In 773 he annexed the Lombard kingdom in Italy.

In 774, he entered Rome and visited the pope. His visit confirmed the earlier Donation of Pepin of 756, which granted political power to the pope over conquered Lombard territories. (This added an entirely new dimension to the pope's spiritual authority.) The stage was set for the alliance of both king and pope, although it would take a quarter century for the seeds to finally take root and germinate. It would be officially sanctioned when the pope crowned Charlemagne emperor in Rome in 800, uniting Heaven and Earth in a single ritual. The Roman Empire had not had an emperor in over three hundred years. Charlemagne absorbed Lombardy into his Frankish Kingdom. Rome had a new earthly master.

It had been 211 years since the Fifth Seal, and the dates intermesh like clockwork. But the power of this seal being opened does not stop there.

Intuition has led me to the conclusion that the real devastation of the Sixth Seal (given the tone of the warning) was to be found in the coming of the Viking Age. The question becomes (and I have spent many hours attempting to put the pieces together here), what events triggered the attacks of the Vikings, and what do they have to do with the year 774?

The Anglo-Saxon Chronicle mentions a Viking raid in the British Isles in 787. A group of men from Norway sailed to Portland in Dorset and there murdered a royal official when he tried to get them to pay a tax on trade. Six years later there was an assault on the Church that rocked the continent when word got out. It bears repeating.

> AD 793. This year came dreadful fore-warnings over the land of the Northumbrians, terrifying the people most woefully: these were immense sheets of light rushing through the air, and whirlwinds, and fiery dragons flying across the firmament. These tremendous tokens were soon followed by a great famine: and not long after, on the sixth day before the ides of January in the same year, the harrowing inroads of heathen men made lamentable havoc in the church of God of Holy-island, by rapine and slaughter.[24]

Clearly, the Viking raids had begun. It is highy probable that the first raids in the historical records may not have been the first ones that actually occurred—but that's only speculation at this point. In any case, the Sixth Seal was opened in 774, and the first recorded Viking raids took place thirteen and nineteen years later.

24 *Anglo-Saxon Chronicle* translation by Rev. James Ingram (1823), Everyman Press, London, 1912. http://www.britannia.com/history/docs/asintro2.html

There are various theories involving the causes of the Viking invasions. Some have proposed that because they lived along the sea, it
was natural for them to look for new lands by sea; but this theory
offers no help as to why they launched their forays at this time. Others
have suggested that because the British Isles were filled with different
warring kingdoms, their internal disarray made them easy prey. This
theory does not explain why the Vikings would then attack France and
the Frankish Kingdom, which was comparatively unified and well-for-
tified.

The first attacks on record along the coast of western Europe took
place between 790 and 800—at the same time as the English raids.
Still another theory suggests that global warming (helping to establish
colonies in Greenland) might have been a factor. Overpopulation is
always a possibility. It was one of principle reasons for Greek colonial
expansion centuries earlier.

> The seacoast towns were naturally the first objects of their raids.
> Masters of the sea, they struck where they chose with all the
> advantage that goes with a surprise attack. Their long open boats
> would appear unheralded out of the morning mist, and before a
> force could be collected to ward them off they would have sacked
> the town and carried their plunder off to the safety of the sea. As
> they grew bolder, the Vikings struck inland, rowing their boats up
> the navigable rivers on which the most important towns were sit-
> uated. For centuries these rivers had been the principal highways
> of trade. They now served the northern pirates equally well. Every-
> where the Northmen sought out monasteries and churches, not so
> much through malice against the Christian clergy as because they
> had learned that there was always rich plunder to be found under
> the sign of the cross and that the monks and clergy had become too
> accustomed to the protection offered them by religious veneration
> to have taken the necessary precautions for defense. Great numbers
> of the monasteries were completely destroyed—a serious blow to
> learning, since they were the chief centers of education. The fear
> these rapacious pirates inspired is echoed eloquently in the prayer,
> introduced into the litany,

"From the fury of the Northmen, good Lord, deliver us!"[25]

The question is why? Why does this wave of aggression sail across the seas to be unleashed on distant Christian shores? What's the connection? It turns out it has been staring us in the face all the time.

We recall that the Sixth Seal was opened in 774. In 772 Charlemagne had launched his first attacks against the Saxons, then left Northern Germany to deal with events in Italy. He returned in 775 for a second assault, and a third in 776. These battles between the Frankish king and the Saxons, eighteen in all, were to extend over thirty years, until the year 804. In fact, it is hard to tell how often they were conquered—humbly submitting to Charlemagne's wishes, promising to obey, giving the required hostages, and walking away—only to return to the battlefield after Charlemagne had departed! Hardly a year went by between 772 and 804 without such vacillations.

The spirit behind the resistance was a Saxon leader named Widukind. He was married to Geva of Westfold, daughter of the Danish king Goimo I and sister of the Danish kings Ragnar and Siefried. After the struggles of 777—when Charlemagne had subdued the Saxons once again—Widukind found refuge with his wife's royal family in Denmark. In what almost seems like a shuttle service, Widukind left and returned, left and returned, finding sanctuary when he needed it and coming back to fight when he could. Of the various Viking nationalities, it was principally the Danes and Norwegians who harassed the western coast of France, in other words, members of Widukind's family.

The Saxon wars were initiated by a foreign king whose goal was to forcibly convert pagans to Christianity. Every time Widukind escaped to the Danish court, he carried stories of atrocities and the destruction of his people—seeds of ill omen. After the back and forth of ten years of war, Chalemagne committed an unforgiveable atriocity. In 782, as a result of the broken treaties and Saxon refusal to be converted, Charlemagne had 4,500 Saxon leaders beheaded. Their crime was practicing

---

25 *A Survey of European Civilization, Pt. 1*, by Wallace Klippert Ferguson, p. 156.

their religion after having been converted at the point of a sword. The Aller River in Verden in the Duchy of Saxony was said to have flowed red with blood. Charlemagne becomes known as the "Butcher of the Saxons." He followed with a series of Draconan laws.

When a Saxon rebellion broke out again, Charlemagne deported 10,000 Saxons to northern France, replacing them with Franks. Although 804 is the recorded final conflict, Saxon uprisings continued as late as 841 and 845, more than 70 years after the initial onslaught.

As we survey this brutal period, we find battle, war, destruction, mass murder and deportation. One can only imagine that a number of these Saxons fled north to an environment of considerably less perse-cution—an area where they shared religious sentiments and were not being besieged by warlike Christians bent on their conversion. They brought with them horror stories of death and destruction.

Given this historical context, we must disagree with the statement of Mr. Ferguson, quoted earlier. One could reasonably conclude that there definitely was malice towards the Christians by these Northern pagans, and that it was Charlemagne's attacks on the Saxons that ignited the conflagration. The initial attacks by the Vikings, recorded by the Anglo-Saxon Chronicles, occurred during the same thirty-year period during which the Frankish-Saxon conflict was happening in northern Germany. These attacks escalated through the ninth century. The Vikings grew bolder as time marched on, eventually sailing right up the Seine and demanding tribute from Paris itself.

We assert that Charlemagne's Saxon wars were the principle cat-alyst of the Viking invasions. The first two waves occurred in the year we are looking for—namely 774, the opening of the Sixth Seal. For the next two centuries—through the Northern seas, Europe, Mediter-ranean and across the rivers of Russia—the Vikings made their mark.

CHAPTER SEVEN

Revelation 7

7:1 *Next I saw four angels, standing at the four corners of the earth, holding four winds of the world back to keep them from blowing over the land or the sea or in the trees./ Then I saw another angel rising where the sun rises, carrying the seal of the living God; he called in a powerful voice to the four angels whose duty was to devastate land and sea, / "Wait before you do any damage on land or at sea or to the trees, until we have put the seal on the foreheads of the servants of our God." / Then I heard how many were sealed: a hundred and forty-four thousand, out of all the tribes of Israel.*

7:5 *From the tribe of Judah, twelve thousand had been sealed; from the tribe of Reuben, twelve thousand; from the tribe of Gad, twelve thousand; / from the tribe of Asher, twelve thousand; from the tribe of Naphtali, twelve thousand; from the tribe of Manasseh, twelve thousand; / from the tribe of Simeon, twelve thousand; from the tribe of Levi, twelve thousand; from the tribe of Issachar, twelve thousand; / from the tribe of Zebulun, twelve thousand; from the tribe of Joseph, twelve thousand; and from the tribe of Benjamin, twelve thousand were sealed.*

7:9 *After that I saw a huge number, impossible to count, of people from every nation, race, tribe and language; they were standing in front of the throne and in front of the Lamb, dressed in white robes and holding palms in their hands. They shouted aloud, / "Victory to our God, who sits on the throne, and to the Lamb!" / And all the angels who were standing in a circle around the throne, surrounding the elders and the four animals, prostrated themselves before the throne, and touched the ground with their foreheads, worshiping God with these words, / "Amen. Praise and glory and wisdom and thanksgiving and honor and power and strength to our God for ever and ever. Amen."*

7:13 *One of the elders then spoke, and asked me, "Do you know who these people are, dressed in white robes, and where they have come from?" / I answered him, "You can tell me, my lord." Then he said, "These are the people who have been through the great persecution, and because they have washed their robes white again in the blood of the Lamb, / they now stand in front of God's throne and serve him day and night in his sanctuary; and the One who sits on the throne will spread his tent over them. / They will never hunger or thirst again; neither the sun nor scorching wind will ever plague them, / because the Lamb who is at the throne will be their shepherd and will lead them to springs of living water; and God will wipe away all tears from their eyes."*

* * * * *

7:1 "Next I saw four angels, standing at the four corners of the earth, holding four winds of the world back to keep them from blowing over the land or the sea or in the trees."

Like the majority of our other images here, the four winds are most often linked to the figures of Greek mythology. Boreas is the North Wind, Zephyrus the West, Eurus the East and Notus the South. Each has a distinctive personality, but these do not seem to be separately invoked by these lines, and so we will leave it at that.

"Then I saw another angel rising where the sun rises, carrying the seal of the living God; he called in a powerful voice to the four angels whose duty was to devastate land and sea,"

I saw another angel rising where the Sun rises—in the East. He carries the "seal" of the living God—one of our seals! The seal is aligning with the Vernal Equinox. We stand between the Sixth and the Seventh Seals, and it could be either one.

"Wait before you do any damage on land or at sea or to the trees, until we have put the seal on the foreheads of the servants of our God."

They are being told to wait. Storms are being held at bay. The Vernal Equinox is related to the Cardinal Direction East, Aries, Ascendant and Spring. Aries rules the head. The head is what the ram uses to butt. The servants of God are identified by their sufferings. Which "seal" did you suffer and die under? They're taking a head count. The head and face are the areas that distinguish us from one another. We take pictures of the face and put it on identification documents. We don't take pictures of other body parts as identification, with the possible exception of fingerprints.

Then I heard how many were sealed: a hundred and forty-four thousand, out of all the tribes of Israel.

The servants have been identified and numbered.

7:5 From the tribe of Judah, twelve thousand had been sealed; from the tribe of Reuben, twelve thousand; from the tribe of Gad, twelve thousand;

Once again we return to these themes of seven and twelve. There were seven visible planets equaling *one* week; there were twelve signs of the zodiac equaling *one* year. Each one of these in different ways represents the complete package, the whole unit. The repetitions of the number twelve, now referring to the tribes of Israel: that which is later reflected in the twelve disciples. These lines are building on a mathematical metaphor of 12 times 12 times a thousand. These are ALL the people to have passed the test. When Jesus fed the multitudes and had twelve basketfuls left over, it is a metaphor about giving a sermon on the power of faith, keynote to the Age of Pisces. If you have faith (Pisces) you can heal yourself (Virgo). He spoke. They heard and were healed, making them "whole" again, the message of twelve leftover basketfuls. By making it twelve thousand times twelve thousand, we are increasing the emphasis, making it even more important. This is who has passed the grade over the last two thousand years.

Victory to our God Who Sits on the Throne

*7:9 After that I saw a huge number, impossible to count, of people from
every nation, race, tribe and language; they were standing in front of
the throne and in front of the Lamb, dressed in white robes and holding
palms in their hands. They shouted aloud,*

The 12 times 12 thousand becomes a very big number, but it represents the multitudes from each tribe *within* Judaism. "People from
every nation, race, tribe and language" represents the multitudes from
outside Judaism who have also purified their robes to the point where
their numbers are "impossible to count." You do not have to be Jewish
or Christian to stand up for truth. There are people of every kind who
have passed the tests and earned white robes.

They are the purified souls. Like the triumphal entry of Jesus into
Jerusalem on Palm Sunday, this is the triumphal entry of all the souls
who have succeeded prior to the conclusion of Revelation. In the
Hebrew tradition, the palm is a symbol of triumph or victory. Their
great tribulation was the End Times of the stars in the constellation
Aries. Palm Sunday comes before the ultimate test, his trial (and death)
on the cross. So now, those holding palms are making an appearance
before the final tribulation. In these lines we see the image of the throne
and the Lamb fused as one.

Victory to our God, who sits on the throne, and to the Lamb!

Repetition. Lamb and throne together. What was first symbolized
is now stated.

*And all the angels who were standing in a circle around the throne, sur-
rounding the elders and the four animals, prostrated themselves before
the throne, and touched the ground with their foreheads, worshiping
God with these words,*

All of these powers are subservient to the greater power, the power
of the throne. Notice that they are standing in a circle (a metaphor for

ellipses, slightly "flattened" circles). They prostrate themselves before the throne, touching the ground with their foreheads. Each identity, each individual bows to a greater power.

Amen. Praise and glory and wisdom and thanksgiving and honor and power and strength to our God for ever and ever. Amen.

Amen. So be it. God is triumphant. The seven superlatives (praise, glory, wisdom, thanksgiving, honor, power, and strength) respresent the seven planets.

7:13 One of the elders then spoke, and asked me, "Do you know who these people are, dressed in white robes, and where they have come from?"

The image of the elder is here being used as a wise one. The wise one asks the question.

I answered him, "You can tell me, my lord." Then he said, "These are the people who have been through the great persecution, and because they have washed their robes white again in the blood of the Lamb,

John, our author, turns the question back on the wise one. The great persecution has been the Age of Pisces, the epoch of suffering. These souls have come to Earth, put on mortal robes and taken the test. It's called life. Since the Lamb, the infant form of the Ram, represents the self, it is YOU who must pass the test, YOU who must spill your blood and bear testimony to truth when the times comes, and be willing to die for it. This is how the mortal robes are washed clean and made white again by the blood of the Lamb. Jesus did it for us. He showed what needed to be done. But this does not absolve you from needing to do it. Jesus is setting the example. A pattern has been established. Are *you* willing to walk the path?

they now stand in front of God's throne and serve him day and night in his sanctuary; and the One who sits on the throne will spread his tent over them.

All those who have passed the test share in the powers of Creation. Notice that we are being told, once again, that it is the One who sits on the throne who has the power; and right now, the Lamb is by the throne. The tent being spread over them represents the powers of heaven that continually watch over us, day or night. These are the skies above.

They will never hunger or thirst again; neither the sun nor scorching wind will ever plague them,

These are souls in heaven. Excellent weather is forecast for eternity!

because the Lamb who is at the throne will be their shepherd and will lead them to springs of living water; and God will wipe away all tears from their eyes."

Notice that it is the Lamb AT the throne. The two are One. The Lamb and the throne (the Vernal Equinox at this time) are heading (precessing) towards the constellation Aquarius, the water-bearer. The cardinal direction East is headed towards the Age of Aquarius, the *"springs of living water"* that come from the urn the water bearer holds.

Pisces is a sign that deals with ignorance and faith, darkness and hope, isolation and spiritual connection. Aquarius is an energy of knowledge. As we enter Aquarius the vibration shifts, and much of what has made us sad in the past will no longer hold a power over us as we move into the New Age. This is a theme that will be touched upon again later in Revelation.

God will wipe away all tears from our eyes, as we learn to look at life in a new light. The time of suffering is over. God will wipe away all tears.

CHAPTER EIGHT

Revelation 8

8:1 *The Lamb then broke the seventh seal, and there was silence in heaven for about half an hour. / Next I saw seven trumpets being given to the seven angels who stand in the presence of God. / Another angel, who had a golden censer, came and stood at the altar. A large quantity of incense was given to him to offer with the prayers of all the saints on the golden altar that stood in front of the throne; / and so from the angel's hand the smoke of the incense went up in the presence of God and with it the prayers of the saints. / Then the angel took the censer and filled it with the fire from the altar, which he then threw down on to the earth; immediately there came peals of thunder and flashes of lightning, and the earth shook.*

8:6 *The seven angels that had the seven trumpets now made ready to sound them. / The first blew his trumpet and, with that, hail and fire, mixed with blood, were dropped on the earth; a third of the earth was burned up, and a third of all the trees, and every blade of grass was burned. / The second angel blew his trumpet, and it was as though a great mountain, all on fire, had been dropped into the sea; a third of the sea turned into blood, / a third of all the living things in the sea were killed, and a third of all ships were destroyed. / The third angel blew his trumpet, and a huge star fell from the sky, burning like a ball of fire, and it fell on a third of all rivers and springs; / this was the star called Wormwood, and a third of all water turned to bitter wormwood, so that many people died from drinking it. / The fourth angel blew his trumpet, and a third of the sun and a third of the moon and a third of the stars were blasted, so that the light went out of a third of them and for a third of the day there was no illumination, and the same with the night.*

8:13 *In my vision, I heard an eagle, calling aloud as it flew high overhead, "Trouble, trouble, trouble, for all the people on earth at the*

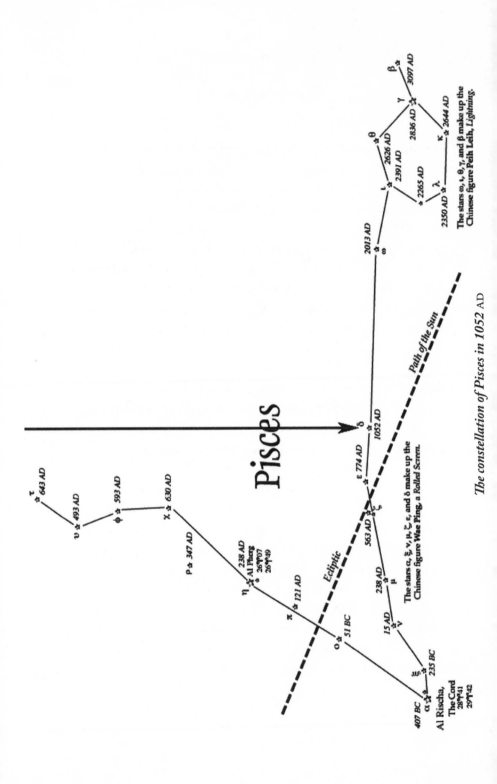

The constellation of Pisces in 1052 AD

Pisces

The stars α, ξ, ν, μ, ζ, ε, and δ make up the Chinese figure Wae Ping, a Rolled Screen.

The stars ω, ι, θ, γ, and β make up the Chinese figure Peih Leih, *Lightning.*

τ 643 AD
υ 493 AD
φ 593 AD
χ 630 AD
ρ 347 AD
η 238 AD
Al Pherg
26ℋ07
26ℋ49
π 121 AD
ο 51 BC
ξ 235 BC
ν 15 AD
μ 238 AD
ζ 563 AD
ε 774 AD
δ 1052 AD
ω 2013 AD
ι 2391 AD
θ 2626 AD
λ 2265 AD
γ 2836 AD
κ 2644 AD
β 3097 AD
2350 AD
α 407 BC
Al Rischa,
The Cord
28ℋ41
29ℋ42

Ecliptic

Path of the Sun

sound of the other three trumpets which the three angels are going to blow."

* * * * *

The Seventh Seal

8:1 The Lamb then broke the seventh seal, and there was silence in heaven for about half an hour.

The Seventh Seal is *Delta Piscium*. It aligned with the Vernal Equinox in AD 1052.

We are being told that there will be no more celestial activity in terms of the Vernal Equinox for quite some time. There was silence in heaven for *"about half an hour."*

The Seventh Seal was the last star in the series that aligned with Spring. There is a large gap before another comes into view. It is the distance between the past and the future, between the last star and the next one that we are attempting to measure. How long does it take for first one to rise, and then to be followed by the other when observed against the horizon in terms of the rotational speed of the Earth? About forty-seven minutes.

This answer works because in antiquity, hours and minutes were not homogenized the way they are today. A half hour today equals exactly thirty minutes because our clocks have been synchronized (a word meaning "with time") and designed that way. We now have standard time zones.

Long ago, hours were measured between sunrise and sunset. In the summer daylight half hours were much larger than our standard 30 minutes, clocking in at about 51 minutes by modern measure, and in the winter they were about 17 minutes long, depending on your degree of latitude (how far north or south you lived).

Forty-seven minutes not only falls within this 17-minute to 51-minute range (depending on the season), it explains why Revelation says "for *about* half an hour."

In today's world we're used to standard time zones. These regi-

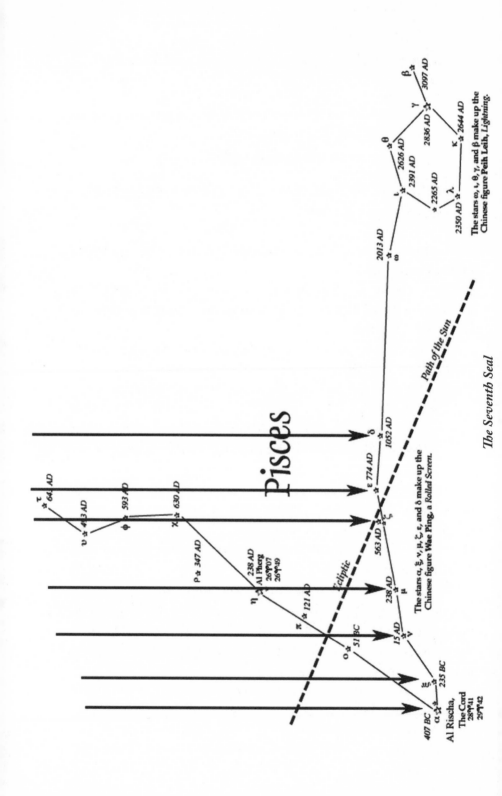

The Seventh Seal

mented segments came about with the development of train travel in the late 19th century. Each town had its own time based on when the Sun reached the "high noon" mark, especially as you traveled along an east-west axis. Interestingly, this is not as much an issue for trains traveling north or south. What time was the train going to pull into Cincinnati? Well, that depends on whose clock you're trying to read. The time zones were created so that everyone in the same geographic area would have clocks that would read the same time at the same moment. The train schedules, our fastest mode of travel at the time, needed to be consistent for everyone and their development forced us to come up with a new system.

There would be a silence for about half an hour.

There were no celestial "voices" about to be triggered, no Piscean stars along the precessional path of the ecliptic to "speak" to the Earth. The Vernal Equinox, the marker of Spring, was silent on the subject following the opening of the Seventh Seal.

Is this interval so different from what had been happening with the previous six stars? How much time passed between each?

The seven stars we have been examining are collectively known as the "Scroll." These seven stars are fairly evenly spaced from first to last. They look like they belong together; which is one reason they're an asterism. They seem to make up part of a visual pattern. If we break it down in years, there are 172 years between the First and the Second Seal, 250 years between the second and the third, etc. Here are the six intervals it takes for the Vernal Equinox to move from one star to the next by precessional motion: 172 years, 250 years, 223 years, 325 years, 211 years and 278 years.

They average out to a little over 243 years. One of them is over three hundred, one under 200, but their intervals are all relatively evenly spaced to each other.

When compared to what? When compared to how long it takes for the interval between the Seventh Seal and the star that follows it. How long is that: 961 years.

How many minutes elapse between the risings of each of these seven stars? Here is the sequence, just as above, from *Alpha* (the First

Seal) to *Delta* (the Seventh Seal), only this time we're not measuring the motion in precessional speed (how long it takes for the Vernal Equinox to move), we're measuring it in rotational speed, the time that is measured on your clock: 9 minutes, 12 minutes, 11 minutes, 16 minutes, 11 minutes and 14 minutes.

Again, for comparison, what is the next "interval" between the Seventh Seal (*Delta Piscium*) and, for the sake of continuity, let's call it the "Eighth Seal": 47 minutes.

It's a sizeable jump, and it's apparent when you look at them in the night sky.

There was silence "*in heaven*" for about half an hour.

From AD 1052 when *Delta Piscium* was the east star until recently, there has not been another star in the constellation Pisces that has aligned with the Vernal Equinox. We have had no new eastern star for almost a thousand years.

That's the metaphor. If this is the Seventh Seal, what happened in 1052? This was the year the seeds were planted to politically and spiritually split the Christian Kingdom in half.

With the succession of foreign invasions and administrative work involved in running the Roman Empire, it was finally decided to have two centers and two emperors to help share the load. Diocletian originally set the precedent by splitting his rule with a co-emperor in 286. Constantine later solidified this split by moving the capitol from Rome to Byzantium, which he called *Nova Roma* in 330. Roman artisans, architecture, and culture were brought in to augment the reconstruction of the new and improved capital.

After Constantine's death the city became known as Constantinople, the City of Constantine. In 395 the physical empire was permanently split into eastern and western halves following the death of Theodosius I, but, while the civil and administrative power of the empire had moved to Constantinople, the spiritual authority of the papacy remained in Rome.

Fast forward to the 11th century. The two sections of the empire had become ingrained in their own ways of doing things over the centuries. The Western empire was in a bad state of affairs, but was still linked to and protected by the East. Southern Italy and Sicily had traditional ethnic links with the east, having been settled by the Greeks in the 6th century BC. One early name for southern Italy was *Magna Graecia*, Greater Greece. The social and spiritual bonds between these colonies and Constantinople had not been forgotten.

When the Normans (descendants of the Saxons who had both been deported to Normandy and later intermingled with the Vikings who migrated there) began to settle in Sicily in the second decade of the 11th century, they stirred jealousies between the Greek Orthodox and Roman Catholic Church over control of the area. Both agreed they wanted the Normans out. These Normans were expanding their holdings from Sicily into southern Italy. Norman raiding parties had few qualms about attacking papal properties. In their marauding they plundered churches and monasteries.

In 1052 Pope Leo IX traveled to Saxony to meet with Henry III, the Western emperor, and asked for his help against the Normans in a military campaign. But Henry turned Leo down. In 1053, on the heels of this rejection, Leo cobbled together a volunteer army and took on the Normans in the battle of Civitate in Italy. Although facing the numerically superior papal forces, whose Eastern Roman allies were on their way, the Normans soundly defeated the papal forces. Leo was held prisoner for nine months in Benevento. While in captivity he was forced to ratify a number of treaties favorable to the Normans, further entrenching them in Italy.

> These were acts of great historical importance, inasmuch as the Normans legitimized their conquests, past and future, and the popes established their feudal sovereignty over all of southern Italy and Sicily.[1]

The problem was that this effectively cut the Eastern Romans out of the loop. Having come to the aid of the West many times previously, Constantinople was not thrilled.

---

1 *Encyclopedia Britannica*, 1986, v. 22, p. 200.

At the beginning of the second millennium of Christian history, the church of Constantinople, capital of the East Roman (or Byzantine) Empire, was at the peak of its world influence and power. Neither Rome, which had become a provincial town and its church an instrument in the hands of political interests, nor Europe under the Carolingian and Ottonian dynasties could really compete with Byzantium as centres of Christian civilization. The Byzantine emperors of the Macedonian dynasty had extended the frontiers of the empire from Mesopotamia to Naples (Italy) and from the Danube River (central Europe) to Palestine. The church of Constantinople not only enjoyed a parallel expansion but also extended its missionary penetration, much beyond the political frontiers of the empire, to Russia and the Caucasus.[2]

Pope Leo IX was held prisoner until March 1054, but was allowed to receive visitors while in captivity. While he was detained he arranged for a legation to go to Constantinople headed by Humbert de Silva Candida. The legation, armed with a papal bull of excommunication against the Eastern patriarch, left for Constantinople in April of 1054 shortly after Leo's release.

Humbert de Silva Candida was Leo's secretary and the head of the legation, a man who shared the Pope's ecumenical zeal. When the legation arrived in Constantinople, the Eastern emperor greeted them warmly, but the patriarch of the Greek Orthodox church spurned them by refusing to meet.

The Greek Orthodox patriarch at this time was Michael Cerularius, the eastern "Pope." Both he and Humbert were stubborn men with tempers to match. While the legation, Eastern Emperor, and Patriarch later attempted negotiations, Pope Leo IX died in Rome, leaving the papal chair vacant for a year. His health had suffered while in captivity. Almost three months after the pope's death, Humbert and the legation took matters into their own hands, entered the Hagia Sophia during the celebration of the liturgy on the 16th of July 1054, and laid the

---

2 *Encyclopedia Britannica*, 1986, v. 17, p. 868.

papal bull of excommunication on the high altar. In return, Cerularius convened a Holy Synod and excommunicated the three Latin legates.

Although Eastern Roman historians took little notice of the event, this marked the final ecumenical division between the two churches in what has become known as the East-West or Great Schism. Technically, the excommunications had been directed at individuals, not the churches; and the Latin excommunication was invalid, since the pope who had authorized it died before it was enacted.

As *The New Catholic Encyclopedia* says:

> The consummation of the schism is generally dated from the year 1054, when this unfortunate sequence of events took place. This conclusion, however, is not correct, because in the bull composed by Humbert, only Patriarch Cerularius was excommunicated. The validity of the bull is questioned because Pope Leo IX was already dead at that time. On the other side, the Byzantine synod excommunicated only the legates and abstained from any attack on the pope or the Latin Church.[3]

Nevertheless, legal or illegal, valid or invalid, the act stuck and history recorded it. The legation left two days later with a city in near riots. Their work was done.

The Seventh Seal is dated to 1052, the year that Henry III turned down Leo's request for military help, and the year that Cerularius forced all Latin churches in his diocese to use the Greek language and liturgical practices. When they refused to do so, he ordered them closed. Cerularius was kicking the Roman influences out of Constantinople, while the Norman incursions erased the Eastern Roman influences in Italy.

It is interesting that the only symbolic reference to this seal is the silence in heaven for half an hour. Hannibal, Tiberius, the civil wars, Lombards, and Vikings all came, had their moment, and moved on. Strictly speaking, the Seventh Seal would be in effect from 1052 until

---

3 *The New Catholic Encyclopedia* edited by The Catholic University of America, McGraw-Hill, 1967

December 7th, 1965 when Pope Paul VI and Patriarch Athenagoras I finally cancelled the original excommunications. Nevertheless, even with the millennial thorn finally removed, the two churches have continued to be fundamentally divided ever since that time.

With the possible exception of the first of the original Seven Seals—which gave birth to the military hegemony of Rome throughout the known world—the Great Schism between the Eastern and Roman Catholicism was to leave the longest lasting impression, during the silence in heaven.

With Rev. 8:1, we have the completion of the opening of the Seven Seals. If we step back for a moment and look at the events involved in Roman history that coincide with the Seals, their historical importance quickly becomes apparent.

With the First Seal, the military ascendancy of Rome is begun. In their history, the Romans themselves called the war with Veii a second founding of Rome, a new beginning.

Immediately a white horse appeared, and the rider on it was holding a bow; he was given the victor's crown and he went away, to go from victory to victory.

With the Second Seal, Hannibal takes his oath and attacks. Livy (59 BC–AD 17), armed with all the advantages of hindsight, and writing more than one hundred and fifty years after the event, had this to say about it.

Most historians have prefaced their work by stressing the importance of the period they propose to deal with; and I may well, at this point, follow their example and declare that I am now about to tell the story of the most memorable war in history: that, namely, which was fought by Carthage under the leadership of Hannibal against Rome.

A number of things contributed to give this war its unique character: in the first place, it was fought between peoples unrivalled throughout previous history in natural resources, and themselves at the peak of their prosperity and power; secondly, it was a struggle between old antagonists, each of whom learned, in the first Punic War, to appreciate the military capabilities of the other; thirdly, the final issue hung so much in doubt that the eventual victors came nearer to destruction than their adversaries. Moreover, high passions were at work throughout, and mutual hatred was hardly less a sharp weapon than the sword ...[4]

... out came another horse, bright red, and its rider was given this duty: to take away peace from the earth and set people killing each other. He was given a huge sword.

With the Third Seal Tiberius became emperor, and the tone of Revelation shifts. It is not war and external conflict that now fans the twin flames of fear and panic: it is internal political tumult. The apple is rotten at the core. Both law and morality must kneel to the will of the emperor. Tiberius set the example by divorcing himself from the senate, Rome, and pantheon. Morality, the sanctuary of the temples, and the influence of the priestesses of Delphi (and other sacred sites) all took a back seat to the Julio-Claudian Emperors. Spiritual channels have been diverted.

Immediately a black horse appeared, and its rider was holding a pair of scales ...

Dark days and dark deeds, indeed.

With the Fourth Seal, Rome was at its nadir, during a period that saw emperor after emperor murdered for personal advancement. It was a time of conflict, strife and civil war. Attacks on the empire from within and without, loss of the historical record, and plague were all part of the mosaic being formed here. This was a period of living hell.

Immediately another horse appeared, deathly pale, and its rider was called Plague, and Hades followed at his heels. They were given authority

---

4 *The War with Hannibal,* Livy, Book XXI.

over a quarter of the earth, to kill by the sword, by famine, by plague and wild beasts.

The Fifth Seal witnessed the coming of the Lombards—a foreign invasion during which, according to the historians, the continuity of Roman civilization was finally broken. The only people who escaped were those who left for the swamps—or the coastal cities where the Eastern Roman (Byzantine) navy could protect them. The landowners and mainland were overwhelmed.

Holy, faithful Master, how much longer will you wait before you pass sentence and take vengeance for our death on the inhabitants of the earth?

The Sixth Seal heralded the coming of the Vikings, who struck without warning from the sea in nearly every geographic corner of the empire.

Then all the earthly rulers, the governors and the commanders, the rich people and the men of influence, the whole population, slaves and citizens, took to the mountains to hide in the caves and among the rocks. They said to the mountains and the rocks, "Fall on us and hide us away from the One who sits on the throne and from the anger of the Lamb. For the Great Day of his anger has come, and who can survive it?"

With the Seventh Seal, what is left of the empire is politically and spiritually split.

The Seven Seals are pivotal points in Roman history. Like a dropped bottle of wine, each seal spills forth its contents through the portal and across time, framing the period and lasting until the next seal. While these historical events are initiated with the opening of each of the seals they are not limited to this, and their influences are felt in the years, decades and centuries following the Seals' opening.

The First Seal established the pattern and growth of the Roman Republic right up until the time they faced their supreme martial test against Hannibal. Once Carthage was out of the way, there was no stopping the Romans until they finally turned on themselves, and Augustus put an end to the civil wars—forging the Empire on the ashes of the Republic. Augustus handed the baton to Tiberius, the first politically appointed Roman Emperor. From the Third Seal and the establishment of the Empire, we moved to Rome's nadir. The Fifth Seal was the Lombards, the Sixth the Vikings, the Seventh the Great Schism.

Each was an important turning point in Roman history. The Seven Seals have come and gone. They were all part of a series, born first of the asterism the "Scroll," secondarily of the constellation Pisces. Following the opening of the Seventh Seal, there is a gap in the heavenly record.

Next in line is what we will call the Eighth Seal (Revelation refers to it once under this name), because it was next in the sequence; but the Eighth Seal represents part of a new dispensation, a new asterism, a new Age. Following the opening of the Seventh Seal, with its silence in heaven, we begin to look ahead to what was about to happen next in our Vernal Equinox series.

Next I saw seven trumpets being given to the seven angels who stand in the presence of God

From the Seventh Seal we move to the next "seven" in our series. The seven *"angels who stand in the presence of God"* are the same "seven" from Chapter 4, wherein it states, *"there were seven flaming lamps burning, the seven spirits of God . . . in front of the throne."* There is a chorus of events that is getting ready to unfold with this next star. The seven angels (the seven visible planets who "dispense" God's justice and are the "eyes" that circle the world doing reconnaissance each day) stand ready for the next round.

"Another angel, who had a golden censer, came and stood at the altar. A large quantity of incense was given to him to offer with the prayers of all the saints on the golden altar that stood in front of the throne;"

We are back at the "altar," but the altar has moved from the Seventh to the Eighth Seal. The golden altar is half of the throne, the ecliptic (Solar) half. All these seals, whether one looks to the Seventh Seal or the First, have represented times of suffering. History records the continuing saga of man's inhumanity to man. God has taken a back seat through the entire Age of Pisces, allowing "man" to run the show without divine council, like the Steward of Gondor awaiting the Return of the King. But suffering generates hopes and prayers, and the prayers have been stored for the day that is coming. These are the prayers of the saints, and all those souls waiting "beneath the altar" in Rev. 6:9, who were forced to make a choice between their beliefs and death.

All this brings us to the opening of the Eighth Seal. This is what Jesus is collectively referring to in Matthew 10:34. All the seals have been difficult, to say the least.

"Do not suppose that I have come to bring peace to the earth: it is not peace I have come to bring, but a sword."

The Age of Pisces, of which Jesus was the herald, is (to be repetitious) a time of suffering, loss, illusion, confusion, betrayal and a lack of understanding. People have lost touch with their divine roots, their spiritual heritage. The priests have no star by which to guide their congregations. One of the reasons Constantinople and the Eastern Roman Empire disengaged from the Western Roman Empire was because of the corruption and political manipulation involved in the legacy of the papacy. It is not a new story. The Eighth Seal brings this spiritual weave to a conclusion. The Eighth Seal marks the end of both Age and asterism; the end of Pisces and the beginning of Aquarius, the end of the Scroll and the beginning of Lightning.

and so from the angel's hand the smoke of the incense went up in the presence of God and with it the prayers of the saints.

God is listening.

Then the angel took the censer and filled it with the fire from the altar,
which he then threw down on to the earth; immediately there came peals
of thunder and flashes of lightning, and the earth shook

This is the lightning referenced in Matthew 24: 27, but there is
another image—that of fire from the altar being thrown down to the
earth—that we will come back to after the next few lines.

… because the coming of the Son of Man will be like lightning striking
in the east and flashing far into the west.

This is an easy translation. The coming of the Age of Aquarius will
happen when the East Point, the Vernal Equinox, aligns with the star
(and asterism) known as *"Lightning."*

Beta (Piscium), a 4½-magnitude (star), is given by Al Achsasi as
Fum al Samakah, the Fish's mouth, descriptive of its position near
that feature in the westernmost of the two (fish). With gamma,
theta, iota and omega (stars of Pisces in the southern fish) it was
the Chinese Peih Leih, Lightning.[5]

The Lathe of Heaven is kicking into gear. The celestial line-up is
underway, and the power of the "Eighth Seal" is getting ready to be
discharged.

8:6 The seven angels that had the seven trumpets now made ready to
sound them.

This is called a fanfare. A celestial announcement is about to be
made. Seven is one of the more difficult metaphors in Revelation, not
necessarily because of the depth of its mysteries, but rather that it is
used to enumerate so many different symbols in the text.

---

5 *Star Names, Their Lore and Meaning,* Richard Hinckley Allen, Dover Press,
p. 343.

The default link to this metaphor is the seven visible planets. As we have already seen, these were represented in terrestrial form through the churches. It's their influence for those of us here upon the Earth.

Seven was also represented as the seven stars of the Scroll, having nothing whatsoever to do with the seven planets (that I'm aware of). Now we are being given "seven" as a number of completeness, of wholeness. The seven planets, as we have seen, make up the seven days of the week. Seven days = one week. Seven = one. A single entity composed of various functioning parts working together. After we review a few more lines of Revelation, this should become apparent.

The First Trumpet

The first blew his trumpet and, with that, hail and fire, mixed with blood, were dropped on the earth; a third of the earth was burned up, and a third of all the trees, and every blade of grass was burned.

This is the first in the series of the seven trumpets and it introduces us to the theme of "thirds." It is the thirds that bind together the seven trumpets into one. The idea of the thirds helps to establish the seven trumpets as different facets of the same crystal. The imagery in the above lines is obvious. The question is: is it literal or metaphorical?

The Second Trumpet

The second angel blew his trumpet, and it was as though a great mountain, all on fire, had been dropped into the sea; a third of the sea turned into blood,

Here we have a second image being introduced that we will see repeated several times. It describes a "fireball" being dropped to the Earth. In this second line we have a fiery mountain being dropped into the sea, in the first we had a third of the Earth burning up. In the opening lines (Rev 9:5), it is fire from the altar that is thrown to the Earth. From heaven, they're all singing about the fire down below.

Let's continue.

a third of all the living things in the sea were killed, and a third of all ships were destroyed.

This completes the earlier sentence and sentiment. The "thirds" continue to be woven into the tapestry.

The Third Trumpet

The third angel blew his trumpet, and a huge star fell from the sky, burning like a ball of fire, and it fell on a third of all rivers and springs;

Here is the motif of a fireball hitting the Earth and its aftermath again. Either the author's mythological reservoir is running dry or he is trying to underscore an important point.

this was the star called Wormwood, and a third of all water turned to bitter wormwood, so that many people died from drinking it.

Wormwood was known for its repulsive bitterness. It figures in several places in the Bible (Jer. 9:15, 23:15; Deut. 29:18; Lam. 3:19; Prov. 5:4). It was, as it is here, used figuratively for a curse or calamity. Its Latin name is *Artemisia Absinthium*, and it has been used for centuries as a general pesticide, or as a tea or spray to repel slugs and snails. Culpeper's *Complete Herbal* calls it a martial plant, meaning that it can be caustic and abrasive. The absinthin is water-soluble, it washes off with sprays or rain, leaches into the soil and can interfere and stunt the growth of surrounding plants. As the name implies, it was once used as a worming medicine for both people and animals before its toxicity was fully realized. The reference above, therefore, is herbally consistent.

Artemisia, after whom the genus was named, was the wife and sister of King Mausolous, from which we derive the term mausoleum. Upon his death she not only had the mausoleum built (another of the seven wonders of the ancient world), she also drank her husband's ashes daily. She is reported to have pined away and died two years later.

The association between this queen and Wormwood is a reflection wherein one is totally immersed in grief, suffering, and despair—especially following death.

The Fourth Trumpet

The fourth angel blew his trumpet, and a third of the sun and a third of the moon and a third of the stars were blasted, so that the light went out of a third of them and for a third of the day there was no illumination, and the same with the night.

Since this still lies in the future, we can only speculate about its meaning, but it is possible that some natural event, such as a volcanic eruption, would throw enough particulate matter into the atmosphere such that, literally, the powers of the sun and the moon could be darkened. Naturally, if this were the case, the time frame of a third of a day would be metaphorical.

The theme of "thirds" continues, uniting these trumpets in a common chorus.

8:13 In my vision, I heard an eagle, calling aloud as it flew high overhead, "Trouble, trouble, trouble, for all the people on earth at the sound of the other three trumpets which the three angels are going to blow."

Following the earlier passages, does this need any explanation? Rev. 9 picks up where Rev. 8 leaves off.

CHAPTER NINE

Revelation 9

9:1 *Then the fifth angel blew his trumpet, and I saw a star that had fallen from heaven on to the earth, and he was given the key to the shaft leading down to the Abyss. / When he unlocked the shaft of the Abyss, smoke poured up out of the Abyss like the smoke from a huge furnace so that the sun and the sky were darkened by it, / and out of the smoke dropped locusts which were given the powers that scorpions have on the earth: / they were forbidden to harm any fields or crops or trees and told only to attack any men who were without God's seal on their foreheads. / They were not to kill them, but to give them pain for five months, and the pain was to be the pain of a scorpion's sting. / When this happens, men will long for death and not find it anywhere; they will want to die and death will evade them.*

9:7 *To look at, these locusts were like horses armored for battle; they had things that looked like gold crowns on their heads, and faces that seemed human, / and hair like women's hair, and teeth like lions' teeth. / They had body-armor like iron breastplates, and the noise of their wings sounded like a great charge of horses and chariots into battle. / Their tails were like scorpions', with stings, and it was with them that they were able to injure people for five months. / As their leader they had their emperor, the angel of the Abyss, whose name in Hebrew is Abaddon, or Apollyon (Destruction) in Greek.*

9:12 *That was the first of the troubles; there are still two more to come.*

9:13 */ The sixth angel blew his trumpet, and I heard a voice come out of the four horns of the golden altar in front of God. / It spoke to the sixth angel with the trumpet, and said, "Release the four angels that are chained up at the great river Euphrates." / These four angels had been put there ready for this hour of this day of this month of this year, and now they were released to destroy a third of the human race. I learned how*

many there were in their army; twice ten thousand times ten thousand
mounted men. / In my vision I saw the horses, and the riders with their
breastplates of flame color, hyacinth blue and sulphur yellow; the horses
had lions' heads, and fire, smoke and sulphur were coming out of their
mouths, that the one third of the human race was killed. / All the horses'
power was in their mouths and their tails: their tails were like snakes,
and had heads that were able to wound. / But the rest of the human
race, who escaped these plagues, refused either to abandon the things they
had made with their own hands—the idols made of gold, silver, bronze,
stone and wood that can neither see nor hear nor move—or to stop wor-
shipping devils. / Nor did they give up their murdering, or witchcraft,
or fornication or stealing.

The Fifth Trumpet

9:1 Then the fifth angel blew his trumpet, and I saw a star that had
fallen from heaven on to the earth, and he was given the key to the shaft
leading down to the Abyss.

Here is the same image of our fireball from heaven hitting the
Earth. The key, shaft and Abyss are new images, appearing for the first
time. The association seems to be that this fireball is connected to the
Abyss, having caused it on impact.

When he unlocked the shaft of the Abyss, smoke poured up out of the
Abyss like the smoke from a huge furnace so that the sun and the sky were
darkened by it,

This line repeats the earlier reference in Rev. 8:12 to the third of
the sun, moon and stars being blasted, darkening the skies.

and out of the smoke dropped locusts which were given the powers that
scorpions have on the earth:

Naturally, the power of scorpions is to sting and sometimes kill with their venom. Locusts are known to swarm, a condition now understood as a response to overcrowding. It has been estimated that some of the largest swarms have covered hundreds of square miles, destroying fields and crops, stripping the land clean in their wake.

Socrates had a different take on locusts. From his *Phaedrus* he claims that when the Muses first brought song to the world, their enchantment so captivated some that they forgot to eat and drink until they died. The Muses turned these souls into locusts, singing their entire lives away. What is interesting is that this is similar to the mythological association to *Artemisia* which we glimpsed under Wormwood. She pined away until she died.

> *they were forbidden to harm any fields or crops or trees and told only to attack any men who were without God's seal on their foreheads.*

This devastation is going to be turned against humanity, not vegetation. Those who have followed a spiritually aligned path will be spared.

> *They were not to kill them, but to give them pain for five months, and the pain was to be the pain of a scorpion's sting*

Here it is made clear that yes, these are indeed the attributes of the scorpion that is being referenced. The rest is self-evident.

> *9:7 To look at, these locusts were like horses armored for battle; they had things that looked like gold crowns on their heads, and faces that seemed human,*

We are climbing into a composite mythological image here, similar to the Chimera. This same image continues to build for the next three lines, so we will include them in their entirety here.

> *and hair like women's hair, and teeth like lions' teeth. They had body-armor like iron breastplates, and the noise of their wings sounded like a*

great charge of horses and chariots into battle. Their tails were like scor-
pions', with stings, and it was with them that they were able to injure
people for five months.

It seems fairly evident that we are looking at an engine of war. They
are armored for battle, and they sound like the charge of horses and
chariots into battle. One might consider a plague (one of the plagues
of Egypt referenced in Exodus is a swarm of locusts), but swarms of
insects don't need a leader.

As their leader they had their emperor, the angel of the Abyss, whose
name in Hebrew is Abaddon, or Apollyon (Destruction) in Greek.

A cataclysimic battle is foreshadowed.

At this point we need to stop, back up, and review some of the
images in Revelation 6, 8, and 9.

Thirds

First of all there is the repeating images of thirds. Do each of these
mean a series of calamities, each of which takes out a third of the
Earth, so that on the first day you have a third taken out, and then the
next day another third of what is left is taken, and then another third
after that. Or are all of these, which seems more likely, talking about
the same event which hammers the Earth in some manner? Are the
seven angels each doing their part in a single cause, a cause that is being
underscored by celestial endorsement?

Also, the fireball being dropped to Earth is an image that is
repeated several times. It gets our attention. In the first instance, hail
and fire—mixed with blood—are dropped to the Earth. In the second,
a mountain of fire is dropped into the sea. In the third, a huge star,
burning like a fire, falls into all the rivers and springs. In the fourth, a
third of the sun, moon, and stars are blasted. There is a dramatic heav-
en-to-earth connection here that is being emphasized.

This is not the last time we will see Revelation refer to a huge celestial force striking the Earth. The smoke from the furnace mentioned in Rev. 9 suggests the smoke resulting from this collision. We would have to wonder what kind of a collision would generate smoke like this if it strikes the sea? Other images hold up well under this metaphor (earth, trees, grass, rivers, springs). It is possible that a meteor could strike or impact a coastline, in which case all the references would work. There is every indication that this is precisely what happened 65 million years ago. An object from space hit the Gulf of Mexico/Yucatan peninsula leaving a huge crater, wiping out the dinosaurs.

Having said this, it's possible that we are simply looking at celestial metaphor. The opening lines (Rev. 8:5) state that the angel took fire from the altar or path of the Sun (the Vernal Equinox) and threw it down onto the Earth. This is astronomical allusion, marked by time. It is telling us *when* this event is going to take place, when the Vernal Equinox, the altar, aligns with the fire, the spark of the star.

Stars are fire. What the priests of their day would have been watching for was when this alignment approached. The peals of thunder and flashes of lightning could be a mythological image for what transpires on Earth. It will shake things up. This was the case with the Sixth Seal, which carried some particularly dark imagery. It's all history now.

6:12 In my vision, when he broke the sixth seal, there was a violent earthquake and the sun went as black as coarse sackcloth; the moon turned red as blood all over, and the stars of the sky fell on to the earth like figs dropping from a fig tree when a high wind shakes it; the sky disappeared like a scroll rolling up and all the mountains and islands were shaken from their places. Then all the earthly rulers, the governors and the commanders, the rich people and the men of the influence, the whole population, slaves and citizens, took to the mountains to hide in caves and among the rocks. They said to the mountains and the rocks, "Fall on us and hide us away from the One who sits on the throne and from the anger of the Lamb. For the Great Day of his anger has come, and who can survive it?"

We are able to view this seal from the safe vantage point of history. Distant history.

If there literally was a huge earthquake, it was not recorded for us from across the centuries. If sediment was injected into the air, such as a huge volcanic explosion turning the Moon red in the same way our industrial pollution now makes for some spectacular sunsets, we don't know about it. If the stars fell to the Earth, we have no knowledge of that event.

But what we do know is that the Vikings instilled terror and fear in the European population for two full centuries following the opening of the Sixth Seal. We know that the local coastal populace did run away to hide beneath the skirts of nature whenever they could find them, whatever their class. People in many cities across Europe never saw a Viking raid, especially if they weren't located on a major waterway. But it was a time when fear was in the air; and there were certainly places where you *didn't* want to be.

The author or authors of the Book of Revelation usually speak in mythic terms, although some of the references seem to be literal.

9:12 That was the first of the troubles; there are still two more to come.

We have heard the first five trumpets. There are two more to sound.

The Sixth Trumpet

9:13 The sixth angel blew his trumpet, and I heard a voice come out of the four horns of the golden altar in front of God.

The Vernal Equinox, the throne, the altar, the source of power, is getting ready to address the angel of the sixth trumpet. The voice, the spirit of the four horns from the stars in the head of the Ram, is the spirit of war.

It spoke to the sixth angel with the trumpet, and said, "Release the four angels that are chained up at the great river Euphrates."

It is clear that events will take place in the Middle East in general, and in particular in Iraq and Kuwait where the great river runs. It will start there.

These four angels had been put there ready for this hour of this day of this month of this year, and now they were released to destroy a third of the human race. I learned how many there were in their army; twice ten thousand times ten thousand mounted men.

That's 200,000,000. Like each of the Seven Seals that have gone before, these events will take place in the designated hour. Here the "one third" seems to be clearly outlined. It will represent a destruction of one-third of the human race, not a third, and then another third, and another. The clouds of locusts are being morphed into the twice ten thousand times ten thousand mounted men. Combine the images. They will swarm.

In my vision I saw the horses, and the riders with their breastplates of flame color, hyacinth blue and sulphur yellow; the horses had lions' heads, and fire, smoke and sulphur were coming out of their mouths, that the one third of the human race was killed.

A weapon of war, wielded by this army, will devastate populations.

All the horses' power was in their mouths and their tails: their tails were like snakes, and had heads that were able to wound.

Their power was coming out of their mouths, smoke and sulphur from Lion's heads. Commanding words, strong convictions. Hellfire and lightning were composed of it. Their snake-tails were venomous. One third of the human race is being taken out.

The imagery we are observing draws from a singular scene of the heavens, where the bow of the constellational centaur, Sagittarius, points its arrow at the body and heart of the Scorpion. It is a highly volatile area of heaven, not only for the martial attributes attributed to this region and these two signs of the zodiac—but also because the Milky Way spills between the two, catching the souls, according to indigenous populations all around the globe, of those who die and pass over. It is a stairway to heaven.

The Milky Way is the celestial river between heaven and earth, the transport of the souls, the River Styx that Charon must ferry. But it is also the Lethe, from which we drink, forgetting all that went before until we pass over again. It is the Lethe, Phlegethon, Acheron and Cocytus all in one, all rivers of the Greek Underworld. It has born many names over the course of time. There are five rivers, but according to mythology they all meet and merge into a great swamp in the middle of the land of the dead.

They are five and they are one.

But the rest of the human race, who escaped these plagues, refused either to abandon the things they had made with their own hands—the idols made of gold, silver, bronze, stone and wood that can neither see nor hear nor move—or to stop worshipping devils.

Here we are being shown a slightly different picture. The locusts, the smoke, the army that dispenses these actions; all may have been part of a plague. But even after some of these terrible events transpire, those in other areas will observe from afar and hang onto their material things and continue to do unhealthy things.

Nor did they give up their murdering, or witchcraft, or fornication or stealing.

Those kinds of unhealthy things like murder, mass murder, casting spells on people and having them believe in things that aren't true, lac-iviousness, and stealing. Who do you think you're doing it to? We are all God's children. Such behavior is wrong.

CHAPTER TEN

Revelation 10

10:1 *Then I saw another powerful angel coming down from heaven, wrapped in a cloud, with a rainbow over his head; his face was like the sun, and his legs were pillars of fire. / In his hand he had a small scroll, unrolled; he put his right foot in the sea and his left foot on the land / and he shouted so loud, it was like a lion roaring. At this, seven claps of thunder made themselves heard / and when the seven thunderclaps had spoken, I was preparing to write, when I heard a voice from heaven say to me, "Keep the words of the seven thunderclaps secret and do not write them down." / Then the angel that I had seen, standing on the sea and the land, raised his right hand to heaven, / and swore by the One who lives for ever and ever, and made heaven and all that is in it, and earth and all it bears, and the sea and all it holds. "The time of waiting is over; / at the time when the seventh angel is heard sounding his trumpet, God's secret intention will be fulfilled, just as he announced in the Good News told to his servants the prophets."*

10:8 *Then I heard the voice I had heard from heaven speaking to me again. "Go," it said, "and take that open scroll out of the hand of the angel standing on sea and land." / I went to the angel and asked him to give me the small scroll, and he said, "Take it and eat it; it will turn your stomach sour, but in your mouth it will taste sweet as honey. / So I took it out of the angel's hand, and swallowed it; it was as sweet as honey in my mouth, but when I had eaten it my stomach turned sour. / Then I was told, "You are to prophesy again, this time about many different nations and countries and languages and emperors.*

* * * * *

10:1 Then I saw another powerful angel coming down from heaven, wrapped in a cloud, with a rainbow over his head; his face was like the sun, and his legs were pillars of fire.

The rainbow re-identifies our Aquarian multi-colored spectrum. This is the Age following Pisces, the Age of our time, a new asterism or vibration "written" in the stars coming down from heaven. The exaltation of the Sun in Aries (which remains consistent from Age to Age) is being invoked again with *"his face was like the Sun."*

> *In his hand he had a small scroll, unrolled; he put his right foot in the sea and his left foot on the land*

The "small Scroll" is similar to the Scroll we saw in Rev. 5:1. It is not as big as the first, and John is studying the prophecies that will come with the next asterism, the one still in our future, that of the western Fish of Pisces or the asterism Lightning. The angel is balanced—both sea (emotionally) and land (practically). He bridges the old and the new.

> *and he shouted so loud, it was like a lion roaring. At this, seven claps of thunder made themselves heard*

The shout will be hard to miss. There have been several references to lightning and thunder as Spring (the Lamb) aligns with the Eighth Seal. This is one of them.

The Seven Thunderclaps

> *and when the seven thunderclaps had spoken, I was preparing to write, when I heard a voice from heaven say to me, "Keep the words of the seven thunderclaps secret and do not write them down."*

This secrecy is a part of a pattern that will be covered more fully later. But we mentioned it earlier in reference to the Hebrew prophets, End Times, and the Scroll. Revelation does not say more about it.

> *Then the angel that I had seen, standing on the sea and the land, raised his right hand to heaven, and swore by the One who lives for ever and*

ever, and made heaven and all that is in it, and earth and all it bears,
and the sea and all it holds. "The time of waiting is over"

He doesn't have to swear. The timing is fairly evident. This is the event that heaven has been waiting for—from God on high to the angels and all the souls under the altar. The Age of Pisces, with its model of spiritual surrender, is coming to a close. Pisces is over and the constellation of the Son of man begins.

This is when the East Point parallels the Eighth Seal and officially enters Aquarius.

at the time when the seventh angel is heard sounding his trumpet, God's
secret intention will be fulfilled, just as he announced in the Good News
told to his servants the prophets.

The seventh angel of the trumpets marks the end of the score. The final piece is falling into place. It corresponds to the end of the *"silence in heaven."* This is the opening of a new era, the time of the Eighth Seal.

It is clear from this and other lines that the entire Age of Pisces has been a test. With the sounding of the seventh trumpet the timing is right. From a heavenly perspective this will be the time of the Good News, because the time of sadness is coming to a conclusion. Isaiah foresaw the coming of the "good news" long before.

> *How beautiful on the mountains,*
> *are the feet of the messenger announcing peace,*
> *of the messenger of good news,*
> *who proclaims salvation*
> *and says to Zion,*
> *"Your God is king!"*[1]

Isaiah continues that the watchmen will shout for joy and God will

---

1 Isaiah 52:7.

protect us from both the front and the rear. With the return of the sign of the "Son of Man," there will usher in a new period of peace—the Good News. In Isaiah, this new period is called Jerusalem, but it comes from Heaven, not from Earth.[2] It will be a time, not a location. The whole planet is the location.

> *10:8 Then I heard the voice I had heard from heaven speaking to me again. "Go," it said, "and take that open scroll out of the hand of the angel standing on sea and land."*
>
> *I went to the angel and asked him to give me the small scroll, and he said, "Take it and eat it; it will turn your stomach sour, but in your mouth it will taste sweet as honey*

Chew on this. The words that will issue from it will sound sweet, because it describes the "Good News" that is coming our way. It will be a time of cooperation for humanity. But the reality of the trials and tribulations that must first be overcome in order to get to this period will be (have been) difficult. It may make you sick, and there are a number who will still have to die in order to purify their robes through suffering.

What Revelation is about to describe in the next few chapters is not a pretty picture. The small Scroll is re-using this image, to describe the period we are about to enter, beyond the Seven Seals, and points the way to what must happen at the end.

> *So I took it out of the angel's hand, and swallowed it; it was as sweet as honey in my mouth, but when I had eaten it my stomach turned sour.*
>
> *Then I was told, "You are to prophesy again, this time about many different nations and countries and languages and emperors."*

Having taken the transmission, consumed and digested it, many things about this time and *our* future will be understood. The political

---

2 See Isaiah 52:8–12.

events that unfold will be made known. You are to proclaim them, and prophesy what will be. Talk about them openly. Tell people more about the mundane conditions that will arise around the world at this time. It may not be pleasant.

Speak heaven's truth. For Earth.

Temperance Card of the Rider/Waite Tarot

CHAPTER ELEVEN

Revelation 11

11:1 *Then I was given a long cane as a measuring rod, and I was told, "Go and measure God's sanctuary, and the altar, and the people who worship there; / but leave out the outer court and do not measure it, because it has been handed over to pagans—they will trample on the holy city for forty-two months. / But I shall send my two witnesses to prophesy for those twelve hundred and sixty days, wearing sackcloth. / These are the two olive trees and the two lamps that stand before the Lord of the world. Fire can come from their mouths and consume their enemies if anyone tries to harm them; and if anybody does try to harm them he will certainly be killed in this way. / They are able to lock up the sky so that it does not rain as long as they are prophesying; they are able to turn water into blood and strike the whole world with any plague as often as they like. When they have completed their witnessing, the beast that comes out of the Abyss is going to make war on them and overcome them and kill them. Their corpses will lie in the main street of the Great City known by the symbolic names Sodom and Egypt, in which their Lord was crucified. Men out of every people, race, language and nation will stare at their corpses, for three and a half days, not letting them be buried, / and the people of the world will be glad about it and celebrate the event by giving presents to each other, because these two prophets have been a plague to the people of the world."*

11:11 *After the three and a half days, God breathed life into them and they stood up, and everybody who saw it happen was terrified; / then they heard a loud voice from heaven say to them, "Come up here." and while their enemies were watching, they went up to heaven in a cloud. / Immediately, there was a violent earthquake, and a tenth of the city collapsed; seven thousand persons were killed in the earthquake, and the survivors, overcome with fear, could only praise the Lord of heaven.*

11:14 *That was the second of the troubles; the third is to come quickly after it.*

11:15 *Then the seventh angel blew his trumpet, and voices could be heard shouting in heaven, calling, "The Kingdom of the world has become the kingdom of our Lord and his Christ, and he will reign for ever and ever." / The twenty-four elders, enthroned in the presence of God, prostrated themselves and touched the ground with their foreheads worshipping God with these words, "We give thanks to you, Almighty Lord God, He-Is-and-He-Was, for using your great power and beginning your reign. / The nations were seething with rage and now the time has come for your own anger, and for the dead to be judged, and for your servants the prophets, for the saints and for all who worship you, small or great, to be rewarded. The time has come to destroy those who are destroying the earth."*

11:19 *Then the sanctuary of God in heaven opened, and the ark of the covenant could be seen inside it. Then came flashes of lightning, peals of thunder and an earthquake, and violent hail.*

* * * * *

11:1 Then I was given a long cane as a measuring rod, and I was told, "Go and measure God's sanctuary, and the altar, and the people who worship there;

The works of John Michell delved into sacred measurements, and Peter Tompkins in his work, *Secrets of the Great Pyramid* also speaks of different units of measure and how they were derived by the Egyptians, but we are not being given specific information in these lines of Revelation, other than measuring the "inner court," the alter and its environments, as opposed to the outer court, presumably the heavens themselves.

Nothing directly is known about the people who first established the symbolic centres of ancient countries. Analogy suggests that they were priestly diviners who were trained, as Caesar says of the Druids, in astronomy, astrology, geodesy and land measurement. These are also the traditional subjects of geomancy, together with number, cosmology and the subtle arts of aesthetics and divination.[1]

We're getting ready to measure God's sanctuary, the altar, and the people who worship there. Traditionally we turn to heaven for advice and wisdom, and the priests interpret what is "written" there for the general populace. Over time, the priests have forgotten how to read the heavenly judgment (which may or may not be changing in its particulars all the time, while the Commandments continue to hold their luster).

> *but leave out the outer court and do not measure it, because it has been handed over to pagans—they will trample on the holy city for forty-two months.*

The pagans are the unbelievers, or those outside the Temple who have no clue about the relationship between Heaven and Earth, between the divine and the mundane. Forty-two months is important as a theme that is about to start repeating itself under various guises.

> *But I shall send my two witnesses to prophesy for those twelve hundred and sixty days, wearing sackcloth.*

There will be two who successfully predict what will happen during the "twelve hundred and sixty days," which is forty-two months. They will be humble souls, subservient to the will of God. In what is becoming an understandable device, Revelation is using repetition to

---

1 *At the Centre of the World,* John Michell, Thames and Hudson, 1994, p. 22.

underscore the importance of key events, as if underlining the text or adding exclamation points. We will see this timetable yet again.

> *These are the two olive trees and the two lamps that stand before the Lord of the world. Fire can come from their mouths and consume their enemies if anyone tries to harm them; and if anybody does try to harm them he will certainly be killed in this way.*

Olives are the "fruit" of Athena, the goddess of wisdom. These two are the wise ones of their time. The World will come to know them. The fire coming from their mouths are powerful words translated into action. What they say, happens. They are in touch with the divine. They can anticipate danger and take measures to deal with it.

If we dig a little deeper into the Bible, the Old Testament itself gives us an explanation to this symbolism in the Book of Zechariah. In a vision, Zechariah saw a lampstand with seven lamps. Two olive tress were on either side of it.[2] He asked the angel who was guiding him to explain the meaning of these signs. The angel answered,

> *"These seven are the eyes of Yahweh; they cover the whole world."*[3]

Zechariah then asked about the meaning of the two olive trees to the right and left of the lampstand. The angel replied,

> *"These are the two anointed ones who stand before the Lord of the whole world."*[4]

Returning to Revelation.

> *They are able to lock up the sky so that it does not rain as long as they are*

---

2 Zechariah 4:2–3.
3 Zechariah 4:10.
4 Zechariah 4:14.

prophesying; they are able to turn water into blood and strike the whole
world with any plague as often as they like.

They are knowledgeable in the workings of heaven and command
the powers of nature. This is our second reference to a plague, and
so once again, we may assume that this is the result of the stream of
locusts that emanate from out of Iraq. Like the plagues we have seen
under various seals, plague seems to be at least part of the picture of
the Eighth Seal.

When they have completed their witnessing, the beast that comes out
of the Abyss is going to make war on them and overcome them and kill
them.

After they have finished speaking God's truth, the forces of the
beast will take them out.

Their corpses will lie in the main street of the Great City known by the
symbolic names Sodom and Egypt, in which their Lord was crucified.
Men out of every people, race, language and nation will stare at their
corpses, for three and a half days, not letting them be buried,

The bodies (or their metaphorical facsimiles) of those that have
been destroyed will become a spectacle before the general public for
three and a half days. Normal rituals will be suspended.

and the people of the world will be glad about it and celebrate the event
by giving presents to each other, because these two prophets have been a
plague to the people of the world.

The people of the world are happy to see the prophets go. They did
not like their predictions, God's truth or not. With the prophets dead,
it might seem that their prophecies will die with them, but such is not
the case. If people are giving presents to each other, some tribulation
must have come to an end, some burden relieved. These prophets pre-

dicted plague, whether symbolic or literal, and folks were not happy with them.

The problem is that if the Lord commands it from heaven, it is Divine Will—whether the blasphemers like it or not.

11:11 After the three and a half days, God breathed life into them and they stood up, and everybody who saw it happen was terrified;

But lo and behold the people are deceived. The prophets are not dead, frightening people into believing that maybe their predictions will come to pass. All who bore witness to the event are frightened and don't know what to do.

then they heard a loud voice from heaven say to them, "Come up here." and while their enemies were watching, they went up to heaven in a cloud.

The prophets willingly relinquished life, having had it restored, to demonstrate that death holds no fear for those in tune with the Divine Will.

Immediately, there was a violent earthquake, and a tenth of the city collapsed; seven thousand persons were killed in the earthquake, and the survivors, overcome with fear, could only praise the Lord of heaven.

This is the second time an earthquake has been referenced. In Rev. 8:5, just as the Eighth Seal is being introduced,

... and then the earth shook.

The rest of the lines seem to be fairly self-explanatory.

11:14 That was the second of the troubles; the third is to come quickly after it.

The Seventh Trumpet

11:15 Then the seventh angel blew his trumpet, and voices could be heard shouting in heaven, calling, "The Kingdom of the world has become the kingdom of our Lord and his Christ, and he will reign for ever and ever."

This is the same story again. The Age of Pisces, here described as the "Kingdom of the world," has precessed into the Age of Aquarius, the "kingdom of our Lord." This new vibration will last forever. It heralds a new era for those on Earth.

The twenty-four elders, enthroned in the presence of God, prostrated themselves and touched the ground with their foreheads worshipping God with these words, "We give thanks to you, Almighty Lord God, He-Is-and-He-Was, for using your great power and beginning your reign.

The hours of the day, subservient to this greater power, do homage to the Eternal One (*He-Is-and-He-Was*). The Vernal Equinox has entered Aquarius and begins the new reign. The heaven-sent messenger arrives with Good News.

The nations were seething with rage and now the time has come for your own anger, and for the dead to be judged, and for your servants the prophets, for the saints and for all who worship you, small or great, to be rewarded.

The people of the world, the nations of the world, will not be happy with the Eighth Seal and the changes it will bring. But here, in contemporary terminology, is a very clear statement.

The time has come to destroy those who are destroying the earth."

This is one you need to figure out on your own. It's not a metaphor.

11:19 Then the sanctuary of God in heaven opened, and the ark of the covenant could be seen inside it. Then came flashes of lightning, peals of thunder and an earthquake, and violent hail.

When Aquarius arrives, the sanctuary of God in heaven will open, and the device once used to measure the skies in order to determine God's Will will be found in the *Arc* of the Covenant. As the Vernal Equinox triggers this new eastern star, there will be flashes of lightning, peals of thunder, an earthquake, and violent hail. This is our third reference to an earthquake. The lightning and thunder we have seen before. The hail is new.

The Age of Aquarius is going to start with a bang. An Eighth Seal bang. So suggests Book 11.

CHAPTER TWELVE

Revelation 12

12:1 *Now a great sign appeared in heaven: a woman, adorned with the sun, standing on the moon, and with the twelve stars on her head for a crown. She was pregnant, and in labor, crying aloud in the pangs of childbirth. / Then a second sign appeared in the sky, a huge red dragon which had seven heads and ten horns, and each of the seven heads crowned with a coronet. / Its tail dragged a third of the stars from the sky and dropped them to the earth, and the dragon stopped in front of the woman as she was having the child, so that he could eat it as soon as it was born from the mother. / The woman brought a male child into the world, the son who was to rule all the nations with an iron scepter, and the child was taken straight up to God and to his throne, / while the woman escaped into the desert, where God had made a place of safety ready, for her to be looked after in the twelve hundred and sixty days.*

12:7 *And now war broke out in heaven, when Michael with his angels attacked the dragon. The dragon fought back with his angels, / but they were defeated and driven out of heaven. / The great dragon, the primeval serpent, known as the devil or Satan, who had deceived all the world, was hurled down to the earth and his angels were thrown with him. / Then I heard a voice shout from heaven, "Victory and power and empire for ever have been won by our God, and all authority for his Christ, now that the persecutor, who accused our brothers day and night before our God, has been brought down. / They have triumphed over him by the blood of the Lamb and by the witness of their martyrdom, because even in the face of death they would not cling to life. / Let the heavens rejoice and all who live there; but for you, earth and sea, trouble is coming—because the devil has gone down to you in a rage, knowing that his days are numbered."*

12:13 *As soon as the devil found himself thrown down to the earth, he sprang in pursuit of the woman, the mother of the male child. / but* *she was given a huge pair of eagle's wings to fly away from the serpent into the desert, to the place where she was to be looked after for a year and twice a year and half a year. So the serpent vomited water from its mouth, like a river, after the woman, to sweep away in the current, but the earth came to her rescue; it opened its mouth and swallowed the river thrown up by the dragon's jaws. / Then the dragon was enraged with the woman and went away to make war on the rest of her children, that is, all who obey God's commandments and bear witness for Jesus.*

12:18 *I was standing on the seashore.*

* * * * *

A Great Sign appeared in Heaven

12:1 Now a great sign appeared in heaven: a woman, adorned with the sun, standing on the moon, and with the twelve stars on her head for a crown. She was pregnant, and in labor, crying aloud in the pangs of childbirth.

A great sign appeared in heaven, a new eastern star, heralding a new epoch! This is important stuff in the celestial record. It's been anticipated and observed for literally Ages. This is one of the twelve signs of the Zodiac. On the position of power it is a Great Sign.

The canopy of heaven, the stars and body of the night sky were thought of by the Egyptians as Nut. Creation, in the form of a woman, is giving birth to the New Age. She is highlighted by Sun and Moon, the archetypes of children (Sun) and birth (Moon). She is the eternal feminine, whether she gives birth to mortal, mammal or millennium.

She is also Juno (Roman) or Hera (Greek), the feminine, Earth-based system (parallels of declination or equatorial base, in astronomical terms), which will give birth to the New Age. If we calibrate the difference between the two triggers (parallels of declination or conjunctions of longitude) for, say, this Eighth Seal, there is a 198-year difference between them.

The New Age is getting ready to be born. The twelve stars are symbolic references to the twelve constellations of the zodiac. They are both her crown and her offspring through the year. We are all her children. In these lines the Age is being born. Labor pains are difficult. The child swept up to heaven is an iron-fisted warlord. Creation is giving birth to a new way of doing things.

A Huge Red Dragon

Then a second sign appeared in the sky, a huge red dragon that had seven heads and ten horns, and each of the seven heads crowned with a coronet.

First we are being told that the Vernal Equinox will be entering Aquarius, now we are being given a reference to what the dragon is doing—Draco—the traditional astronomical guardian of the North Celestial Pole throughout antiquity. The equinox is the cardinal direction East. Draco guards (or guarded) the North Point.

In 2788 BC, Draco was the pole star when Thuban, the heart of the dragon (*Alpha Draconis*) marked heaven's center. This was the year it was at its closest approach to the exact North Celestial Pole, but it was recognized as the constellational guardian for many centuries both leading into, and coming out of this date. No other constellation came close. There was an ancient tradition in many cultures of linking together the astronomical North and East points into heaven's Creation myths.

That weave is being repeated here.

Ptolemy recorded the stars of Draco as being of a martial character. Mars is the red planet. This is the red dragon. He has been king of his realm, the night-time sky, for many, many centuries. "Highest Judge" the Egyptians called him. We should not be surprised to find him turning up at the birth of a new heavenly member, whether represented as a new bride, or a new birth.

Its tail dragged a third of the stars from the sky and dropped them to the earth, and the dragon stopped in front of the woman as she was having the child, so that he could eat it as soon as it was born from the mother.

The opening line is an accurate astronomical representation. Draco is huge. Its stars are not bright, after the fashion of Ursa Major or Orion, but they were extremely important, for it established north after the Sun set for literally thousands of years. Its length is huge, so much so that it entwines both celestial Bears in its coils, while continuing to keep his head held high. Besides, this verse is bringing up the theme of the "thirds" once again.

Because Draco is long and his coils lie so close to the pole, they astronomically command one third of the circular arc of heaven. If you looked at this constellation's position relative to the pole in the 1st century AD, Draco's tail (what else is there to a serpent?) dragged out a third of the stars of the sky. If we think of this dragon as a sentient being lying far above us on his solitary perch, watching all that goes on below, he has had plenty of time to study the prophecies regarding this new epoch and understand their implications.

If that sounds a little too imaginative, try this interpretation.

Like Herod, our leaders are interested in what the future holds—largely for reasons that have to do with their own self-preservation. They have traditionally invested heavily to gain insights on the future. This can be anything that advances their interests. In Revelation, Draco (those in power when these events take place) wants to consume the newborn. Herod is told during his visit with the wise men that prophecy says there is a new king being born in Herod's realm, in the town of Bethlehem, and they are on their way to honor the newborn child. Herod is king of the land. He doesn't want a new upstart to interfere with his dynasty, thank you very much. He suggests that the wise men return to tell him precisely where to find this child, but the wise men are warned in a dream not to return, and so they don't. In order to preserve his interests and without the help of the three kings, Herod decides to have all the children of Bethlehem murdered.

These lines of Revelation suggest the same set up here, over two thousand years later. When the Queen of Heaven is about to give birth to the New Age, the serpent—those who are a part of the old administration—do not want the old ways to change. They are therefore ready to kill this creation in its infancy, before it grows into its strength and power.

Draco is a universal symbol and is therefore a doorway into many realities. Our markets are based upon selling to the senses; what smells good, looks good, sounds good, tastes good, or feels good. Those who run the show introduce the need, fan the passions and bait the market. One of the most obvious is its phallic association—those who are a slave to their senses. It's been that way for a long time. Draco has been guardian of the pole for as far back as we can collectively remember. It's all about the money. The traditional spirit of doing business is wanting to "catch the wind" of the new era. Draco wants to posses the child, to embrace the child, to consume the child.

> *The woman brought a male child into the world, the son who was to rule all the nations with an iron scepter, and the child was taken straight up to God and to his throne,*

Aquarius is born. This male child with an iron scepter is taking his place on the throne, just as the Ram had before him. Each Age has a herald of the new period. The herald of Aquarius will come in the form of a martial lord (iron scepter), a warlord. The child will be empowered by Time, and the heavens will proclaim the birth. Once the Age is here, it will be seen in the skies. There is no way to stop it. The tribulations will be strong and powerful.

These will be the labor pains of civilization at the advent of the New Age.

> *while the woman escaped into the desert, where God had made a place of safety ready, for her to be looked after in the twelve hundred and sixty days.*

The conditions that give birth to the New Age will be looked after in the twelve hundred and sixty days. This is forty-two months. And it is the second time Revelation has referenced this time period.

This is the outer court, the time leading into Aquarius when the pagans will overrun the court, which is to say that the unbelievers are in charge. The Age may have begun, but there's going to be a three-and-a-half year buffer period between epochs.

During this time things may get a little wooly.

12:7 And now war broke out in heaven, when Michael with his angels attacked the dragon. The dragon fought back with his angels,

Here's the war for which the warlord was born. Heaven's child must now live up to his destiny. The two sides polarize, with those opting for the senses lining up on one side, and those who pull for the planet lining up on the other.

but they were defeated and driven out of heaven.

It isn't a good day for the forces of darkness. Precessional motion is carrying Draco's power further and further from the power position, the North Celestial Pole. His power is waning, moving off-center in the pictorial sky record.

The great dragon, the primeval serpent, known as the devil or Satan, who had deceived all the world, was hurled down to the earth and his angels were thrown with him.

His defeat assured, the Dragon is thrown to the Earth. He now rises and sets.

Then I heard a voice shout from heaven, "Victory and power and empire for ever have been won by our God, and all authority for his Christ, now that the persecutor, who accused our brothers day and night before our God, has been brought down.

We're heading into Aquarius. The change of era means a change of everything. We will make new contacts and learn to work in new ways as never before. There is a recognition of our own and each other's divinity. It means victory and power and empire, a new Age and a new realm. Those who were out will now be those who are in. The old guard will change. The Dragon will be brought down.

> *They have triumphed over him by the blood of the Lamb and by the witness of their martyrdom, because even in the face of death they would not cling to life.*

This is the ultimate test of standing up for what you believe.

> *Let the heavens rejoice and all who live there; but for you, earth and sea, trouble is coming—because the devil has gone down to you in a rage, knowing that his days are numbered."*

The heavens themselves will proclaim his glory. Aquarius will make and honor the promises of the water-bearers, but it's going to begin with a struggle. The Dragon is down, but he's not out. He's got three and a half years.

> *12:13 As soon as the devil found himself thrown down to the earth, he sprang in pursuit of the woman, the mother of the male child.*

Since the male child has been taken up to heaven and is out of harm's way, the Dragon goes after the mother, the source of the energy that gave birth to this new way of being.

Once those who run the show know that they're being replaced, they will go after those who seem to represent the new time. They will call them the children of the Revolution. They want to stop the waters that are beginning to flow from the celestial stream, but it will be like trying to sweep back the tide. The astronomical stream and its precessional motion will not be denied.

but she was given a huge pair of eagle's wings to fly away from the serpent into the desert, to the place where she was to be looked after for a year and twice a year and half a year.

That's three times this same time frame has been used—once as days, once as months and once as years. Twelve hundred and 60 days, forty-two months, and a year and twice a year and half a year, three and a half years. The outer court, over which the pagans trample, is the no-man's land of Aquarius. Folks are going to have to wait for a while yet. The dragon must first be tended to.

So the serpent vomited water from its mouth, like a river, after the woman, to sweep away in the current, but the earth came to her rescue; it opened its mouth and swallowed the river thrown up by the dragon's jaws.

Mythologically, dragons have a long history of vomiting floods. Heracles wrestled with a dragon that was causing floods. Emperor Yu spent a lifetime harnessing the floods. Dragons cause floods, rains, tsunamis and other forms of storm damage—from Typhon to Ti'amat, from Tatsu to Lung. The dragon anticipated the birth of the child, but the child was taken up to heaven. It then went after the mother, who is saved by the earth. Next will be the children.

Then the dragon was enraged with the woman and went away to make war on the rest of her children, that is, all who obey God's commandments and bear witness for Jesus.

This is a Red Dragon. Red is the attribute of Mars, the God of War. Of course he's angry. He's always angry! He can find no satisfaction in a target that can't be caught (the Giants of old once attempted to assault Olympus, but were cast down. Bellerophon tried to ride on the back of Pegasus to Olympus, but was thrown when the winged horse was stung by a gadfly). The dragon now turns its attention to all those that support the incoming regime and attempt to nurture it into being. In the transitional days between these two energies, those who obey spiritual truths will be persecuted for their beliefs.

12:18 I was standing on the seashore.

A common metaphor for the stellar seas and islands to be found there, especially with a maritime culture such as the Greeks. We're getting ready to take a long look at something that is *'from the sea.'*

CHAPTER THIRTEEN

Revelation 13

13:1 *Then I saw a beast emerge from the sea: it had seven heads and ten horns, with a coronet on each of its ten horns, and its heads were marked with blasphemous titles. / I saw that the beast was like a leopard, with paws like a bear and a mouth like a lion; the dragon had handed over to it his own power and his throne and his world-wide authority. / I saw that one of its heads seemed to have had a fatal wound but that this deadly injury had healed and, after that, the whole world had marveled and followed the beast. They prostrated themselves in front of the dragon because he had given the beast his authority; and they prostrated themselves in front of the beast, saying, "Who can compare with the beast? How could anybody defeat him?" / For forty-two months the beast was allowed to mouth his boasts and blasphemies and to do whatever it wanted; / and it mouthed its blasphemies against God, against his name, his heavenly Tent and all those who are sheltered there. / It was allowed to make war against the saints and conquer them, and given power over every race, people, language and nation; / and all people of the world will worship it, that is, everybody whose name has not been written down since the foundation of the world in the book of life of the sacrificial Lamb. / If anyone has ears to hear, let him listen: / Captivity for those who are destined for captivity; the sword for those who are to die by the sword. That is why the saints must have constancy and faith.*

13:11 *Then I saw a second beast; it emerged from the ground; it had two horns like a lamb, but made a noise like a dragon. / This second beast was servant to the first beast, and extended its authority everywhere, making the world and all its people worship the first beast, which had had the fatal wound and had been healed. / And it worked great miracles, even to calling down fire from heaven on to the earth while people watched. / Through the miracles which it was allowed to do on behalf of the first beast, it was able to win over the people of the world and persuade them to put up a statue in honor of the beast that had been* *wounded by the sword and still lived. / It was allowed to breathe life into the statue, so that the statue of the beast was able to speak, and to have anyone who refused to worship the statue of the beast put to death. / He compelled everyone—small and great, rich and poor, slave and citizen—to be branded on the right hand or on the forehead, / and made it illegal for anyone to buy or sell anything unless he had been branded with the name of the beast or with the number of its name.*

13:18 *There is need for shrewdness here: if anyone is clever enough he may interpret the number of the beast: it is the number of a man, the number 666.*

* * * * *

The Beast

13:1 Then I saw a beast emerge from the sea: it had seven heads and ten horns, with a coronet on each of its ten horns, and its heads were marked with blasphemous titles.

From out of the depths, a beast appears. The sky has in various cultures been used as a symbol for the watery depths. For instance, in Genesis.

In the beginning God created the heavens and the earth. / Now the earth was a formless void, there was darkness over the deep, and God's spirit hovered over the water.[1]

Indeed, we don't even have to go back to the Old Testament to see this portrayal used in this manner. Here in the 4th chapter of Revelation the author used the sea as a metaphor for the sky. As we saw in Rev. 4:6,

---

1 Genesis 1:1–2.

Between the throne and myself was a sea that seemed to be made of glass, like crystal

The planets, comets and constellations must be up there suspended in something, lest they fall from the sky. In any event, this beast had seven heads and ten horns. It's been bequeathed power over the course of time, authority over others. But it used its power not for the common good, but for selfish purposes. The blasphemous titles were past deeds marked on the head, just as the seal of those who succeeded were marked on the forehead. Like Thoth checking the scales weighing the souls of the deceased against that of a feather, like the Akashic Record, the Law of Karma and the Golden Rule,

A coronet is a simple crown, as a prince or princess with royal responsibilities might wear, designating royalty, but not competing with the king's crown for status or power. These are seven heads whose horns have given them victories, the military muscle to get things done. They have strength and importance.

I saw that the beast was like a leopard, with paws like a bear and a mouth like a lion; the dragon had handed over to it his own power and his throne and his world-wide authority.

We are being drawn a composite mythological figure once again; a leopard with the paws of a bear and a mouth like a lion. A leopard/lion with bear paws.

This is Ursa Minor, Little Bear. Its bear paws give it away. It's strength, power and importance derive from the feline imagery, as well as its central role in the sky.

The dragon handed over his worldwide power to Ursa Minor, once considered to be not a bear but the wing of the Dragon. The precessional position of the *North Celestial Pole*—the shaft that forms the axis of the Earth—has shifted from Draco to Ursa Minor, from the Dragon to the Bear, from Dragon to the beast.

In the last eight thousand years there have only been two pole stars: Polaris is the one we have now. It will achieve it's greatest northern lat-

208 THE EIGHTH SEAL

itude in AD 2100 at the end of the current century. The other pole star reached its greatest height in 2788 BC, a couple of centuries before the construction of the Great Pyramid in Giza.

To repeat,

the dragon had handed over to it his own power and his throne and his world-wide authority

Here the throne is being used as an image, not for the Vernal Equinox (cardinal direction East), but for the North Celestial Pole (the North Point). These ancient stargazers could see that precession was carrying an imaginary point in space from one cardinal position on the compass to another. These are two of the four (East and North) power points of our world.

Worldwide authority. Literally. It is seen by every nation above the equator.

The Dragon has handed his power, throne, and worldwide authority over because the North Celestial Pole crowns the cardinal direction North for half the planet. North is unique in its abilities. East, South and West all involve motion. East, planets rise, West, planets set. South, they transit across their highest arc in a wave of ephemeral supremacy each day.

But in the North and only in the North is there a position that can be marked by a single star, around which all others rotate. Only the North Star holds true, neither rising nor setting, fixed within a half degree, immobile, while chained by time to the hub of heaven. It is a testament to God's eternal truth, his eternal laws. This is why the Egyptians called it (when Thuban held the position) the eternal judge. The Great Pyramid was built to channel Thuban's image down a long, darkened corridor so that its light could be seen even during the day in the middle of a bright sunlit Egyptian desert. Thuban, the heart of the Dragon, climbed to within *3 minutes* of arc or about one thirtieth of a degree from the summit of Creation. Polaris is brighter, Thuban climbed higher.

The entire construction of the Pyramid of Cheops was oriented

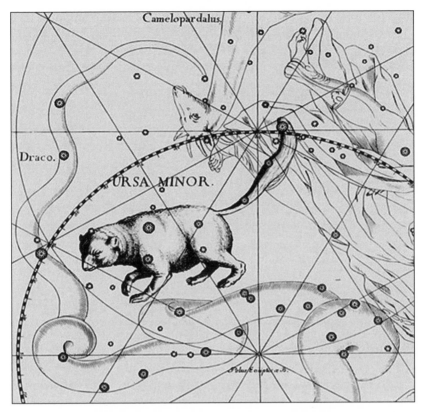

*The Beast of Revelation to whom the Dragon
gives authority (see the serpent wrapping Ursa)*

to the North Star the last time there was one. The ONLY other time in
thousands of years that there has been one, until now. That was almost
five thousand years ago. After all these eons, another star is getting
ready to assume that position.

The Dragon has protected this secret through the centuries. That's
the story the myths tell. He is guardian of the center of Time and Creation, the illusive egg of the Orient. With Polaris at the Pole, the center
of heaven is marked by a star. In Revelation's time, it didn't look that
way. Centuries from now, it won't look that way. Revelation foresees
the day when Draco will relinquish its hold and pass the celestial baton
to the Little Bear. That day is now. They foresaw where it was headed.

This is strong stellar stuff. It's the culmination of heaven around which all Creation turns. After almost five thousand years, a star again crowns the material universe.

> The last star in the tail of Little Bear,
> where he is pinned fast to a stake.
> You can still find him there,
> Wondering what it'll take?
> Pacing, tracing, spacing
> night after night,
> in tiny, tight
> circles
>
> .

I saw that one of its heads seemed to have had a fatal wound but that this deadly injury had healed and, after that, the whole world had marveled and followed the beast.

In the pagan world, the North Celestial Pole (NCP) was marked on a regular basis, because it moved each year. The astronomer/priests (astrologers) would be part of a ceremony that would cut, stab, or shoot an arrow into the Dragon, and each year he (or she) would heal and be stabbed, pierced or shot again. My previous book, *When the Dragon Wore the Crown*, covers this ritual in great detail. Myths from around the world all sought to find the center of Creation, to mark time and their calendars. It starts here.

They prostrated themselves in front of the dragon because he had given the beast his authority; and they prostrated themselves in front of the beast, saying, "Who can compare with the beast? How could anybody defeat him?"

He is attacked and triumphs year after year, in ceremony after ceremony, in culture after culture. The Chinese honor the Dragon on New Year's to this day.

For forty-two months the beast was allowed to mouth his boasts and blasphemies and to do whatever it wanted;

We're back to the mudroom between one Age to the next. These are its dimensions. It's forty-two months large, which, once again, could be literal or metaphorical. The power of the old school, the Dragon and the Beast has taken a hit, but they have come out on top.

and it mouthed its blasphemies against God, against his name, his heavenly Tent and all those who are sheltered there.

These folks have their own self-interests in mind, of corruption and greed, and they're taking it out on the people who are trying to succeed. They're using propaganda in the media to generate lies. The "heavenly Tent" is another reference to the skies above and their divine influence. We are all sheltered beneath this Tent. It covers the Earth.

It was allowed to make war against the saints and conquer them, and given power over every race, people, language and nation;

The forces of the Dragon and the Beast will initially win out. While it is still in power it can say whatever it wants, painting vile pictures of its adversaries.

and all people of the world will worship it, that is, everybody whose name has not been written down since the foundation of the world in the book of life of the sacrificial Lamb

Everybody who simply believes what they see and hear through the media will be taken in by the Big Lie. Everybody that has not awakened to his or her divine connection. After many lifetimes, have you given yourself back to God? Have you spilled the blood of your own sacrificial Lamb? If you're tuned in, you probably have. Many have returned to help.

If anyone has ears to hear, let him listen:

Think about it.

Captivity for those who are destined for captivity; the sword for those who are to die by the sword. That is why the saints must have constancy and faith.

Like the real saints of our Age—the Kennedys, Martin Luther King, and Gandhi, each of whom died by a bullet while attempting to make things better for people—we have to be willing to lose in order to win. It's the secret behind the veil. The end of Pisces and beginning of Aquarius will include prison, confinement, isolation, loss, betrayal, lust, corruption, and greed. Some will give up their lives in defense of the truth. These are the keynotes of the time of transition.

The "mudroom," the three and a half year period that Revelation repeatedly brings us back to, will be a time of persecution, the Great Persecution. It represents the transition between the two Ages, when things will still be in a state of flux and those in the Bear's lair will initially continue to hold the high ground.

Those in positions of authority will desperately work to hold onto power with no regard for morality. But the daily propaganda spread forth by their liars will be telling us why we need to obey for our own safety.

It had a mouth like a lion. It has command of the language. It rules what we read and hear.

The Second Beast

13:11 Then I saw a second beast; it emerged from the ground; it had two horns like a lamb, but made a noise like a dragon.

This beast emerged from the ground, not from heaven. These lines attempt to describe the earthly manifestation of what it will mean when the Eighth Seal triggers the power of Ursa Minor. As we will learn later (Revelation tells us so) ... the beast is a man.

Notice that as in so many other myths of antiquity, we have the

weaving of the North and the East Points, in this case the dragon and
the lamb.

*This second beast was servant to the first beast, and extended its authority
everywhere, making the world and all its people worship the first beast,
which had had the fatal wound and had been healed.*

Earth is subservient to Heaven. The earthly beast is the material
manifestation of what is happening in the sky. He champions the cause
of the first beast. This earthly beast spread his power everywhere on the
planet, making people tow the party line, because people were utterly
convinced by what they had already seen happen. It had been witnessed by all.

*And it worked great miracles, even to calling down fire from heaven on
to the earth while people watched.*

The "fireball from heaven" that we have seen underscored so often
before is back again. The Beast (or its administration) may have foreknowledge of this event, and successfully parley its power into propaganda, taking advantage of worldly wisdom.

*Through the miracles which it was allowed to do on behalf of the first
beast, it was able to win over the people of the world and persuade them
to put up a statue in honor of the beast that had been wounded by the
sword and still lived.*

Again, another possibility is that the Beast will come to take the
blows, year after year, in assuming the power of the Dragon. This is
what the mythology of the Dragon records, even more so than "flood-
vomiter." In tradition after tradition, the Dragon is attacked. There's
Marduk, Apollo, St. George, St. Michael, Sigurd and Heracles to name
a few.

Each of these cultures are pinpointing the new precessional
center, the North Celestial Pole, every few years with a new myth. The

Chinese were more elegant. They used a common pin and the five-colored thread to bind their dragon. Much simpler, and, they continue to honor the dragon in a New Year's parade to this day.

These are astronomical markings. The cut, whether it be by dagger, arrow, sword, spear, lance or common household pin, is the point that is being brought to our attention. Gilgamesh is told to insert the sword between the head and the neck; Nebuchadnezzer cuts the head off the Ram. The piercing of the Dragon at the New Year by each of the heroes listed above refer to the astronomical points of importance, which change over time. These are when the cardinal points of Creation are being triggered. It is what people are seeing in the sky.

The dragon was constantly being wounded every year at New Year, but recovers for the next round. We have the dragon delegating his power and authority to the beast who "emerged from the sea." This is Ursa Minor. The second beast emerges from the ground. He is Earth-born, a person who was a servant to the principles and philosophies of the first beast and furthers them. With Draco being displaced from his central role, his Draconian policies are a part of what are being passed on.

It is possible that one point being referenced here is Polaris reaching its summit in AD 2100. In mythological terms, the ancients would "mark" this moment with some kind of "cut" and then tell a story about it to reflect what they saw in a memorable manner. In terms of the Ages, this is not a large swath of time. One century out of twenty-one. For those following the stars, this would have been noted and anticipated.

It would also be translated into how they thought it would manifest for those of us here on Earth. This is the principle objective of the Book of Revelation—to anticipate, observe and interpret what was to come in the future.

It was allowed to breathe life into the statue, so that the statue of the beast was able to speak, and to have anyone who refused to worship the statue of the beast put to death.

The statue is the power and pomp of the state, where all must come on bended knee. Breathing life into the statue is pumping life into the party line, whatever that may be. It will rule with an iron fist through Draconian Law. Offer obedience to an earthly lord, or face death.

He compelled everyone—small and great, rich and poor, slave and citizen—to be branded on the right hand or on the forehead,

Think of it as Identification Papers. They take a picture of your face; they take your fingerprints. Hand and forehead, you are a marked man or woman.

and made it illegal for anyone to buy or sell anything unless he had been branded with the name of the beast or with the number of its name.

In this manner, the entire economic system can be controlled.

666

13:18 *There is need for shrewdness here: if anyone is clever enough he may interpret the number of the beast: it is the number of a man, the number 666.*

John is here speaking to us directly and giving his readers a numerological tip. Numerological hints are not generally provided in dreams; they are products of the mind. This is a mental insert, a puzzle to be logically figured out.

The beast is the man is 666.

Six is ruled by Venus. Six is balance and peace, harmony and rhythm, but it is also these elements when they are out of balance. Every planet, every number, every sign and constellation has both a positive and a negative side. As mortals, our choice is what do we do with these qualities? The number six can be peace and justice, with balance in the land, and even a little music.

The flip side to Venus is that it's all for pleasure. What feels good, tastes good, looks good, smells good, and sounds good takes precedence over what *is* good. The three levels of six (666) are the thirds of Creation—physical, mental and spiritual, a Holy Trinity. When you place pleasure at the helm in the physical, mental, and spiritual levels, fun is your guiding star, inside and out. You're a teenager.

In reverse order, the layers are what you're drawn to, what you think about, and what you do.

Venus is a beautiful lady and has many gifts, but she shouldn't ALWAYS be at the helm, on every level. We will see this image and theme being repeated later in Revelation. Pleasure, money and profits—all gifts of the goddess—are the powers of the Beast. There will be one at the helm, running the show, giving to those who will buy a very good time.

Don't get me wrong. This doesn't mean there should be no fun, no enjoyment, no music. But life needs a higher moral compass than simply pleasure.

But there is another layer here. We are being given encouragement. If you're shrewd, if you're clever, here's a clue. This one is a tease. Think about it. Temptation is used to tantalize the reader into going deeper into the Mystery.

CHAPTER FOURTEEN

Revelation 14

14:1 *Next in my vision I saw Mount Zion, and standing on it a Lamb who had with him a hundred and forty-four thousand people, all with his name and his Father's name written on their foreheads. / I heard a sound coming out of the sky like the sound of the ocean or the roar of thunder; it seemed to be the sound of harpists playing their harps. / There in front of the throne they were singing a new hymn in the presence of the four animals and the elders, a hymn that could only be learned by the hundred and forty-four thousand who had been redeemed from the world. / These are the ones who have kept their virginity and not been defiled with women; they follow the Lamb wherever he goes; they have been redeemed from among men to be the first fruits for God and for the Lamb. / They never allowed a lie to pass their lips and no fault can be found in them.*

14:6 *Then I saw another angel, flying high overhead, sent to announce the Good News of eternity to all who live on the earth, every nation, race, language and tribe. / He was calling, "Fear God and praise him, because the time has come for him to sit in judgment; worship the maker of heaven and earth and sea and every water spring."*

14:8 *A second angel followed him, calling, "Babylon has fallen, Babylon the Great has fallen, Babylon which gave the whole world the wine of God's anger to drink."*

14:9 *A third angel followed, shouting aloud, "All those who worship the beast and his statue, or have had themselves branded on the hand or the forehead, / will be made to drink the wine of God's fury which is ready, undiluted, in his cup of anger: in fire and brimstone they will be tortured in the presence of the holy angels and the Lamb / and the smoke of their torture will go up for ever and ever. There will be no respite, night or* *day, for those who worshiped the beast or its statue or accepted branding with its name." / That is why there must be constancy in the saints who keep the commandments of God and faith in Jesus. / Then I heard a voice from heaven say to me, "Write down: Happy are those who die in the Lord! Happy indeed, the Spirit says; now they can rest for ever after their work, since their good deeds go with them."*

14:14 *Now in my vision I saw a white cloud and, sitting on it, one like a son of man with a gold crown on his head and a sharp sickle in his hand. / Then another angel came out of the sanctuary, and shouted aloud to the one sitting on the cloud, "Put your sickle in and reap: harvest time has come and the harvest of the earth is ripe." / Then the one sitting on the cloud set his sickle to work on the earth, and the earth's harvest was reaped.*

14:17 *Another angel, who also carried a sharp sickle, came out of the temple in heaven, / and the angel in charge of the fire left the altar and shouted aloud to the one with the sharp sickle, "Put your sickle in and cut all the bunches off the vine of the earth; all its grapes are ripe." / So the angel set his sickle to work on the earth and harvested the whole vintage of the earth, and put it into a huge winepress, the winepress of God's anger, / outside the city, where it was trodden until the blood that came out of the winepress was up to the horses' bridles as far away as sixteen hundred furlongs.*

* * * * *

144,000 People

Next in my vision I saw Mount Zion, and standing on it a Lamb who had with him a hundred and forty-four thousand people, all with his name and his Father's name written on their foreheads.

They're lining up at the gate, and the gate is the Eighth Seal. These are the good people. They are the twelve by twelve, the whole unit, the big picture, multiplied by thousands. This has been going on for a while. These are the souls who will be redeemed because of their purity.

Interesting that both the good guys and the bad guys have marks on their foreheads. All are identified, whether in the Book of Life or by the beast.

They're preparing for battle. The souls of those who have passed the test are getting ready to enter into the Kingdom of the Lord.

I heard a sound coming out of the sky like the sound of the ocean or the roar of thunder; it seemed to be the sound of harpists playing their harps

They're playing in the band, the music of the spheres. Lightning is getting ready to speak (*the roar of thunder*).

There in front of the throne they were singing a new hymn in the presence of the four animals and the elders, a hymn that could only be learned by the hundred and forty-four thousand who had been redeemed from the world.

There's a new energy, signified by the new hymn, in front of the keepers of time. It's a hymn that only the awakened to spirit will feel like singing, those who truly know the secret of Unity.

These are the ones who have kept their virginity and not been defiled with women; they follow the Lamb wherever he goes; they have been redeemed from among men to be the first fruits for God and for the Lamb

Work hard, and do not be distracted by temptations. Follow the Lamb wherever he goes. Follow the will of God, no matter where it might lead, as determined by the position of the Vernal Equinox (the Lamb). As it aligns with various stars, various situations will present themselves as they have throughout history.

They never allowed a lie to pass their lips and no fault can be found in them.

Be ye therefore perfect in treating everyone as though he or she were part of the body of God.

14:6 Then I saw another angel, flying high overhead, sent to announce the Good News of eternity to all who live on the earth, every nation, race, language and tribe.

The Good News is to be announced, and it will spread to all points on the globe.

He was calling, "Fear God and praise him, because the time has come for him to sit in judgment; worship the maker of heaven and earth and sea and every water spring."

The time of holding back is over. The Age of Pisces is at an end. Pisces sits *"in absentia."* During the Age of Pisces, God has had a "hands off" policy, allowing Free Will to have its own way, regardless of the morality. Pisces' keynote is faith, because faith is what is strengthened in arenas of uncertainty. During Aquarius faith will morph into knowledge. People will come to know God and call him "Friend." In the meantime, St. Peter is standing at the gate, getting ready to take the roll call.

Now it's time to pay up. Why else would He/She/It come to our aid? Note that God is the maker of heaven, earth and sea. No surprises there. But the text adds that God is the maker of every water spring as well. What is this? That's different. We saw it before in Rev. 7:17.

because the Lamb who is at the throne will be their shepherd and will lead them to springs of living water

There's a theme being presented here, and intuition suggests that with the upcoming problems about clean sources of water, and the Earthly vibrational shift, new courses of water will be made available to the populace to nourish and sustain us. It will also simply represent a whole new way of looking at and thinking about life.

It is the birth of the Aquarian Age. The Lamb is leading us to the springs of living water. This is the stream that pours from the Aquarian urn. The Vernal Equinox (the Lamb) is leading us to Aquarius. Note some of the sub-themes here… The time has come for judgment, and to worship every water stream.

The Sea is Pisces and the ocean that it rules. Aquarius is the Stream from the Urn.

14:8 A second angel followed him, calling, "Babylon has fallen, Babylon the Great has fallen, Babylon which gave the whole world the wine of God's anger to drink."

With the coming of the Age of Aquarius, there's going to be a huge, radical shift in how the Earth is run. That's what Aquarius is, change: abrupt, dramatic, sudden, exciting, stimulating, surprised, "out-of-the-blue," "wasn't-in-the-cards," crazy, unorthodox change. Water is going to be a big part of it. The 4th of July chart of the United States has an Aquarian Moon. We were a nation born to change, born in the cradle of independence and revolution. We can learn from some of these clues about Aquarius.

There will be a worldwide revolution, born of war, but for which war will not be the final answer. Those who have run the show, the old school, tradition and status quo will not be running the show during the new heavenly kingdom.

This merchandizing prince has marketed an intoxicating brew to the entire world. We've been drunk on it since the Age began. The Creator is not happy about it.

14:9 A third angel followed, shouting aloud, "All those who worship the beast and his statue, or have had themselves branded on the hand or the forehead, will be made to drink the wine of God's fury which is ready, undiluted, in his cup of anger: in fire and brimstone they will be tortured in the presence of the holy angels and the Lamb

Divine punishment will be the lot of the sinful. The "holy angels and the Lamb" signify when Time and the Vernal Equinox align with the Eighth Seal. It's a huge shift. These are the images they believe to be true.

But fire and brimstone are Old Testament images. Yes, and this one goes all the way back. to Genesis.

Then Yahweh rained down on Sodom and Gomorrah brimstone and fire of his own sending.[1]

What happens next?

and the smoke of their torture will go up for ever and ever. There will be no respite, night or day, for those who worshiped the beast or its statue or accepted branding with its name."

The torments will be painful. The smoke is presumably from the fireball striking the Earth, from the abyss that opens up, and the smoke from their torture. They may all be part of a common origin, a singular event.

That is why there must be constancy in the saints who keep the commandments of God and faith in Jesus. Then I heard a voice from heaven say to me, "Write down: Happy are those who die in the Lord! Happy indeed, the Spirit says; now they can rest for ever after their work, since their good deeds go with them."

Here it is. This is the test. Each of the Ages has a different spiritual (and material) lesson to teach. During the Age of Gemini, humanity learned one set of lessons. During the Age of Taurus, there was a new set. During Aries, etc. During the Age of Pisces, the wisdom, understanding, and rational all hid away where they were not apparent. We must walk the path, even though there are no more signposts.

---

1 Genesis 19:24.

A Son of Man with a Gold Crown on his Head.

14:14 Now in my vision I saw a white cloud and, sitting on it, one like a son of man with a gold crown on his head and a sharp sickle in his hand.

The Son of man, seated on a cloud, has been given the crown. The Vernal Equinox has passed into Aquarius, and now Aquarius is Lord, the power and authority over all. Let there be no other Gods before me. The Son of Man is getting ready to assume the Ascendancy. The sharp sickle in his hand is the same born by Father Time, Cronos or Saturn. Time has come today. It is time for the Age to act, be that what it may. Saturn is the traditional ruler of Aquarius. Here is a Biblical representation, a mythical representation, of Saturn in Aquarius.

Then another angel came out of the sanctuary, and shouted aloud to the one sitting on the cloud, "Put your sickle in and reap: harvest time has come and the harvest of the earth is ripe."

Aquarius is here, and what God promised in his "secret intention" will now be revealed. God has had a hands-off policy until now. Now the Earth is full, teeming with people and ripe for the picking as the image of the harvest suggests. The roll call is complete.

14:17 Another angel, who also carried a sharp sickle, came out of the temple in heaven, and the angel in charge of the fire left the altar and shouted aloud to the one with the sharp sickle, "Put your sickle in and cut all the bunches off the vine of the earth; all its grapes are ripe."

At the time of the Eighth Seal, the Harvest of the Earth will commence.

So the angel set his sickle to work on the earth and harvested the whole vintage of the earth, and put it into a huge winepress, the winepress of God's anger, outside the city, where it was trodden until the blood that came out of the winepress was up to the horses' bridles as far away as sixteen hundred furlongs.

It is clear that the "grapes" of this harvest are the people. The harvest will be a bloodbath.

CHAPTER FIFTEEN

Revelation 15

15:1 *What I saw next, in heaven, was a great and wonderful sign: seven angels were bringing the seven plagues that are the last of all, because they exhaust the anger of God. / I seemed to see a glass lake suffused with fire, and standing by the lake of glass, those who had fought against the beast and won, and against his statue and the number which is his name. They all had harps from God, / and they were singing the hymn of Moses, the servant of God, and of the Lamb:*

> *"How great and wonderful are all your works,*
> *Lord God Almighty;*
> *just and true are all your ways,*
> *King of nations*
> *Who would not revere and praise your name, O Lord?*
> *You alone are holy,*
> *and all the pagans will come and adore you*
> *for the many acts of justice you have shown."*

15:5 *After this, in my vision, the sanctuary, the Tent of the Testimony, opened in heaven, / and out came the seven angels with the seven plagues, wearing pure white linen, fastened around their waists with golden girdles. / One of the four animals gave the seven angels seven golden bowls filled with the anger of God who lives for ever and ever. / The smoke from the glory and the power of God filled the temple so that no one could go into it until the seven plagues of the seven angles were completed.*

* * * * *

15:1 What I saw next, in heaven, was a great and wonderful sign: seven angels were bringing the seven plagues that are the last of all, because they exhaust the anger of God.

The great and wonderful sign is what we've been hearing about all along. It is the change-over from Pisces to Aquarius. As Aquarius begins, God is angry as a result of children who will not listen. The plagues that will occur manifest that anger.

I seemed to see a glass lake suffused with fire, and standing by the lake of glass, those who had fought against the beast and won, and against his statue and the number which is his name. They all had harps from God,

These are the souls beneath the altar once again. They all have harps, because they have all made the descent into the Underworld like Orpheus.

and they were singing the hymn of Moses, the servant of God, and of the Lamb:

> *"How great and wonderful are all your works,*
> *Lord God Almighty;*
> *just and true are all your ways,*
> *King of nations*
> *Who would not revere and praise your name, O Lord?*
> *You alone are holy,*
> *and all the pagans will come and adore you*
> *for the many acts of justice you have shown."*

In his day Moses fulfilled heaven's will—he correctly interpreted the future and followed where it led.

These lines sing the praises of Creation. There is only One God (no matter by what name you might call He, She or It), and it works as part of a system, part of an intelligence. Everyone—Jew, Christian, gentile, and pagan—will come to acknowledge the Great Spirit. There are spiritual checks and balances. There is celestial justice. It's all been a part of the plan. Time has been waiting for this moment.

The Tent of Testimony

15:5 After this, in my vision, the sanctuary, the Tent of the Testimony, opened in heaven,

The Tent is the heavenly canvas we have seen before. Everyone can see it. The dawning of the Age of Aquarius will become common knowledge to everyone.

and out came the seven angels with the seven plagues, wearing pure white linen, fastened around their waists with golden girdles.

And as it begins, the chastisements come. Seven plagues are released on the world, the labor pains of the New Age.

One of the four animals gave the seven angels seven golden bowls filled with the anger of God who lives for ever and ever.

Here is a reference to the earlier plagues and torments that were unleashed at the sounding of the seven trumpets in Revelation chapters 8–11. The bowls are the sufferings that are to be discharged when the New Age begins. For with the start of the New Age, the system is knocked out from under us, nature, man, or the stars intervene.

The smoke from the glory and the power of God filled the temple so that no one could go into it until the seven plagues of the seven angles were completed.

We have already seen the smoke tied in with the locusts and their leader. We have seen the smoke pour from the Abyss, possibly as a result of the "fireball" that struck the Earth. In various images, we are seeing similar themes repeating. Repetition underscores the importance of the message.

CHAPTER SIXTEEN

Revelation 16

16:1 *Then I heard a voice from the sanctuary shouting to the seven angels, "Go, and empty the seven bowls of God's anger over the earth."*

16:2 *The first angel went and emptied his bowl over the earth; at once, on all the people who had been branded with the mark of the beast and had worshipped its statue, there came disgusting and virulent sores.*

16:3 *The second angel emptied his bowl over the sea, and it turned to blood, like the blood of a corpse, and every living creature in the sea died.*

16:4 *The third angel emptied his bowl into the rivers and water springs and they turned into blood. / Then I heard the angel of water say, "You are the holy He-Is-and-He-Was, the Just One, and this is a just punishment: / they spilled the blood of the saints and the prophets, and blood is what you have given them to drink; it is what they deserve." / And I heard the altar itself say, "Truly, Lord God Almighty, the punishments you give are true and just."*

16:8 *The fourth angel emptied his bowl over the sun and it was made to scorch people with its flames; / but though people were scorched by the fierce heat of it, they cursed the name of God who had the power to cause such plagues, and they would not repent and praise him.*

16:10 *The fifth angel emptied this bowl over the throne of the beast and its whole empire was plunged into darkness. Men were biting their tongues for pain, /but instead of repenting for what they had done, they cursed the God of heaven because of their pains and sores.*

16:12 *The sixth angel emptied his bowl over the great river Euphrates; all the water dried up so that a way was made for the kings of the East to come in, / Then from the jaws of the dragon and beast and false* *prophet I saw three foul spirits come; they looked like frogs / and in fact were demon spirits, able to work miracles, going out to all the kings of the world to call together for the war of the Great Day of God the Almighty—/ This is how it will be: I shall come like a thief. Happy is the man who has stayed awake and not taken off his clothes so that he does not go out naked and expose his shame—/ They called the kings together at the place called, in Hebrew, Armageddon.*

16:17 *The seventh angel emptied his bowl into the air, and a voice shouted from the sanctuary, "The end has come." / Then there were flashes of lightning and peals of thunder and the most violent earthquake that anyone has ever seen since there have been men on the earth. / The Great City was split into three parts and the cities of the world collapsed; Babylon the Great was not forgotten: God made her drink the full wine cup of his anger. / Every island vanished and the mountains disappeared; / and hail, with great hailstones weighing a talent each, fell from the sky on the people. They cursed God for sending a plague of hail; it was the most terrible plague.*

* * * * *

16:1 Then I heard a voice from the sanctuary shouting to the seven angels, "Go, and empty the seven bowls of God's anger over the earth."

The Time has come. The horrors begin.

The First Bowl

16:2 The first angel went and emptied his bowl over the earth; at once, on all the people who had been branded with the mark of the beast and had worshipped its statue, there came disgusting and virulent sores.

This is what seems to be the first plague. There is an expression about someone putting "a plague on your house." This can either be an idle comment, or it can be part of a nefarious act wherein some ill-will is coupled to the sentiment. In the same manner, this can be "a plague on your nation." This could be coupled to a foreign policy mandate, such as a trade embargo that is imposed so vital components of a society's needs are denied like medicines or food. As a result, innocent people and children die; suffering is often used as a political tool, to leverage mineral or material resources.

When it is exposed that those branded with the mark of the beast have been involved in schemes of ill-gotten gain, their social and political pain will be considerable. They will seem to be affiliated with "disgusting and virulent sores." The guilty parties, and those who love them will be placed in considerable anguish. We will see this theme repeated in the fifth bowl.

The Second Bowl

16:3 The second angel emptied his bowl over the sea, and it turned to blood, like the blood of a corpse, and every living creature in the sea died.

Remember that at the sounding of the second trumpet, the fireball fell into the Sea and one-third died. The second bowl is now being dumped into the sea, causing the death of every living creature in the sea. This is another appalling reminder of the consistency of the prophesy.

Intuition suggests that the molten core of the planet is changing. I believe it is for this reason, and not those proposed by others, that we are seeing environmental changes taking place—more powerful storms and the activization of the Pacific "Ring of Fire" among others.

Our magnetic core has a great deal to do with the oceanic currents, and this core is getting ready to shift. We are seeing signs of its increased activity. As the core shifts, the oceanic currents will shift, impacting not only all sea life and the coastlines, but also our weather patterns and everything that is tied to the "ebb and flow" of the tides. The oceans will not die, but will enter what seems to be a "coma." Its blood will be "*like* the blood of a corpse," and not, "the blood *of* a corpse." It will seem to stop. The Earth and her oceans will *seem* to be dead, but will revive, although on a different series of cycles.

Our planetary pulse will be different from that of the past.

The Third Bowl

16:4 The third angel emptied his bowl into the rivers and water springs and they turned into blood.

The third trumpet called forth a fireball to fall on rivers and springs. It was called Wormwood. The springs and rivers are important because Aquarius will bring new "waters," new springs as a result of the earthquake, referenced four times in Revelation.

Then I heard the angel of water say, "You are the holy He-Is-and-He-Was, the Just One, and this is a just punishment

The heavenly verdict is that the "hands-off" period is over, and retribution is being exacted. The angel of water is the angel of the Age of Pisces, our mutable water sign. Pisces is getting ready to flush out the imbalances at the end of the system. It is Heracles flushing out the stables as one of his twelve labors. Each in a single day. The angel didn't say it was going to be easy. She said it was going to be just.

they spilled the blood of the saints and the prophets, and blood is what you have given them to drink; it is what they deserve.

The establishment, the authority, the system has been run by those at the top. Those that have defended and who have died for truth are the blood of the saints and the prophets. The evening of the scales is the beginning of a fair verdict.

And I heard the altar itself say, "Truly, Lord God Almighty, the punishments you give are true and just."

The Altar, the Vernal Equinox and the power of the Lamb confirm the judgment.

But there is a flip side to this "bowl." With the stirring of the planetary currents, from the molten core of the Earth to the oceans to the coastlines and weather patterns, there will be a stirring up of the vital "internal organs" of the planet—like stirring up all the silt at the bottom of a mighty river before it spills into the sea. With this stirring, new streams and rivers will appear in diverse places, and the "blood" (here in part related to the blood of the Lamb, what is happening in life at the moment) will represent mineral and nutrient vitality. All those places where these new (and in some cases old) watercourses start to flow will each be like an oasis in the desert, enabling new plants and animals to flourish.

For those who make it through to the "Wedding of the Lamb (and the bride of Aquarius)," this will be a marvelous land indeed, and much will grow. As the Vernal Equinox (Spring) passes into the constellation Aquarius, the stream represented by the Water-Bearer that flows from the urn will be greatly re-vitalized, and our waters will run afresh, with renewed vigor and vitality.

Isaiah speaks about this in several places. Here are several especially inspiring verses.

> *The oppressed and needy search for water, and there is none,*
> *their tongue is parched with thirst.*
> *I, Yahweh, shall answer them,*
> *I, God of Israel, shall not abandon them.*
> *I shall open up rivers on barren heights*
> *and water-holes down in the ravines;*
> *I shall turn the dry ground into a lake*
> *and dry ground into springs of water.*
> *I shall plant the desert with cedar trees,*
> *acacias, myrtles and olives;*
> *in the wastelands I shall put cypress trees,*
> *plant trees and box trees side by side;*
> *so that all people may see and know*

so that they may all observe and understand
that the hand of Yahweh has done this,
that the Holy One of Israel has created it.[1]

These are the revitalized rivers and waters, filled with a new vitality, like fresh blood in the veins and arteries of a Spring Lamb. But in this case the body of the Lamb is Mother Earth.

For Yahweh says this:
"Look, I am going to send peace
flowing over her like a river,
and like a stream in spate
the glory of the nations."[2]

In the changing times, fresh drinking water will first be compromised but will reappear in a new and revitalized fashion. Praise-be to the Name of the Lord!

The Fourth Bowl

16:8 The fourth angel emptied his bowl over the sun and it was made to scorch people with its flames

During the sounding of the fourth trumpet a third of the light of the Sun, Moon, and stars were blasted.

but though people were scorched by the fierce heat of it, they cursed the name of God who had the power to cause such plagues, and they would not repent and praise him.

Times of tribulation are ahead. One of the tricks is going to be

---

1 Isaiah 41:17–20. See also several related verses in Isaiah 30:25; 35:1–3; 35:5–8,
2 Isaiah 66:12,

to embrace the changes, approve of the divine wisdom in spite of the problems. Sing praise for the changes that are coming. They, too, are God's plan. There's a reason for all of it.

Not all of the changes (the bowls) are limited to criteria here on Earth. This one represents the "jarring" of the Sun into solar flare activity, and its resulting "heating up" of space weather, not only for the Earth, but for our entire solar system. We could be burned. Space weather (solar winds generated by solar flare activity) has a dramatic effect on communications here on the planet, and on those dependent upon those communications: like air traffic control, and people who monitor the transmissions, such as astronomers, guidance systems, weather and military intelligence, etc. Cell phone reception could be dramatically impacted.

The Fifth Bowl

16:10 *The fifth angel emptied this bowl over the throne of the beast and its whole empire was plunged into darkness. Men were biting their tongues for pain,*

The throne of the beast was, as we have seen, the location of the North Celestial Pole. The fifth trumpet was the smoke from the furnace, out of which dropped the locusts.

> *Their tails were like scorpions', with stings, and it was with them that they were able to injure people for five months.*[3]

Say hello to darkness.

> *but instead of repenting for what they had done, they cursed the God of heaven because of their pains and sores.*

Like the cursing of the sinners in the text of the Fourth Bowl, this

---

3 Rev. 9:10.

is wrong. Events that are heaven-sent have divine sanction and are not to be argued with. They are to be honored as the Will of God.

This one is an oxymoron, beautiful in its simplicity. The fifth angel is telling the truth, and this small amount of truth has great power, power to expose the throne of the beast and its whole dark empire. People will see it for what it is. Those who were responsible will be in great pain for what must be said, the admission of their own guilt. These are painful, cutting words. What's worse is that they're self-incriminating.

You need the light to see the darkness. It is a core of goodness that magnifies the evil by contrast. There are those who have descended so far into the darkness that a light blinds them, and they cannot see.

For these, the goodness becomes a self-torture. The more they resist the goodness, the more the pain persists. It is a time of great difficulty for the minions of the beast.

The Sixth Bowl

16:12 The sixth angel emptied his bowl over the great river Euphrates; all the water dried up so that a way was made for the kings of the East to come in,

What do you think the sixth trumpet heralded?

"Release the four angels that are chained up at the great river Euphrates."

The kings of the East are waiting for the stars to align with the East Point, the Vernal Equinox.

Then from the jaws of the dragon and beast and false prophet I saw three foul spirits come; they looked like frogs

The jaws of the dragon in many traditions have been the mythic dispensers of noxious fumes, fires and floods. In fact, there is a star, *26 Draconis*, located beneath the head of the great serpent, called *"Dragon's breath.*" The image is not a new one. The *Uraeas*, the serpent poised on Pharaoh's brow was a "flame-spiting cobra."

The foul spirits spewing forth a line of miracles and propaganda intoxicated the masses with hypnotic words.

> *and in fact were demon spirits, able to work miracles, going out to all the kings of the world to call together for the war of the Great Day of God the Almighty—*

The "world" is clearly in the realm of the dragon, beast and demon spirits. They are getting ready for the upcoming battle.

> *This is how it will be: I shall come like a thief. Happy is the man who has stayed awake and not taken off his clothes so that he does not go out naked and expose his shame—*

This notion of the thief as villain in part derives from Obadiah. In his work, history records how the Edomites took advantage of the sack of Jerusalem to invade southern Judaea while the country was in a militarily weakened condition. This betrayal cut deeply into the soul of a nation already humbled and on its knees. This notion of endorsed, legitimatized, nationalistic theft infuriated the remaining Jews who witnessed these acts.

People won't know at what time to expect these changes. Happy are those who are ready. Keeping his clothes on is a metaphor for being ready when the time comes, of having a pure soul.

With the coming Earth-changes, there will be rivers and water-courses that dry up as well as those that appear. The Earth is getting ready to shift, to "readjust" her position. Some areas, such as lakes, will rise, causing the lakes to dramatically drain down their traditional spillways, and in some cases, along new courses. In other areas, the lands will be depressed, allowing water to cover areas that were not covered before. As a general rule, coastal areas will be dramatically impacted, and are not good locations to "ride through the storm." There will be a series of smaller earthquakes and volcanic activity. Each of these has already begun, of land rising and land falling. The shifting mantles will make traditional water sources more problematic, with new ones unexpectedly appearing. This shifting mantle (there will a series of earth tremors in anticipation of the climatic event) will also cause shifting political conditions—paving the way for the kings of the East to enter. Presumably to Europe and the West.

Jesus refers to the time at the end of the Age in Matthew, chapter 24.

> *"You see all these? (referring to the walls of the Temple) In truth I tell you, not a single stone here will be left on another: everything will be pulled down."*[4]

He continues after the disciples seek more specific information.

> *"You will hear of wars and rumors of wars; see that you are not alarmed, for this is something that must happen, but the end will not be yet. For nation will fight against nation, and kingdom against kingdom. There will be famines and earthquakes in various places. All this is only the beginning of the birth pangs."*[5]

First, all the stones will be leveled, and second, there will be a series of earthquakes building into this period. But it is during these times that the greatest opportunity for humanity presents itself. How things unfold and how we treat each other when the infrastructure collapses can allow us to start a new independent order—a political revolution, a brave new world.

In those days, great leaders will be required. We are not talking just about "power" here, but rather leadership in its finest sense. It will be those who make the difficult choices in what is best for the children of God, for all of us.

---

4 Matthew 24:2
5 Matthew 24:6–8.

Armageddon

They called the kings together at the place called, in Hebrew, Arma-
geddon.

Once again, John is speaking directly to the reader and offering
a clue, "Here is a Hebrew word!" This is not generally the "voice" of
dreams, but rather one of literary compositions and footnotes.

The Hebrew translation of Armageddon is *Har-Magedon*, the
Mount of Megiddo. There are several intersections with Armageddon
that could be plumbed here. One is geographic. Like the Greek
churches located in the Decapolis of Turkey, the Mount of Megiddo
is important because it is located on a trade route. Control the mount
and you control the flow of trade and traffic in and out of the city.
Megiddo is located along the southwestern edge of Jezreel Valley in
Israel, beyond the Carmel ridge and the Mediterranean. The fortress
at Megiddo controlled the main trade route between Egypt and Syria.

Megiddo is not large even though the name could be literally
translated as "Mountain of Megiddo." It is a small, elevated plateau
close to a large coastal plain big enough to accompany a substantial
body of troops. It was not a mountain fortress, but was useful as a garrison and a staging area for campaigns on the coast. It was also a good
water source.

Another connection with *Har-Magedon* is historic. There have
been no less than three battles fought there—each of epic proportions
in its own right.

The first battle in *Har-Magedon* is thought to be history's oldest,
accurate depiction of a modern battle supplied in reliable detail. A royal
scribe by the name of Tjaneni recorded it in the year 1457 BC as a
monument to Egypt's glory. As a result of the battle, the Canaanite
rebels were crushed, even though the siege and final fall of the city took
somewhat longer.

The second battle of *Har-Magedon* is probably the one that the
lines of Revelation reference, as they are part of the Judaic historical
record. It was the Battle of Megiddo in 609 BC, fought between Egypt

and the Kingdom of Judah, the last of the tribes of Israel. This battle is referenced in both the second book of Kings (2 Kings 23:28–35) and Chronicles (2 Chronicles 35:19–26).

This battle carries with it a curious storyline. Josiah, the king of Judah, had broken with a long tradition undertaken by the kings of Judah (including his own father). They had not done what Yahweh asked, but reverted to the older, more enticing pagan practices. As king of Judah, Josiah tore down the high places, destroying the altars and killing the priests of the surrounding religions. He even went so far as to dig up the bones of the old priests and burned them together with their altars. Both the books of Kings and Chronicles are pleased with Josiah's devotion toward Yahweh.

Then, as the Pharaoh of Egypt was passing through on his way to do battle with a "different dynasty," Josiah taunted the Egyptians. He and his army were promptly defeated—his gratuitous arrogance being the cause. For all intents and purposes, this ended the sporadic line of "Yahweh-conscious" kings of Judah. Josiah's son ruled briefly (Jehoahaz), but was replaced with a new Egyptian king. Jehoahaz was then taken captive to Egypt, where he held the unique distinction of being the first king of Judah to die in exile.

The tragedy of Josiah's death in the second battle of Megiddo was crushing. There is a tradition in Judaism that looks forward to the return, the re-birth of Josiah, the last king to kneel before the will of Yahweh. Part of that hope is planted here, in the hope for the return of the spirit of Jesus.

The final battle of Megiddo took place in AD 1918, during the waning months of World War I. It is important, as some have pointed to it being part of the fulfillment of the prophecy for the end times. It was the culminating victory for the British in the conquest of Palestine. The Ottoman Turks lost 75,000 men. They were crushed.

Each of the three battles was lopsided, with fatal consequences for the losers. Such are the association with and implications for the final battle at Armageddon.

The Seventh Bowl

16:17 The seventh angel emptied his bowl into the air, and a voice shouted from the sanctuary, "The end has come."

And the seventh trumpet?

"The kingdom of the world has become the kingdom of our Lord and Christ, and he will reign for ever and ever... The time has come to destroy those who are destroying the earth."[6]

Revelation 16 continues.

Then there were flashes of lightning and peals of thunder and the most violent earthquake that anyone has ever seen since there have been men on the earth.

The great shift between the two Ages will be an earthquake, such as—if this book of prophecy is to be believed—will be the most violent earthquake the world has ever known. This great event, whatever it is, will define the arrival of the New Age.

The Great City was split into three parts and the cities of the world collapsed; Babylon the Great was not forgotten: God made her drink the full wine cup of his anger.

God has been biding "His" time, waiting for the fulfillment of "His" plan. Notice that we are back to our "thirds" again. The Great City is the cities of the world, our urban cosmopolitan culture. It is the web of civilization, all under one roof, under one heavenly tent. One third of the Earth will suffer through the times of the final shift from Pisces, and all it represents, into Aquarius.

God has held back throughout the entire Age, *in absentia* for the

---

6 Rev. 11:15, 18.

last two thousand years, watching and waiting. All this changes with the Eighth Seal.

Every island vanished and the mountains disappeared;

There's a really big earthquake. This is what one might expect.

and hail, with great hailstones weighing a talent each, fell from the sky on the people. They cursed God for sending a plague of hail; it was the most terrible plague,

According to Exodus, this has happened before; and it sets the stage for what may be about to happen under the Eighth Seal. The power of a dark star discharged on Earth. We are hearing about a string of calamities, orchestrated by a larger, singular event.

Moses used a string of calamites to good effect with the Hebrews. He was raised in the Egyptian courts. He knew the Egyptian stellar wisdom. His "staff," which changed into a "serpent," was a sighting stick used to help read the heavens. The serpent guarded the North Celestial Pole. All the other Egyptian priests could do it with their staffs too, but the staff of Moses consumed the others. His precision, his wisdom, outmatched theirs. His celestial mechanics were better. He saw and successfully interpreted the successive layers of plagues that would unfold as the celestial trigger was discharged.

The Seven Sprits before the throne of God divide Creation up amongst themselves. The head is ruled by one, the throat another, the arms, the legs, etc. But we need all of these elements working together while we are living. It doesn't matter if you're good or bad. Your heart has to pump; your lungs need air; your stomach food. They are seven separate parts all working together as a whole, as the seven days work together to complete the week. They are one and they are two. They are one and they are seven.

They are all One. There is only One. The Holy One, whatever name people use.

CHAPTER SEVENTEEN

Revelation 17

17:1 *One of the seven angels that had the seven bowls came to speak to me, and said, "Come here and I will show you the punishment given to the famous prostitute who rules enthroned beside abundant waters, / the one with whom all the kings of the earth have committed fornication, and who has made all the population of the world drunk with the wine of her adultery." / He took me in spirit to a desert, and there I saw a woman riding a scarlet beast which had seven heads and ten horns and had blasphemous titles written all over it. This woman was dressed in purple and scarlet, and glittered with gold and jewels and pearls, and she was holding a gold wine cup filled with the disgusting filth of her fornication; / on her forehead was written a name, a cryptic name: "Babylon the Great, the mother of all the prostitutes and all the filthy practices on the earth." / I saw that she was drunk, drunk with the blood of the saints, and the blood of the martyrs of Jesus; and when I saw her, I was completely mystified. / The angel said to me, "Don't you understand? Now I will tell you the meaning of this woman, and the beast she is riding, with the seven heads and the ten horns.*

17:8 *"The Beast you have seen once was and now is not; he is yet to come up from the Abyss, but only to go to his destruction. And the people of the world, whose names have not been written since the beginning of the world in the book of life, will think it miraculous when they see how the beast once was now is not and is still to come. / Here there is need for cleverness, for a shrewd mind; the seven heads are the seven hills, and the woman is sitting on them.*

17:10 *"The seven heads are also seven emperors. Five of them have already gone, one is here now, and one is yet to come; once here, he must stay for a short while. / The beast, who once was and now is not, is at the same time the eighth and one of the seven, and he is going to his destruction.*

17:12 *"The ten horns are ten kings who have not yet been given their royal power but will have royal authority only for a single hour and in association with the beast. / They are all of one mind in putting their strength and their powers at the beast's disposal, / and they will go to war against the Lamb; but the Lamb is the Lord of lords and the King of all kings, and he will defeat them and they will be defeated by his followers, the called, the chosen, the faithful."*

17:15 *The angel continued, "The waters you saw, beside which the prostitute was sitting, are all the peoples, the populations, the nations and the languages. / But the time will come when the ten horns and the beast will turn against the prostitute, and strip off her clothes and leave her naked; then they will eat her flesh and burn the remains in the fire. / In fact, God influenced their minds to do what he intended, to agree together to put their royal powers at the beast's disposal until the time when God's words would be fulfilled. / The woman you saw is the great city which has authority over all the rulers on earth."*

* * * * *

17:1 One of the seven angels that had the seven bowls came to speak to me, and said, "Come here and I will show you the punishment given to the famous prostitute who rules enthroned beside abundant waters,

We're being given a description of the themes introduced by 666 (Rev. 13:18).

the one with whom all the kings of the earth have committed fornication, and who has made all the population of the world drunk with the wine of her adultery."

The prostitute is mercantilism. She sits enthroned by the multitudes (the abundant waters), and she does business where she chooses. The Earth has been seduced by a frenzy of consumption.

*He took me in spirit to a desert, and there I saw a woman riding a
scarlet beast which had seven heads and ten horns and had blasphemous
titles written all over it.*

This woman has power, but it is power over a wasteland. There is no
nourishment here, there is no future here.

*This woman was dressed in purple and scarlet, and glittered with gold
and jewels and pearls, and she was holding a gold wine cup filled with
the disgusting filth of her fornication;*

This is a passionate woman of power. She indulges her sensuality.
She has seduced many.

*on her forehead was written a name, a cryptic name: "Babylon the Great,
the mother of all the prostitutes and all the filthy practices on the earth."*

Many of the pagan rites were fertility rites, and the prostitutes
are being related to Venus (or Aphrodite, Istarte, Ishtar, and others).
The world was a dangerous place, and survival was anything but guaranteed. Superior numbers enhanced tribal self-protection. Whether
the cattle, flock, or populace, go forth, be fruitful and multiply. It made
for security in numbers.

*I saw that she was drunk, drunk with the blood of the saints, and the
blood of the martyrs of Jesus; and when I saw her, I was completely mystified.*

Looking at the images, John doesn't understand, but the spirit of
Revelation is about to explain it.

*The angel said to me, "Don't you understand? Now I will tell you the
meaning of this woman, and the beast she is riding, with the seven heads
and the ten horns.*

17:8 "The Beast you have seen once was and now is not; he is yet to come up from the Abyss, but only to go to his destruction. And the people of the world, whose names have not been written since the beginning of the world in the book of life, will think it miraculous when they see how the beast once was now is not and is still to come.

For many millennia in mythological terms, only two creatures have occupied the celestial pole position, the Dragon and the Beast. As discussed at length in my earlier book *When the Dragon Wore the Crown*, the Dragon retained this position for thousands of years. For centuries the North Celestial Pole passed between the Dragon and Beast (where it was when Revelation was being written). The Beast assumed this astronomical crown, but only so that it could fulfill its rendezvous with destiny.

When Revelation was written, there was no pole star, no constellational guardian. Yet the author or authors of Revelation were familiar enough with the motions of heaven to perceive where it was headed, and they are describing these astronomical motions in mythological terms.

Here there is need for cleverness, for a shrewd mind; the seven heads are the seven hills, and the woman is sitting on them.

This line is saying the prostitute's power emanates from Rome. Once again John is speaking directly to the reader. This is not part of a vision, it's a clue provided by a logical mind. If the seven heads are the seven hills, the prostitute is riding, controlling, and has seduced Rome, and through Rome, the world.

17:10 "The seven heads are also seven emperors. Five of them have already gone, one is here now, and one is yet to come; once here, he must stay for a short while.

Of the many lines in Revelation, this one eludes me. Writing in the

1st century AD. Five gone, one here, one to come (but only for a short while). I have no idea.

At the Same Time the Eighth and One of the Seven

The beast, who once was and now is not, is at the same time the eighth and one of the seven, and he is going to his destruction.

This makes sense. With the completion of the Seven Seals, there's a break. This is the *"once was and now is not"* (the silence in heaven for about half an hour). It is the Eighth Seal, the next in line that marks the end of the initial series and the start of a new one. This is the celestial marker we've been waiting for. When will God's Curse come to an end?

The eighth is the Eighth "Seal," the Seven Seals plus the next one in line. In this clause Revelation is including the eighth star/seal as part of the group of seven, just as we have done. The first seven were relatively evenly spaced. The "eighth" is part of the picture only after a sizeable jump that differentiates it from the others, yet is part of the others, marking a new start. In the above quote, the beast (aligned with the North Celestial Pole) and the star (*Omega Piscium*) are center and circle, a continuing mythological theme generally reserved for Creation Myths. Now that *Alpha Ursa Minor* is aligning with the North Celestial Pole, these are future sky patterns that the authors of Revelation are anticipating, and they are the stellar positions we currently see marked by Spring in our night skies.

Revelation is suggesting that the power of the Eighth Seal is opening and the North Celestial Pole is changing at nearly the same time. The star *Omega Piscium* coincided with the Vernal Equinox in 2013; and Alpha Ursa Minor will reach its highest degree of latitude in AD 2100—there is only an eighty-seven year difference between the two astronomical events. In stellar time (in precessional time), that's not much at all.

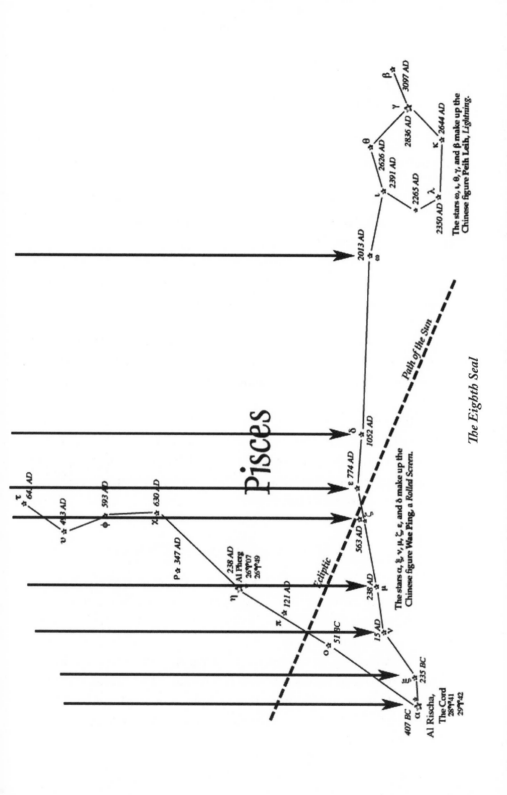

Pisces

Path of the Sun

Ecliptic

τ 64 AD
υ 483 AD
φ 593 AD
χ 630 AD

ρ 347 AD

238 AD
Al Pherg
26°♈07
26°♈49
η

π 121 AD

o 51 BC

407 BC
α
Al Rischa,
The Cord
28°♈41
29°♈42

ξ 235 BC

ν 15 AD

μ 238 AD

563 AD
ζ

ε 774 AD

δ 1052 AD

ω 2013 AD

ι 2391 AD

θ 2626 AD

λ 2265 AD

2350 AD

γ 2836 AD

β 3097 AD

κ 2644 AD

The stars α, ξ, ν, μ, ζ, ε, and δ make up the Chinese figure Wae Ping, a Rolled Screen.

The stars ω, ι, θ, γ, and β make up the Chinese figure Peih Leih, Lightning.

The Eighth Seal

17:12 The ten horns are ten kings who have not yet been given their royal power but will have royal authority only for a single hour and in association with the beast.

This is fairly clear. There will be ten kings, whether of nationality or industry, that are lieutenants to the beast (woman, dragon, beast, man, 666, etc.).

They are all of one mind in putting their strength and their powers at the beast's disposal,

They will all be pulling in the same direction as one. This is a unified effort, a mutual cooperation between the evil ones.

and they will go to war against the Lamb; but the Lamb is the Lord of lords and the King of all kings, and he will defeat them and they will be defeated by his followers, the called, the chosen, the faithful."

The forces of the Earth, the powers of the past are about to con-front the wave of the future. The Lamb—zero degrees of Aries in the tropical Western zodiac—is shifting constellations, leaving Pisces and entering Aquarius. The two opposing political spectrums will each square off against each other.

The Waters You Saw Are All the Peoples

17:15 The angel continued, "The waters you saw, beside which the pros-titute was sitting, are all the peoples, the populations, the nations and the languages.

The waters are the entire length of the Age, the water sign Pisces, and all those who have lived under its Heavenly Tent during that time. They are the common, indigenous people all around the world, the simple people, the little people, the humble people, the poor people, the lonely people.

"But the time will come when the ten horns and the beast will turn against the prostitute, and strip off her clothes and leave her naked; then they will eat her flesh and burn the remains in the fire.

Corruption begets corruption. These fair weather allies will turn on those in power and strip them of what valuables they have, consuming completely any signs of her past.

"In fact, God influenced their minds to do what he intended, to agree together to put their royal powers at the beast's disposal until the time when God's words would be fulfilled.

This is an interesting statement. God pre-conditioned the lieu-tenants to serve the beast in order that the divine plan might be ful-filled. God hardened Pharaoh's heart to affect the Exodus. How many other "lieutenants" could claim these moral precedents as grounds for exoneration? God programmed them to do it.

Are they then morally responsible for the actions performed while in the beast's service? If they are responsible for crimes committed while in the employ, are they then guilty of said crimes?

"The woman you saw is the great city which has authority over all the rulers on earth."

If there is a power behind the civic administration, she's it. Her name is Roma.

We'll learn more about her in the chapters ahead.

CHAPTER EIGHTEEN

Revelation 18

18:1 *After this, I saw another angel come down from heaven, with great authority given to him; the earth was lit up with his glory. / At the top of his voice he shouted, "Babylon has fallen, Babylon the Great has fallen, and has become the haunt of devils and a lodging for every foul spirit and dirty, loathsome bird. / All the nations have been intoxicated by the wine of her prostitution; every king in the earth has committed fornication with her, and every merchant grown rich through her debauchery."*

18:4 *A new voice spoke up from heaven; I heard it say, "Come out, my people, away from her, so that you do not share in her crimes and have the same plagues to bear. / Her sins have reached up to heaven, and God has her crimes in mind; she is to be paid in her own coin. She must be paid double the amount she exacted. She is to have a doubly strong cup of her own mixture. / Every one of her shows and orgies is to be matched by a torture or a grief. I am the queen on my throne, she says to herself, and I am no widow and shall never be in mourning. / For that, within a single day, the plagues will fall on her; disease and mourning and famine. She will be burned right up. The Lord God has condemned her, and he has great power.*

18:9 *There will be moaning and weeping for her by the kings of the earth who have fornicated with her and lived with her in luxury. They see the smoke as she burns, "while they keep at a safe distance from fear of her agony. They will say:*

> *"Mourn, mourn for this great city,*
> *Babylon, so powerful a city,*
> *doomed as you are within a single hour."*

/ There will be weeping and distress over her among all the traders of the earth, when there is nobody left to buy their cargoes of goods; / their stocks of gold and silver, jewels and pearls, linen and purple and silks and scarlet; all the sandalwood, every piece in ivory or fine wood, in bronze or iron or marble; / the cinnamon and spices, the myrrh and ointment and incense; wine, oil, flour and corn; their stocks of cattle, sheep, horses and chariots, their slaves, their human cargo.

18:14 *"All the fruits you had set your hearts on have failed you; gone for ever, never to return, is your life of magnificence and ease."*

18:15 *The traders who had made a fortune out of her will be standing at a safe distance from fear of her agony, mourning and weeping. / They will be saying:*

> *"Mourn, mourn for this great city;*
> *for all the linen and purple and scarlet that you wore,*
> *for all your finery of gold and jewels and pearls;*
> *your riches are all destroyed within a single hour."*

All the captains and seafaring men, sailors and all those who make a living from the sea will be keeping a safe distance, "watching the smoke as she burns, and crying out, "Has there ever been a city as great as this!" / They will throw dust on their heads and say, with tears and groans:

> *"Mourn, mourn for this great city*
> *whose lavish living has made a fortune*
> *for every owner of a seagoing ship;*
> *ruined within a single hour.*

18:20 *"Now heaven, celebrate her downfall, and all you saints, apostles and prophets: God has given judgment for you against her."*

18:21 *Then a powerful angel picked up a boulder like a great millstone, and as he hurled it into the sea, he said, "That is how the great city of Babylon is going to be hurled down, never to be seen again.*

18:22   *"Never again in you, Babylon,*
will be heard the song of harpists and minstrels,
the music of flute and trumpet:
never again will craftsmen of every skill be found
or the sound of the mill be heard;
/ never again will shine the light of the lamp,
never again will be heard
the voices of bridegroom and bride.
Your traders were the princes of the earth,
all the nations were under your spell.

/In her you will find the blood of the prophets and saints, and all the blood that was ever shed on the earth."

* * * * *

18:1 After this, I saw another angel come down from heaven, with great authority given to him; the earth was lit up with his glory.

This is one of the Lords of Heaven coming down with great authority, probably the Angel of Aquarius, with great power and authority. He is lighting up the Earth as the Vernal Equinox infuses it with its Spring-like vitality. Those living here are very excited about it.

Babylon has Fallen

At the top of his voice he shouted, "Babylon has fallen, Babylon the Great has fallen, and has become the haunt of devils and a lodging for every foul spirit and dirty, loathsome bird.

Babylon, whether this is a location, philosophy or people that support a particular style of living, is seeing the end of its days. It is a place and a time when anything goes. Loathsome birds relate to the element AIR, which is communications and ideas. There are some nasty notions at work here.

All the nations have been intoxicated by the wine of her prostitution; every king in the earth has committed fornication with her, and every merchant grown rich through her debauchery."

Pleasures on a silver platter, all there for the taking. Market it, sell it. Sell what, you ask?
Sell everything.

18:4 A new voice spoke up from heaven; I heard it say, "Come out, my people, away from her, so that you do not share in her crimes and have the same plagues to bear.

"Babylon" has been in power for the previous two thousand years. Divine retribution is getting ready to fall on "Babylon" as we move from the Age of Pisces to the Age of Aquarius.

Her sins have reached up to heaven, and God has her crimes in mind; she is to be paid in her own coin. She must be paid double the amount she exacted. She is to have a doubly strong cup of her own mixture.

God has been waiting. This is what you served up? Now it is ripe with the fermentation of centuries.

Every one of her shows and orgies is to be matched by a torture or a grief. I am the queen on my throne, she says to herself, and I am no widow and shall never be in mourning.

This queen is married to the source of her power and feels its vitality. This union is so strong and vital, the most powerful in the land, that she is confident no Earthly power could knock it off its hinges. She is supremely self-confident.

For that, within a single day, the plagues will fall on her; disease and mourning and famine. She will be burned right up. The Lord God has condemned her, and he has great power.

A single day may be metaphorical, but it may not. It is in line with both the nature of the Age into which we're heading. It may well be strong, sudden, unexpected, different, and of a wildly unsuspected origin. A shot in the dark, a strike from out of the blue. It will hit and she (Rome and the power that emanates from there) will be consumed.

This is the result of the fireballs hitting the earth and/or sea, and it will change the political, social and military balance radically and suddenly.

Like a lightning strike, the name of the new asterism the Vernal Equinox is entering according to Chinese mythology. Or it could be a collective computer crash, affecting world-wide markets, or a natural event like a world-wide earthquake that brings everyone to their knees.

Within a day, it will change everything.

18:9 There will be moaning and weeping for her by the kings of the earth who have fornicated with her and lived with her in luxury. They see the smoke as she burns, "while they keep at a safe distance from fear of her agony. They will say:

"Mourn, mourn for this great city,
Babylon, so powerful a city,
doomed as you are within a single hour."

A single day is now being reduced to a single hour. They are not mutually exclusive. The money that was made in the system won't be in the system anymore. Whatever the location of the lair of the beast, it all goes down in a single hour! Most of the Earth was on the side of the Beast—which would suggest that most of the populace is not going to like the initial changeover. (Remember that we are only attempting to read the interpretation of what Revelation is trying to tell us here. We will comment on its implications later.)

It is entirely possible that the entire economic system and all it supports is getting ready to collapse.

> "I have lived here before, the days of Ice,
> and of course this is why, I'm so concerned;
> and I come back to find, the stars misplaced
> and the smell of a world, that is burned ...
> ... that is burned.[1]

All the Traders of the Earth

There will be weeping and distress over her among all the traders of the earth, when there is nobody left to buy their cargoes of goods;

The trade network is going to collapse. For some, this is called our "standard of living."

their stocks of gold and silver, jewels and pearls, linen and purple and silks and scarlet; all the sandalwood, every piece in ivory or fine wood, in bronze or iron or marble; the cinnamon and spices, the myrrh and ointment and incense; wine, oil, flour and corn; their stocks of cattle, sheep, horses and chariots, their slaves, their human cargo.

It's simply going through the list of the articles that will no longer be available.

18:14 "All the fruits you had set your hearts on have failed you; gone for ever, never to return, is your life of magnificence and ease."

When you think about it, we modern Westerners do have an abundant lifestyle in terms of material goods when compared to any other time in human history, as well as when compared to the lives of citizens in many other countries today.

---

1 *Up from the Skies*, J. Hendrix.

beast, and diverting it through the golden road that runs via the city of the New Jerusalem.

18:21 Then a powerful angel picked up a boulder like a great millstone, and as he hurled it into the sea, he said, "That is how the great city of Babylon is going to be hurled down, never to be seen again.

We're back to our fireball image, but this time without the fire. This is the 22nd time we're seen it alluded to, and we're only part way through Revelation 18. Here's the list so far:

Rev. 8:5 (Then the angel took the censer and filled it with the fire from the altar, which he then threw down on to the earth), 8:7 (hail and fire, mixed with blood, were dropped on the earth), 8:8 (and it was as though a great mountain, all on fire, had been dropped into the sea), 8:10 (a huge star fell from the sky, burning like a ball of fire), 8:11 (this was the star called Wormwood, and a third of the people turned to bitter wormwood, so that many people died from drinking it), 8:12 (were blasted), 9:1 (I saw a star that had fallen from heaven on to the earth), 9:2 (smoke from a huge furnace), 9:3 (out of the smoke dropped), 9:17 (with their breastplates of flame color... the horses had lions' heads, and fire, smoke and sulphur were coming out of their mouths), 9:18 (It was by these three plagues, the fire, the smoke and the sulphur coming out of their mouths, that the one third of the race was killed), 13:13 (even to calling down fire from heaven on to the earth while people watched), 14:10 (made to drink the wine of God's fury which is ready, undiluted, in his cup of anger; in fire and brimstone they will be tortured), 14:11 (and the smoke of their torture will go up for ever and ever), 15:8 (The smoke from the glory and the power of God filled the temple so that no one could go into it until the seven plagues of the seven angels were completed), 16:8 (The fourth angel emptied his bowl over the sun and it was made to scorch people with its flames), 16:21 (and hail, with great hailstones weighing a talent each fell from the sky on the people. They cursed God for sending a plague of hail; it was the most terrible plague), 17:16 (and burn the remains in the fire), 18:1 (the earth was lit up with his glory), **18:8** *(within a single day, the plagues will fall on her: disease and mourning and famine. She will be burned right up),* **18:9** *(They see the smoke as she burns), and* **18:18** *(watching the smoke as she burns).*

They are all variations on a theme.

> *"Never again in you, Babylon,*
> *will be heard the song of harpists and minstrels,*
> *the music of flute and trumpet:*
> *never again will craftsmen of every skill be found*
> *or the sound of the mill be heard;*[2]

Babylonian culture was vibrant, whether artistic or industrial, work or play. The songs of civilization are being stilled.

> *never again will shine the light of the lamp,*
> *never again will be heard*
> *the voices of bridegroom and bride.*
> *Your traders were the princes of the earth,*
> *all the nations were under your spell.*

Once the Age of Pisces is over, life is no longer "married" to that Seaborn "bride." What was the equinoctical axis of this bride (represented by heaven at the commencement of the Age) and bridegroom (represented by Jesus). The Pisces (vernal) Virgo (autumnal) axis; the Fish and the wheat-holding Virgin.

If you have *faith*, you can *heal* yourself. It is the inherent message behind the feeding of the multitudes with the Fish and the loaves of bread. Pisces is obvious. Pisces is Latin for Fish. The opposite polarity is Virgo, generally depicted holding the *sheaf of wheat* representative of bread.

The voice of this bride and bridegroom spoke of traders, who, with

---

2 Rev. 18:22.

divine sanction became the princes of the earth. They still are as of this writing. This is the spell all the nations are under.

In her you will find the blood of the prophets and saints, and all the blood that was ever shed on the earth."

In the name of advertising, in the name of commercial enterprise, in the name of capitalization, material resources (Virgo), and colonialism have the wars of this epoch been fought—in spite of what the history books say. I believe we fight, in order that we may own things cheaply, not for any righteous, misguided morality.

CHAPTER NINETEEN

Revelation 19

19:1 *After this I seemed to hear the great sound of a huge crowd in heaven, singing, "Alleluia! Victory and glory and power to our God! He judges fairly, he punishes justly, and he has condemned the famous prostitute who corrupted the earth with her fornication; he has avenged his servants that she killed." / They sang again, "Alleluia! The smoke of her will go up for ever and ever." / Then the twenty-four elders and the four animals prostrated themselves and worshipped God seated there on his throne, and they cried, "Amen, Alleluia."*

19:5 *Then a voice came from the throne; it said, "Praise our God, you servants of his and all who, great or small, revere him." / And I seemed to hear the voices of a huge crowd, like the sound of the ocean or the great roar of thunder, answering, "Alleluia! The reign of the Lord our God Almighty has begun; / let us be glad and joyful and give praise to God, because this is the time of the marriage of the Lamb. / His bride is ready, and she has been able to dress herself in dazzling white linen, because her linen is made of the good deeds of the saints." / The angel said, "Write this. Happy are those who are invited to the wedding feast of the Lamb," and he added, "All the things you have written are true messages from God." / Then I knelt at his feet to worship him, but he said to me, "Don't do that; I am a servant just like you and all your brothers who are witnesses to Jesus. It is God that you must worship." The witness Jesus gave is the same as the spirit of prophecy.*

19:11 *And now I saw heaven open, and a white horse appear; its rider was called Faithful and True; he is a judge with integrity, a warrior for justice. / His eyes were flames of fire, and his head was crowned with many coronets; the name written on him was known only to himself, / his cloak was soaked in blood. He is known by the name, The Word of God. Behind him, dressed in linen of dazzling white, rode the armies of heaven on white horses. / From his mouth came a sharp sword to strike* *the pagans with; he is the one who will rule them with an iron scepter, and tread out the wine of Almighty God's fierce anger. / On his cloak and on his thigh there was a name written: The King of kings and the Lord of lords.*

19:17 *I saw an angel standing in the sun, and he shouted aloud to all the birds that were flying high overhead in the sky, "Come here. Gather together at the great feast that God is giving. / There will be the flesh of kings for you, and the flesh of great generals and heroes, the flesh of horses and their riders and of all kinds of men, citizens and slaves, small and great."*

19:19 *Then I saw the beast, with all the kings of the earth and their armies, gathered together to fight the rider and his army. / But the beast was taken prisoner, together with the false prophet who had worked miracles on the beast's behalf and by them had deceived all who had been branded with the mark of the beast and worshipped his statue. These two were thrown alive into the fiery lake of burning sulphur. / All the rest were killed by the sword of the rider, which came out of his mouth, and all the birds were gorged with their flesh.*

* * * * *

19:1 *After this I seemed to hear the great sound of a huge crowd in heaven, singing, "Alleluia! Victory and glory and power to our God! He judges fairly, he punishes justly, and he has condemned the famous prostitute who corrupted the earth with her fornication; he has avenged his servants that she killed."*

We're back to the souls beneath the altar (Vernal Equinox), waiting for the time when Pisces would end and the roll call be over. The New Age wins over the old, the new sound resonates over the old; the time of patience has come to an end. It's time for the reaper.

They sang again, "Alleluia! The smoke of her will go up for ever and ever."

This is the twenty-fourth mention in the fireball series.

Then the twenty-four elders and the four animals prostrated themselves and worshipped God seated there on his throne, and they cried, "Amen, Alleluia."

The lords of the hours of the day and the seasons of the year bow and say, "The Vernal Equinox (God on the throne) is the Creator. We'll follow the way of the divine."

19:5 Then a voice came from the throne; it said, "Praise our God, you servants of his and all who, great or small, revere him."

This is the seat of power. All things flow from here. Will you honor that, and do what is required of you in the celestial record, before heaven? Even the planets are but His servants.

And I seemed to hear the voices of a huge crowd, like the sound of the ocean or the great roar of thunder, answering, "Alleluia! The reign of the Lord our God Almighty has begun;

Aquarius is here re-establishing the communicative link between mortal and divine.

The Time of the Marriage of the Lamb

let us be glad and joyful and give praise to God, because this is the time of the marriage of the Lamb.

The Vernal Equinox (zero degrees of Aries—the Lamb) is moving into the celestial area designated as Aquarius. Heaven and Earth, the union of the ecliptic and the equator, represent the marriage of the Divine in our World. This is a magical time. When it moves into Aquarius, the marriage is accomplished, the new bride joined.

His bride is ready, and she has been able to dress herself in dazzling white linen, because her linen is made of the good deeds of the saints."

The spiritual essence of Pisces—all the poor souls who gave their lives in the service of truth and the Divine—is feeding the fires of Aquarius. There are souls of considerable advancement (dazzling white linen) who have returned to the Earth for this sojourn.

The angel said, "Write this. Happy are those who are invited to the wedding feast of the Lamb," and he added, "All the things you have written are true messages from God."

Those that make it through the end of Pisces, through the end of the three and a half years, will do well. True messages from God in heaven.

Then I knelt at his feet to worship him, but he said to me, "Don't do that; I am a servant just like you and all your brothers who are witnesses to Jesus. It is God that you must worship." The witness Jesus gave is the same as the spirit of prophecy

Aquarius is not a time of homage, at least to none save God. We are equals among equals. Caste, class, and gender systems will end as Pisces/Virgo shifts into Aquarius/Leo. The "wheat from the chaff" attitude will pass into the past. Some will see this as a loss of quality (Virgo). As this vibration shifts into Aquarius, we will move from having a "sense" of God (Pisces), to "knowing" God (Aquarius). It will be a huge distinction.

The last clause is telling us that what the Book of Revelation (the spirit of prophecy) is about is what Jesus was telling us about. They bear witness to the same truth. Matthew 24 is a microcosm of the Book of Revelation.

And Now I Saw Heaven Open

19:11 And now I saw heaven open, and a white horse appear; its rider was called Faithful and True; he is a judge with integrity, a warrior for justice.

We're being swept back up to heaven again for the big picture. The Eighth Seal is being opened. Like the First Seal, which was the last time we saw a white horse appearing, this rider also marks the start of a new era, a new age.

As with each of the other seals, the qualities of the events that are to take place under its "council" are being described. The point being that spiritual values are important, they should not be over-looked, shoved aside, or ignored. In the past, this has been allowed.

But the day of reckoning is now here. God's plan is being fulfilled. To this "He" will remain Faithful and True. It will happen. He keeps His Word. The Eighth Seal will manifest as a warrior, a warlord, a martial power who will lay down the law with a sword. This could easily be the sword that Jesus says he is going to bring (and has already brought). The spiritual record will be set straight, the chorus of the Ages acknowledged.

His eyes were flames of fire, and his head was crowned with many coronets; the name written on him was known only to himself,

This is the point of power, the Vernal Equinox has moved into position with the new bride. This is the King, the Lord in his new guise, the new reality. The seven will stand in accompaniment, because life will bestow its moment in time on the heralded entry, the new beginning, the new dawn.

Life begins again. A new civilization, a New Jerusalem born. Not an urban, terrestrial city, but a whole planet ready to acknowledge all life as living under one heavenly Tent. It will have a new name that will be evident once it arrives.

his cloak was soaked in blood. He is known by the name, The Word of

God. Behind him, dressed in linen of dazzling white, rode the armies of heaven on white horses.

We all come back to this planet over and over again. This is the School of Earth. We keep coming back until we deliver a life in service to spirit, unless we volunteer to come back to serve humanity. Obviously, this can take many forms. All those who reside below the altar have passed the test, but have had to wait while the period of the testing was still on. Others had not yet finished their exams.

His cloak soaked in blood is a dual reference. It is both the death of all those who have gone before, and the deaths of those who will die in this opening confrontation that will take place as Aquarius is born.

Even though the name written on him is known only to himself, He is known by the name, "The Word of God." God is giving His word that these things will take place at this time. All those who are united in the new message, in the new revolution, from around the planet will join together under one who assumes a mortal guise (or guises) and comes to fulfill this design.

From his mouth came a sharp sword to strike the pagans with; he is the one who will rule them with an iron scepter, and tread out the wine of Almighty God's fierce anger.

The multitudes are going to find that Draconian law will be the rule at the outset, possibly longer. The iron scepter is a warlord's rod of rule. The anger of the Almighty will be expressed through this warlord, the war, and the time of martial law that follows. This tsunamic explosion of moral indignation will impact fully one-third of the planet. It will rule with a vengeance.

On his cloak and on his thigh there was a name written: The King of kings and the Lord of lords.

We're back to the name. The Vernal Equinox is the commander-in-chief, the CEO, the emperor, and president all rolled into one. The thigh is the part of the body ruled by Sagittarius and Jupiter. Jupiter is the King of the Gods, the Lord of Lords, the Father of gods and men. He is the Big Picture, the sky and all that's in it.

Modern astronomy focuses on the Sun as our elliptical center. It is the largest member of our solar system, a true star and the foundation stone (so to speak) of our modern mathematical models, of astronomy itself. Basing our planetary formulas on the ecliptic, the path of the Sun, is the ellipse from which celestial mechanics spiraled through space.

However, if you live on the Earth, Jupiter rules the sky and all that's in it, Sun included. Zeus (Jupiter) *is* the Sky and all that's in it, including the Sun and Moon. He is the Father of Gods and Men.[1] Given the realm of heaven, the most important point, the most concentrated spot, is the Vernal Equinox. The Sun represents the mathematical model, the foundation stone (and therefore the center) of spherical trigonometry and science. The Vernal Equinox, where the path of the Sun and the path of equator cross, represent the foundation stone of the mytho-logical and astrological models whose focus is celestial interpretation. It is therefore depicted as riding the White horse.

19:17 I saw an angel standing in the sun, and he shouted aloud to all the birds that were flying high overhead in the sky, "Come here. Gather together at the great feast that God is giving.

The Sun, to the Greeks, meant prophecy. Apollo was the Lord of Prophecy. He was the one who spoke through the oracle at Delphi, so that she might speak truth. He was the one who successfully "divined" that Hermes (Mercury) had stolen his cattle as a one-day-old infant.

To stand in the Sun and make a pronouncement is to speak from the seat of truth. While you may want to attend the wedding, the feast may be another matter.

---

1 "Now when Morning, clad in her robe of saffron, had begun to suffuse light over the earth, Zeus called the gods in council on the topmost crest of serrated Olympus. Then he spoke and all the other gods gave ear. "Hear me," said he, "gods and goddesses, that I may speak even as I am minded. . . . So far am I above all others either of gods or men." Homer, *The Iliad*, Book VIII.

There will be the flesh of kings for you, and the flesh of great generals and heroes, the flesh of horses and their riders and of all kinds of men, citizens and slaves, small and great."

This is the expected carnage from the battle.

19:19 Then I saw the beast, with all the kings of the earth and their armies, gathered together to fight the rider and his army.

Here is the preparation for the battle that lies ahead.

But the beast was taken prisoner, together with the false prophet who had worked miracles on the beast's behalf and by them had deceived all who had been branded with the mark of the beast and worshipped his statue. These two were thrown alive into the fiery lake of burning sulphur.

Those responsible for the falsehoods will be captured and dealt with. Presumably the fiery lake of burning sulphur is the result of the fireball, abyss and smoke that the locusts brought to the Earth.

All the rest were killed by the sword of the rider, which came out of his mouth, and all the birds were gorged with their flesh.

By martial decree the losers will be dealt with, their bodies left as carrion.

CHAPTER TWENTY

Revelation 20

20:1 *Then I saw an angel come down from heaven with the key of the Abyss in his hand and an enormous chain. / He overpowered the dragon, that primeval serpent which is the devil and Satan, and chained him up for a thousand years. / He threw him into the Abyss, and shut the entrance and sealed it over him, to make sure he would not deceive the nations again until the thousand years had passed. At the end of that time he must be released, but only for a short while.*

20:4 *Then I saw some thrones, and I saw those who are given the power to be judges take their seats on them. I saw the souls of all who had been beheaded for having witnessed for Jesus and for having preached God's word, and those who refused to worship the beast or his statue and would not have the brand mark on their foreheads or hands; they came to life, and reigned with Christ for a thousand years. / This is the first resurrection; the rest of the dead did not come to life until the thousand years were over. / Happy and blessed are those who share in the first resurrection; the second death cannot affect them but they will be priests of God and of Christ and reign with him for a thousand years.*

20:7 *When the thousand years are over, Satan will be released from his prison and will come out to deceive all the nations in the four quarters of the earth, Gog and Magog, and mobilize them for war. His armies will be as many as the sands of the sea; / they will come swarming over the entire country and besiege the camp of the saints, which is the city that God loves. But fire will come down on them from heaven and consume them. / Then the devil, who misled them, will be thrown into the lake of fire and sulphur, where the beast and the false prophet are, and their torture will not stop, day or night, for even and ever.*

20:11 *Then I saw a great white throne and the One who was sitting on it. In his presence, earth and sky vanished, leaving no trace. / I saw* *the dead, both great and small, standing in front of his throne, while the book of life was opened, and other books opened which were the record of what they had done in their lives, by which the dead were judged.*

20:13 *The sea gave up all the dead who were in it; Death and Hades were emptied of the dead that were in them; and every one was judged according to the way in which he had lived. Then Death and Hades were thrown into the burning lake. This burning lake is the second death; / and anybody whose name could not be found written in the book of life was thrown into the burning lake.*

* * * * *

20:1 Then I saw an angel come down from heaven with the key of the Abyss in his hand and an enormous chain

More of the same. The angel is the Spirit of Aquarius getting underway. He has the key to the Abyss in his hand because it's marking on the sky map when Aquarius commences. It commences when the Vernal Equinox aligns with the Eighth Seal.

The Thousand Years

He overpowered the dragon, that primeval serpent which is the devil and Satan, and chained him up for a thousand years.

Peace will reign for a thousand years and our passions will be held in check for that period of time. The thousand years is an image that we will come back to in the final chapter.

He threw him into the Abyss, and shut the entrance and sealed it over him, to make sure he would not deceive the nations again until the thousand years had passed. At the end of that time he must be released, but only for a short while.

This repeats the sentiment of the earlier line.

*20:4 Then I saw some thrones, and I saw those who are given the power
to be judges take their seats on them. I saw the souls of all who had been
beheaded for having witnessed for Jesus and for having preached God's
word, and those who refused to worship the beast or his statue and would
not have the brand mark on their foreheads or hands; they came to life,
and reigned with Christ for a thousand years.*

With the changing of the guard with the new bride, New Age,
and new epoch comes a new set of rules. This is the new "vibration" we
keep talking about. All of those who passed the "test" of the last period
will now be able to enjoy this new realm, this new period of time, for a
thousand years. Like the hands on the face of a clock that move from
one hour to another, we're still on the same clock, but are moving to a
different hour.

The reference to "they came to life" makes a strong argument to
embrace reincarnation. The souls under the Fifth Seal (the dead), have
now come back to life.

*This is the first resurrection; the rest of the dead did not come to life until
the thousand years were over.*

This star marks the first "release" point for the souls, but they will
have a second chance. Approximately a thousand years later, *Beta
Piscium*, the last star in the *constellation* Pisces is triggered; greed and
corruption are released, and souls get a second chance.

*Happy and blessed are those who share in the first resurrection; the
second death cannot affect them but they will be priests of God and of
Christ and reign with him for a thousand years.*

Those who make it through the test, through to the marriage ceremony of the Lamb, will have reason to celebrate. They will be able to
fully appreciate the *"sign of the times"* and gain positions of power and
influence through its reign on Earth.

20:7 When the thousand years are over, Satan will be released from his prison and will come out to deceive all the nations in the four quarters of the earth, Gog and Magog, and mobilize them for war. His armies will be as many as the sands of the sea;

A one thousand year break, and then it's back to business as usual, for a while. These are the conditions that have become so familiar to us during the period of "God's Curse."

they will come swarming over the entire country and besiege the camp of the saints, which is the city that God loves. But fire will come down on them from heaven and consume them.

A revolt will rise up, but it will be put down. It seems to happen in the same manner that takes place under the Eighth Seal. Another "Star Gate" is getting ready to be discharged.

Then the devil, who misled them, will be thrown into the lake of fire and sulphur, where the beast and the false prophet are, and their torture will not stop, day or night, for ever and ever.

Then the Dragon, the devil, and those who pursue falsehoods and untruths will get their just desserts.

A Great White Throne and the One Sitting on It

20:11 Then I saw a great white throne and the One who was sitting on it. In his presence, earth and sky vanished, leaving no trace.

As Aquarius begins, all trace of the former regime quickly disappears. Notice that it is a white throne, just as it was a white horse (First Seal) that opened the Age of Pisces, and a white horse that opened the start of Aquarius in Rev. 19:11. Now this "white" element is being used for the throne, and it's color link to the start of the Age.

The turn-around time will be surprisingly short.

I saw the dead, both great and small, standing in front of his throne, while the book of life was opened, and other books opened which were the record of what they had done in their lives, by which the dead were judged.

The same theme we have seen repeated many times. The coming of Aquarius will fulfill God's master plan, at which time He makes a dramatic re-entry into the atmosphere, and life is once again realized as theater to heaven's design, to God's will.

20:13 The sea gave up all the dead who were in it; Death and Hades were emptied of the dead that were in them; and every one was judged according to the way in which he had lived. Then Death and Hades were thrown into the burning lake. This burning lake is the second death;

The sea, in this reference, is Pisces. It is all the souls who have been waiting under the altar, which has been passing through the constellation Pisces. All of those who have died through this period of time now return in a massive collective judgment. Following this judgment, there was no longer a need for the abodes of the dead, as none would be confined there. The illusion of death will fade from the equation.

and anybody whose name could not be found written in the book of life was thrown into the burning lake.

Those who have not "passed the test" are thrown into the burning lake.

CHAPTER TWENTY-ONE

Revelation 21

21:1 *Then I saw a new heaven and a new earth; the first heaven had disappeared now, and there was no longer any sea. / I saw the holy city, and the new Jerusalem, coming down from God out of heaven, as beautiful as a bride all dressed for her husband. / Then I heard a loud voice call from the throne, "You see this city? Here God lives among men. He will make his home among them; they shall be his people, and he will be their God; his name is God-with-them. / He will wipe away all tears from their eyes; there will be no more death, and no mourning or sadness. The world of the past is gone."*

21:5 *Then the One sitting on the throne spoke: "Now I am making the whole of creation new," he said. "Write this: that what I am saying is sure and will come true." / And then he said, "It is already done. I am the Alpha and the Omega, the Beginning and the End. I will give water from the well of life free to anybody who is thirsty; / it is the rightful inheritance of the one who proves victorious; and I will be his God and he a son to me. But the legacy for cowards, for those who break their word, or worship obscenities, for murderers and fornicators, and for fortunetellers, idolaters or any other sort of liars, is the second death in the burning lake of sulphur."*

21:9 *One of the seven angels that had the seven bowls full of the seven last plagues came to speak with me, and said, "Come here and I will show you the bride that the Lamb has married." / In the spirit, he took me to the top of an enormous high mountain. / It had all the radiant glory of God and glittered like some precious jewel of crystal-clear diamond. / The walls of it were of a great height, and had twelve gates; at each of the twelve gates there was an angel, and over the gates were written the names of the twelve tribes of Israel, / on the east there were three gates, on the north three gates, on the south three gates, and on the west* *three gates. /The city walls stood on twelve foundation stones, each one of which bore the name of one of the twelve apostles of the Lamb.*

21:15 *The angel that was speaking to me was carrying a gold measuring rod to measure the city and its gates and wall. / The plan of the city is perfectly square, its length the same as its breadth. He measured the city with his rod and it was twelve thousand furlongs in length and in breadth, and equal in height. / He measured its wall, and this was a hundred and forty-four cubits high—the angel was using the ordinary cubit. / The wall was built of diamond, and the city of pure gold, like polished glass. / The foundations of the city wall were faced with all kinds of precious stone: the first with diamond, the second with lapis lazuli, the third turquoise, the fourth crystal, the fifth agate, the sixth ruby, the seventh gold quartz, the eighth malachite, the ninth topaz, the tenth emerald, the eleventh sapphire and the twelfth amethyst. / The twelve gates were twelve pearls, each gate being made of a single pearl, and the main street of the city was pure gold, transparent as glass. / I saw that there was no temple in the city since the Lord God Almighty and the Lamb were themselves the temple, / and the city did not need the sun or the moon for light, since it was lit by the radiant glory of God and the Lamb was a lighted torch for it. / The pagan nations will live by its light and the kings of the earth will bring their treasures. / The gates of it will never be shut by day— there will be no night there— / and the nations will come, bringing their treasure and their wealth. / Nothing unclean may come into it: no one who does what is loathsome or false, but only those who are listed in the Lamb's book of life.*

* * * * *

New Heaven New Earth

21:1 Then I saw a new heaven and a new earth; the first heaven had disappeared now, and there was no longer any sea.

Aquarius and the world that it will author will replace Pisces and the world that it authored. There was no longer any sea. The ocean is over. Pisces is done.

I saw the holy city, and the new Jerusalem, coming down from God out of heaven, as beautiful as a bride all dressed for her husband.

Beautiful. Aquarius is a period of time on the planet. It will represent the holy city, the New Jerusalem *"coming down from God out of heaven,"* just like it says. Aquarius (the bride) is ready to marry the Vernal Equinox, the Lamb of God, who will then be seated on the power of the throne. The New Jerusalem, like Eden, is a period of time rather than a specific place. All one image, beautifully expressed. Heaven sings "Hallelujah." "Hallelujah" the Earth replies.

Then I heard a loud voice call from the throne, "You see this city? Here God lives among men. He will make his home among them; they shall be his people, and he will be their God; his name is God-with-them.

The power of heaven, having just found its voice, comes to life and is describing the new epoch. Heaven will be in tune with Earth, as it always has been, but more importantly, Earth will be in tune with Heaven.

He will wipe away all tears from their eyes; there will be no more death, and no mourning or sadness. The world of the past is gone."

Pisces is over. The Water Sign is over. The Sea is over. Death, mourning and sadness are all products of water, of the emotions. Not being able to connect with those who have passed away is one of the most powerful emotional traumas we have to work through. It even has it's own special emotional category; grief. These have been the elements we have been working with in the schoolhouse of the spirit for the last two thousand years. The ultimate development of these watery elements has been faith. Learning to believe in something you can't see and don't know to be true. It is the spiritual crown of both life and death.

Aquarius is correctly depicted as the Waterbearer, but this can be confusing. Aquarius is an AIR sign. It deals with the intellect, community, the people—being both independent and capable of pulling together when we need to. The waters that Aquarius bears are said to be etheric currents, the celestial waters of creation. Aquarius comes closer to the currents flowing through electrical wires than it does to what passes down the drain in the tub. We don't "see" these etheric currents, but neither can we "see" electricity, radio, television or microwaves. In truth, these are the greater seas, the wavelengths found within Creation and the skies themselves. Our minds (part of the realm of Air) are pushing back the shoreline, to include the stellar seas in which we swim, even as we walk the paths of the planet on Mother Earth.

The world of the past is gone.

21:5 Then the One sitting on the throne spoke: "Now I am making the whole of creation new," he said. "Write this: that what I am saying is sure and will come true."

The power (the One) is sitting on the throne. This is the Vernal Equinox in the moment of Creation, a new movement, the celestial baton poised for the downbeat. It all starts again with the Eighth Seal: a new time, a new epoch, a new Age.

And then he said, "It is already done. I am the Alpha and the Omega, the Beginning and the End.

We will cover the *Alpha and the Omega* in the final chapter, Weaving Together Some Loose Threads.

"I will give water from the well of life free to anybody who is thirsty;

This sentence is another identifying characteristic of the Aquarian energy. Any beginning student of Astrology knows this one fairly well. These are the spiritual waters, the etheric waters that Aquarius distributes to any who are "thirsty" for the knowledge it offers. This is the first time we are being introduced to this theme in Revelation. It is the stream.

"it is the rightful inheritance of the one who proves victorious; and I will be his God and he a son to me. But the legacy for cowards, for those who break their word, or worship obscenities, for murderers and fornicators, and for fortunetellers, idolaters or any other sort of liars, is the second death in the burning lake of sulphur."

Again, this is a familiar weave. Those who "pass the test," who prove victorious, will have a new relationship with God, Truth and Life. Those who build their houses on sand are condemned to the sulphuric fires.

21:9 One of the seven angels that had the seven bowls full of the seven last plagues came to speak with me, and said, "Come here and I will show you the bride that the Lamb has married."

In yet another reference to a previous theme, one of the seven angels of the bowls is introducing the bride that the Lamb (the Vernal Equinox) has married. With the end of the tribulation comes the exaltation. The emphasis in Revelation 21 is shifting away from the "labor pains" of the birth of the new Age, and is moving into what it will mean once the initial tumult is over.

In the spirit, he took me to the top of an enormous high mountain.

This mountain has had many names. Olympus has been one. Another is referenced in Ezekiel. Once again, we are being taken up to heaven to see the view from that perspective. This is a mythical mountain, a magical mountain. That is why it is so high. We're going all the way up to where we can see. As high as the sky. And then weave your imagination in on top of that.

Here is an Old Testament rendition of that same mountain, a mountain that "towers above all others." Indeed it does, as the sky always trumps the mountains.

But in days to come
Yahweh's Temple Mountain
will tower above the mountains,
rise higher than the hills.
Then the people will stream to it,
then many nations will come and say,
"Come, we will go up to Yahweh's mountain"[1]

For the Greeks, Olympus, the gods and hallowed halls. For the Hebrews, Yahweh's Temple Mountain, the sky above.

It had all the radiant glory of God and glittered like some precious jewel of crystal-clear diamond.

We're gazing into the heavens themselves, where the glory of God resides like a great jewel, with heavenly fires both great and small.

As we will see, Revelation itself sets up the diamond as the first of the twelve. It is associated with Aries, also the first of the twelve. The diamond is re-focusing our attention onto the "hook" of the Vernal Equinox.

Twelve Gates Twelve Tribes

The walls of it were of a great height, and had twelve gates; at each of the twelve gates there was an angel, and over the gates were written the names of the twelve tribes of Israel,

The new city, the New Jerusalem is being described. Its walls are of great height. They reach to the sky. The gates are twelve in number. You may enter life through any one of the twelve months of the year. Over the gates were the names of the twelve tribes. This is not a new notion. It has been used before.

---

1 Micah 4:1–2.

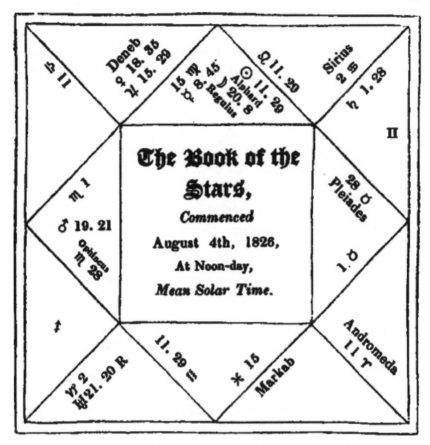

The Book of the Stars,

Commenced

August 4th, 1826,

At Noon-day,

Mean Solar Time.

Medieval-style horoscope with three "gates" on each of its four sides.

on the east there were three gates, on the north three gates, on the south three gates, and on the west three gates.

Given the four cardinal points of the compass, three on each side seems appropriate. This is similar to the charts calculated by astrologers from medieval times through the early twentieth century.

Twelve Foundation Stones Twelve Apostles

The city walls stood on twelve foundation stones, each one of which bore the name of one of the twelve apostles of the Lamb.

Twelve gates, twelve tribes, twelve stones, twelve apostles. They all flow from the same source, from the same celestial stream. These are the foundation stones upon which the fruits of the year are gathered. These are the gates through which each must pass. Time is the law, the sky our heavenly Tent.

21:15 The angel that was speaking to me was carrying a gold measuring rod to measure the city and its gates and wall.

This is probably the angel from Pergamum. They're always measuring, numbering and counting everything there, although the "golden rod" suggests the ecliptic pole.

Twelve Thousand

The plan of the city is perfectly square, its length the same as its breadth. He measured the city with is rod and it was twelve thousand furlongs in length and in breadth, and equal in height.

Twelve times twelve times twelve. One times one times one; the whole unit. This is the same play as the 144,000 who were to march (Rev. 7:4). All of them. We're measuring all of Creation, the only "One" there is. It includes all of us.

Twelve Times Twelve

He measured its wall, and this was a hundred and forty-four cubits high—the angel was using the ordinary cubit.

A third time. Twelve times twelve, one hundred and forty-four cubits high. The ordinary cubit, and units of measure in ancient times, was carefully determined.

To find the length of the cubit that would fit these measures, Jomard again consulted the classics. According to Herodotus 400 cubits made a stadium of 600 ft. Jomard divided the apothem of the Pyramid by 400 and obtained a cubit of .4618 meter. To his surprise this tuned out to be the common cubit of the modern Egyptians.[2]

Exaltations, twelve signs of the zodiac, seven planets, numerology, gemology and even herbology (*and the leaves of which are the cure for the pagans*, Rev. 22:2) in the study of Wormwood are all to be found within these pages; the basics for many of what are now thought to be occult sciences were hidden in the Book of Revelation.

The wall was built of diamond, and the city of pure gold, like polished glass.

Mars (diamond) is in its exaltation in Capricorn (walls). This is the toughest stuff there is. The walls are carved from reality. They promise to last for as long as time. A city of gold? A place where truth is of paramount importance, where actions speak louder than words.

Twelve Foundation Stones Revisited

The foundations of the city wall were faced with all kinds of precious stone: the first with diamond, the second with lapis lazuli, the third turquoise, the fourth crystal, the fifth agate, the sixth ruby, the seventh gold quartz, the eighth malachite, the ninth topaz, the tenth emerald, the eleventh sapphire and the twelfth amethyst.

Here the foundation stones are specified, in order, according to the authors of Revelation. An organized list like this is not usually conjured in dreams, it is constructed by the conscious mind. As we have seen earlier, Revelation is both visionary and didactic. Here, John of Patmos augments his vision with reference to occult systems. This is a book of wisdom, teaching on many levels as it continues to unravel its central mystery.

---

2 *Secrets of the Great Pyramid*, Peter Tompkins, Harper and Row, p. 47.

Table of Zodiacal Gems

the first with diamond,	Aries
the second with lapis lazuli,	Taurus
the third turquoise,	Gemini
the fourth crystal,	Cancer
the fifth agate,	Leo
the sixth ruby,	Virgo
the seventh gold quartz,	Libra
the eighth malachite,	Scorpio
the ninth topaz,	Sagittarius
the tenth emerald,	Capricorn
the eleventh sapphire	Aquarius
and the twelfth amethyst.	Pisces

It is from this list that we see Aries being identified with the "mineral" diamond. This is one of the wisdom books. It is both teaching and training. This is the mineralogical (Earth) set of twelve, the foundation stones. There will be other "dozens" that arise as Revelation continues to instruct.

Twelve Pearls

The twelve gates were twelve pearls, each gate being made of a single pearl, and the main street of the city was pure gold, transparent as glass.

Here we have another celestial gem. Traditionally, pearls are thought to be associated with the Moon due to their luminescence. Moonlight reaching across the water, dancing on the waves, listening to the night. The twelve pearls represent the twelve Full Moons of the year, all on a string and tied together. We have already seen symbolic metaphors for the hours, days of the week and seasons. Now we are including the months.

Pearls on a string. These are the constructs of Creation. In Christian circles, these lines evolve into the "Pearly Gates" of St. Peter. All Revelation is a book of judgment. St. Peter checks his ledger when you get there.

Returning to our lines, the main street of the city is the path of the ecliptic as it runs through the stars of Aquarius. The "metal" of the Sun is gold, and therefore it is a golden road (ecliptic) running through the city of the Water Bearer, "transparent as glass."

"like a Son of man, dressed in a long robe tied at the waist with a belt of gold."[3]

It is a road that runs by a celestial stream. This road can't be seen, however, because the Sun is never up at night when the stars of the constellations can be perceived, with the exception of solar eclipses. This road is indeed *"transparent as glass,"* and yet at the same time very tangible, important and real. It is of heavenly construct, divine design.

I saw that there was no temple in the city since the Lord God Almighty and the Lamb were themselves the temple

Temples were used to observe the heavens. The temples will no longer be needed; people will look to heaven and make the connection from one to the other once again, from heaven to earth as they did in times gone by, learning anew to follow the "stream." Besides, now we have computers and telescopes. Is it possible we do not need temples? The Lamb is the location of the Vernal Equinox. If you wanted to visit the "temple" … where would you go!? Can you suspend yourself in space?

and the city did not need the sun or the moon for light, since it was lit by the radiant glory of God and the Lamb was a lighted torch for it.

There will be a change in the type of energy source, the fuel the

---

3 Rev. 1:13.

planet is using, wherein everyone will have power. It will become a community resource, not the fossilized fuels of oil, coal and gas that are controlled, regulated and metered as they are now.

We have explored this notion of Pisces into Aquarius, Water into Air, before. The gestalt is changing. People are becoming more knowledgeable, more connected. Welcome to the World Wide Web. Welcome to Wiki. But this is only the beginning—these are the training wheels of civilization teaching us what communication can be. We connect with different portions of the globe instantaneously through the Web. Radio, television, satellite reception—these are among the airwaves the Water Bearer channels. Aquarius is electricity. This notion is closer to the Aquarian "waves" and "currents" than are those of physical water. This Aquarian vibration can be "channeled" along wires, as conduits to a multitude of tasks, universal in scope.

The ethers of the Air, the winds of our planet, the storms of our atmosphere will become the new spiritual medium, the new element elevated to rite of passage for the soul. People have met, merged and been schooled through Pisces. This Water Age dispensed with baptism as the spiritual rite-of-passage. This time, an oath and a conscious verbal acknowledgement should get us through.

The age is changing. Air is getting ready to take the baton from Neptune's aquatic nymphs. A new social mind-set is getting ready to guide the planet, one that will be motivated by a common goal. Ultimately, to share peace as One.

As we cross the threshold of Aquarius the world will be shaken to its roots, and from this event a new world order will be born. Like a bolt from the blue, our way of doing things will change—new financial order, new food distribution, new environmental order, new spiritual order, even a new heartbeat, a new rhythm for the planet. A new world with a more cosmopolitan outlook, one that not only appreciates differences in people, but actually cultivates, learns, and is fascinated by those differences.

It will become obvious to the multitudes, to people everywhere, that Earth and Sky move as one in a celestial dance, bobbing and weaving together. It will be like "lightning" striking in the east' because the star "Lightning" has recently aligned with the East, becoming the new Eastern Star. The light of the stars, and their relevance will be seen and understood by all. The power of Aquarius is in the stars, and the mysteries of the stars, the Heavenly Tent, will be opened for all to share. Free.

The whispered codes of the ancients will be openly shared, their powers plumbed. Science has been the embryonic beginning of the new "religion" of the coming age, although it will seem unusual to look back on it in that way once it is here, it will be so obvious.

The pagan nations will live by its light and the kings of the earth will bring their treasures.

This is a testament to a new power source, a new "orientation." We will once again align ourselves with the will of heaven, and *"will live by its light."*

The gates of it will never be shut by day—there will be no night there—

This is a notion easier to grasp in the days of electricity than of whale or olive oil lamp! It has huge implications both economically and politically.

Twenty-four/seven. We will be connected to heaven and heaven to us, *consciously.* This will represent another of the chief distinctions between Pisces and Aquarius and the divine; in Pisces, as a civilization, we have lost the divine, forgotten the divine, ignored the divine. In Aquarius we will come to know the divine, as individuals and as a collective. It will not be a matter of becoming One.

We already are One. The trick is to wake up (Pisces) to it. We need only to become conscious of it. No one can successfully push us to it; we can only come to it from within. No one else can find our center, no matter how hard they may look.

and the nations will come, bringing their treasure and their wealth.

The world brings its resources to the collective nerve center of the Divine Mind.

Nothing unclean may come into it: no one who does what is loathsome or false, but only those who are listed in the Lamb's book of life.

It is a place where truth will be known before you enter, a beacon whose light is so brilliant as to allow no shadow. To do that, it must be a light that is omnipresent, shining from all sides at once. Further information will be made available (on-line, or its metaphorical equivalent!).

CHAPTER TWENTY-TWO

Revelation 22

22:1 *Then the angel showed me the river of life, rising from the throne of God and of the Lamb and flowing crystal-clear / down the middle of the city street. On either side of the river were the trees of life, which bear twelve crops of fruit in a year, one in each month, and the leaves of which are the cure for the pagans.*

22:3 *Then the ban will be lifted. The throne of God and of the Lamb will be in its place in the city; his servants will worship him, / they will see him face to face, and his name will be written on their foreheads. / It will never be night again and they will not need lamplight or sunlight, because the Lord God will be shining on them. They will reign for ever and ever.*

22:6 *The angel said to me, "All that you have written is sure and will come true: the Lord God who gives the spirit to the prophets has sent his angel to reveal to his servants what is soon to take place. / Very soon now, I shall be with you again." Happy are those who treasure the prophetic message of this book.*

22:8 *I, John, am the one who heard and saw these things. When I had heard and seen them all, I knelt at the feet of the angel who had shown them to me, to worship him, / but he said, "Don't do that: I am a servant just like you and like your brothers the prophets and like those who treasure what you have written in this book. It is God that you must worship."*

22:10 *This, too, he said to me, "Do not keep the prophecies in this book a secret, because the Time is close. / Meanwhile let the sinner go on sinning, and the unclean to be unclean; let those who do good go on doing good, and those who are holy continue to be holy. / Very soon now, I shall be with you again, bringing the reward to be given to every man according to what he deserves. / I am the Alpha and the Omega, the First* *and the Last, the Beginning and the End. / Happy are those who will have washed their robes clean, so that they will have the right to feed on the tree of life and can come through the gates into the city. / These others must stay outside: dogs, fortunetellers, and fornicators, and murderers, and idolaters, and everyone of false speech and false life."*

22:16 *I, Jesus, have sent my angel to make these revelations to you for the sake of the churches. I am of David's line, the root of David and the bright star of the morning.*

22:17 *The Spirit and the Bride say, "Come." Let everyone who listens answer, "Come." Then let all who are thirsty come: all who want it may have the water of life, and have it free.*

22:18 *This is my solemn warning to all who hear the prophecies in this book: if anyone adds anything to them, God will add to him every plague mentioned in the book; / if anyone cuts anything out of the prophecies in this book, God will cut off his share of the tree of life and of the holy city, which are described in the book.*

22:20 *The one who guarantees these revelations repeats his promise: I shall indeed be with you soon. Amen; come, Lord Jesus.*

22:21 *May the grace of the Lord Jesus be with you all. Amen.*

* * * * *

The River of Life / The Trees of Life

22:1 Then the angel showed me the river of life, rising from the throne of God and of the Lamb and flowing crystal-clear down the middle of the city street.

This is a beautiful depiction of Aquarius running like a clear stream of stars through the sky, pouring from the throne, the Vernal Equinox and the Lamb, all at the same time. This can only be the picture *after* the Vernal Equinox has moved into Aquarius. Once the Eighth Seal is uncovered, this is our promise for the future, together with its rocky start. Notice that the river of life flows down the middle of the street. The Vernal Equinox falls on the line of the equator. It marks the middle together with the Autumnal Equinox. The two are one, at least along this part of the path. This is a mythically and astronomically correct depiction.

On either side of the river were the trees of life, which bear twelve crops of fruit in a year, one in each month, and the leaves of which are the cure for the pagans.

Now we have the Twelve Trees of Life; Revelation is returning as teacher. This time it's not discussing mineralogical gems. The twelve months each yield a harvest, their own fruit, but the image is not limited to what we eat. The twelve sun signs each produce their fruit of the womb, giving each person his or her personality. This includes herbal wisdom of how to heal body and soul, and points a gentle green finger in that direction. Some of the oldest stellar memories derive from agricultural rituals, such as sowing or reaping and the like. Hunting, agriculture and wild-crafting all used the wisdom of their predecessors wrapped in story form. We find a number of these disciplines being listed here.

22:3 Then the ban will be lifted. The throne of God and of the Lamb will be in its place in the city; his servants will worship him,

The "ban" is also translated as "the curse of destruction."

Next to Ezekiel, Zechariah was probably the most influential work on John, the author of Revelation. There is much imagery that Revelation draws upon. Among them is the notion of the "ban."

When that day comes, I shall make Jerusalem a stone too heavy for all the peoples to lift; all those who try to lift it will hurt themselves severely, although all the nations of the world will be massed against her.[1]

---

1 Zechariah 12:3

Many will compete to lift the administrative weight of Jerusalem, but it will be too complex an issue. Later in Zechariah, we find the "ban" being lifted, and it is made clear what it has represented.

"People will make their homes there. The curse of destruction will be lifted; Jerusalem will be safe to live in."[2]

The curse has been the curse of brother not being able to live with brother.

Jerusalem is metaphor for the New City *"coming down out of heaven,"* the stars of the Water Bearer, building on the idea of the Greek *polis* spreading religion and culture. The throne of God and of the Lamb (together again) will be in its place in the city and in Aquarius. His servants will be in touch with the heavenly homilies.

they will see him face to face, and his name will be written on their foreheads.

The keywords of Aquarius are "I know." It derives from the Latin *"scire,"* to know. From knowledge comes the root of our word for sci-ence, a systematized body of collective knowledge. During the Age of Aquarius we will come to know God—a blasphemous concept in the Age of Pisces. For Piscean-era dwellers, God must remain hidden, otherwise faith would falter. The question becomes, however: is faith more important than God? The gentle mists of belief quickly disappear in the bright light of knowing.

His name will be written on their foreheads. We will become aware of working with divinity at all times, not just while sitting in a pew on Sunday morning. It's all sacred. We will see divinity in heaven, and heaven will acknowledge the divinity in us. We're made in God's image. We begin to reflect it back.

It will never be night again and they will not need lamplight or sun-

---

2 Zechariah 14:11

light, because the Lord God will be shining on them. They will reign for ever and ever.

We're back to the new energy source. This new way of looking at things and living life is going to be around for a while.

22:6 The angel said to me, "All that you have written is sure and will come true: the Lord God who gives the spirit to the prophets has sent his angel to reveal to his servants what is soon to take place.

Here we are getting confirmation on the content of the text and its symbolism. God has given this work to the people to distribute it, and it is asked that it be revealed to those who demonstrate a willingness to work. When those who composed Revelation said what would take place very soon, they saw that the clock, the Vernal Equinox moving through the constellation Pisces. The countdown had begun. We now stand on the threshold of a New Age. It has arrived.

Very soon now, I shall be with you again." Happy are those who treasure the prophetic message of this book.

The spirit of the angel of peace returns with the end of Pisces. There is reason to hold dear the information of this book. May it help you prepare, get your "tent" in order.

22:8 I, John, am the one who heard and saw these things. When I had heard and seen them all, I knelt at the feet of the angel who had shown them to me, to worship him,

This is John of Patmos, and when he experienced all this, he was overwhelmed and knelt at the feet of the angel to give thanks and blessings for all these powerful insights.

but he said, "Don't do that: I am a servant just like you and like your brothers the prophets and like those who treasure what you have written in this book. It is God that you must worship."

Aquarius works to break down class distinctions: of class, color, creed and all the other concepts we use to compartmentalize each other. During the Age of Pisces, this was thought necessary. Civilization strove to be all it could, seeking the Autumnal Equinox and the civilizing allure of Virgo. We attempted to separate the wheat from the chaff on a societal level. Selection was the name of the game. Keep the best and leave the rest. Those days are done.

Do Not Keep the Prophecies a Secret

22:10 This, too, he said to me, "Do not keep the prophecies in this book a secret, because the Time is close.

We're on the home stretch. The skies were being watched at least as far back as 8,000 years ago. The arrival of Pisces was well-anticipated, obviously more so as the Time drew closer. The works of Ezekiel, Daniel, and Zechariah are but a few examples. This is a message that wants to be told. Don't keep it a secret. Pisces is almost over. People need to understand what is about to happen so they can have a choice about how to deal with it.

Meanwhile let the sinner go on sinning, and the unclean to be unclean; let those who do good go on doing good, and those who are holy continue to be holy.

The purpose of Revelation is not evangelical. Let people be. Worry about you. Focus within, not without. Peace begins within. Change what it is within your power to change. This has been the path throughout Pisces sojourn, of listening to the song of peace playing quietly within. Venus, for both song and art, is exalted in Pisces.

Very soon now, I shall be with you again, bringing the reward to be given to every man according to what he deserves.

The collective karma of two thousand years—held off until this

time—will be dispensed at the end of the Age. The End. We approach
a new dawn. It is time to wake up.

*I am the Alpha and the Omega, the First and the Last, the Beginning
and the End.*

We will examine this theme in the next chapter.

*Happy are those who will have washed their robes clean, so that they
will have the right to feed on the tree of life and can come through the
gates into the city.*

The Great Persecution has been a time of suffering. Through suffering our souls have been purified, the aura or halo of the saints. You
wear your spiritual report card every day for those who can see. Those
who have clean robes will be able to enter the New Jerusalem, the time
of Aquarius.

*These others must stay outside: dogs, fortunetellers, and fornicators, and
murderers, and idolaters, and everyone of false speech and false life.*

Those who are unclean, whose lives are centered on deceit, must
not enter. Only those whose lives are centered on truth are welcome. It
is time to tell the truth; it always has been.

*22:16 I, Jesus, have sent my angel to make these revelations to you for
the sake of the churches. I am of David's line, the root of David and the
bright star of the morning.*

The spirit of the message of Jesus has been successfully conveyed.
For "the sake of the churches" implies this information has been trans-
mitted to those who have developed their lives around spirituality, and
honoring the sacred attributes of heaven.

There are two possible associations to the Morning Star, one of
which is Venus. Jesus sent his angel? Jesus is the Prince of Peace, and

so is his angel. That's one possibility. The other is that the bright star of the morning is the Sun, and the line would translate: I am of David's line, the root of David, the heavenly ordained *king*.

The kingship of David was the high-water mark of Jewish culture. The relation of David to God was good, and much was promised. Militarily, Israel was at its peak. Additional promises are revealed in the following lines from Samuel.

> *I will give you fame as great as the fame of the greatest on earth. I will provide a place for my people Israel; I will plant them there and they shall dwell in that place and never be disturbed again; nor shall the wicked continue to oppress them as they did, in the days when I appointed judges over my people Israel; I will give them rest from all of their enemies. Yahweh will make you great, Yahweh will make you a House. And when thy days are fulfilled, and thou shalt sleep with thy fathers, I will set up thy seed after thee, that shall proceed out of thy body, and I will establish his kingdom. He shall build a house for My name, and I will establish the throne of his kingdom for ever.* [3]

To be linked to the royal line of David was to be linked to Judaic history at the time of its supremacy. To have one linked to David's line was to continue the seed of these promises.

> *22:17 The Spirit and the Bride say, "Come." Let everyone who listens answer, "Come." Then let all who are thirsty come: all who want it may have the water of life, and have it free.*

The Spirit, the Bride and a new epoch; everyone will share in it. The final sentence is textbook astrology. These are the free waters the Aquarian pours out of the celestial urn for humanity. The well we all will drink from is there for any who are able to attend the wedding feast of the Ram and the bride, any to make it into the New City. It's

---

3 2 Samuel 7:9–12.

there for all of the children of God who have waited out the time of judgment.

> *22:18 This is my solemn warning to all who hear the prophecies in this book: if anyone adds anything to them, God will add to him every plague mentioned in the book*

There are some important messages here. Don't try to improve upon what you don't fully understand. Bad things will happen if we don't get it right!

> *if anyone cuts anything out of the prophecies in this book, God will cut off his share of the tree of life and of the holy city, which are described in the book.*

Everything has its place here. It's all been written in code, and not everyone is going to understand that code. This is an encrypted communication that provides a map of the future.

> *22:20 The one who guarantees these revelations repeats his promise: I shall indeed be with you soon. Amen; come, Lord Jesus.*

Peace between us will be known again, as we warm ourselves by a common divinity. *I will be with you soon is now here.* We have arrived. Soon, indeed.

> *22:21 May the grace of the Lord Jesus be with you all. Amen.*

Amen.

CHAPTER TWENTY-THREE

The Alpha and the Omega

Weaving Together Some Loose Threads

The Eighth Seal

The Age of Pisces commenced with the Vernal Equinox entering the constellation of Pisces by aligning with *Al Rischa*, the Cord. We also proposed that the Age of Pisces will end with the Vernal Equinox aligning with the next star following the seven, which we have been calling the Eighth Seal.

By whose authority are we entitled to say that the Ages begin with *Al Rischa* and ends with the Eighth Seal? By Revelation's authority. The answer has been clearly left in code.

There is a well-known expression in the Book of Revelation with which everyone is familiar, although few really knows what it means. The phrase seems to permeate our culture. We have purposely delayed commenting on it until now—waiting until having worked our way through the entire book before examining this subtle but important key. The expression we're referring to, of course, is, "*The Alpha and the Omega.*"

In the entire Bible, Revelation is the only book that uses this phrase. And it is used three times: Rev. 1:8; 21:6; and 22:13.

I am the Alpha and the Omega, the First and the Last, the Beginning and the End.[1]

The code is being flashed, stellar benchmarks established, a mantra is being chanted three times in Revelation, three times in the entire Bible.

---

1 Rev. 22:13.

Hermes Trismegistus. Hermes, thrice great. Hermes/Mercury, communication.

While praying to the gods (certainly as part of the state run Roman religion), the pagans would repeat the chosen prayers, incantations or rituals three times. The rituals had to be performed perfectly. Like the animal of sacrifice, there must be no flaw or blemish, no stumbling over the phrases or mispronunciations; otherwise you have not given up what is perfect and best. Imperfect prayers to the Divine do not bode well for the fate of that prayer. In other words, if you say a prayer for rain improperly, no rain will fall.

None of this is stated in Revelation. It is merely implied by those watching the ceremonies going on around them at the time and by repeating the phrase *Alpha and Omega* three times in the body of the text. So much of ritual hides truth behind the veil. We're getting God's attention. This is one reason why they repeat the expression in the beginning and the end of Revelation. In itself, this represents the first and the last, the Alpha and the Omega.

When we examine the parallels of latitude, the dates translate to 407 BC and AD 2013, from Victory to Victory, to Good News, from Pisces to Aquarius.

The code establishes visual benchmarks in the sky for a celestial slice of Time, an epoch of history. It starts on this date, it ends on that date. And it gives us the specific stars we are talking about, *Alpha* and *Omega Piscium*.

The code is heard three times. The "courtyard" of the Age of Pisces is being delineated for us. We should listen to what the message has to say.

It starts with the first star *Alpha* and ends with *Omega*, the final star of the series.

The Eighth Seal is *Omega Piscium*. Examine any star map. It falls very close to the current intersection of the Earth's equator and the Sun's ecliptic, the Vernal Equinox. *Omega Piscium* is our new "Eastern Star," the celestial signal for the changeover about to commence.

This is what those under the altar were waiting for.

They were told to be patient a little longer, until the roll was complete...[2]

The roll is now complete. Civilization is in the process of "reorienting." It is realigning along a new celestial, terrestrial and spiritual axis.

I am the Alpha and the Omega, the First and the Last, the Beginning and the End.

The First of Two Problems with our Age of Pisces Timetable

For those of you who have been paying attention and done your homework, you should have noticed there's a fly in the ointment, a problem with the equation. There's something wrong with this Age of Pisces timetable at each end. Did you catch it?

Let's start at the beginning. The Lamb aligned with *Al Rischa* (our *Alpha*) in 407 BC. But Jesus was not born until 7 BC. That's a 400 year difference. The birth and life of Jesus overlap the Third Seal, not the First.

If this is the Messiah, and the Messiah is the harbinger of the New Age, shouldn't he be born together with the first star? Not necessarily. As *Al Rischa* aligned with the Vernal Equinox, there was another spiritual leader by the name of Siddhartha Gautama being born. He was later to become the Buddha. Most historians in the early 20th century believed he lived c. 563 to 483 BC, but many more modern historians believe his death may have occurred some decades later, up to twenty years on either side of 400 BC.[3]

The birth of Gautama Buddha represents the heavenly beginning of the spiritual overtones of Pisces. The Buddha was a prince of a royal line known as Siddhartha Gautama. He grew up as a blue blood with all the benefits and the prerogatives that go along with that class. This was the influence of being born during the period of the overlap. From there, he went on to discover the poverty of the world. He sought

---

2 Rev. 6:11.
3 *https://en.wikipedia.org/wiki/Gautama_Buddha.*

release from worldly attachments and began to walk a new path, experiencing Nirvana beneath the Bodi Tree.

The message of spiritual surrender common to both Buddhism and Christianity is hard to miss. Each represents tides of the same ocean, lapping at different geographic shores of the same Sea of Time. But if the Buddha is the harbinger of the Age of Pisces, why does the spirit of Jesus wait until the Third Seal to bring his message to the West?

Jesus waited because even though Pisces had begun, Aries wasn't yet over.

By a curious celestial coincidence, the brightest star (*lucida*) in Pisces, *Alpha Piscium*, and the brightest star in Aries, *Alpha Arietis*, aligned with the Vernal Equinox within five years of each other. These were two of the twelve *lucida* stars in a 26,000 year cycle. For those anticipating such celestial phenomena, this combination must have caused considerable celestial concern. *Alpha Piscium*, the *lucida* of Pisces, aligned first in 407 BC followed by *Alpha Arietis* in 402 BC. This is the reverse of what one might expect under precessional direction. The stars of Aries, followed by Pisces, seems to be the way it's supposed to work. But not in this case.

Remember that seasonally the order of the signs is Aries, Taurus, Gemini, etc. That is the direction the Sun passes through the zodiac while moving from spring to summer to autumn to winter. But during the precession of the equinoxes, the Vernal Equinox, the "Ages," move in the opposite direction, from Gemini to Taurus to Aries to Pisces to Aquarius. In two thousand years, we'll be moving into Capricorn.

So *Alpha Arietis* aligned in 402 BC, followed by *Beta* and *Gamma Arietis* in 182 and 168 BC. These three stars of the Ram's horns are the brightest in the entire constellation, and their spiritual message for Earth had yet to be imparted. After the horns of the Ram were finished being "triggered" by the Vernal Equinox the Arian essence ended.

The Time of the Fish had finally fully arrived. Heaven baptized the new Fishers of men. The multitudes (the schools of Fish) were about to be netted.

By the time the last star of Aries finished being triggered by the Vernal Equinox (*Gamma* in 168 BC), the Second Seal of the Scroll in Pisces had already come and gone (235 BC), leaving the Third Seal (AD

15) next in line. Having fully cast off the Golden Mantle of Aries, life could now fully embrace the "unpolluted" lessons of Pisces.

Enter Jesus, whom John calls "The Lamb of God." He represented the archetype, the role model for the coming Age. "Follow me," whispered Jesus through his actions. "I will show you what you need to do."

That is what harbingers do. They announce what is to follow. As the Lamb of God (John 1:29, 35), Jesus is Earthly sacrifice for the coming epoch—the first wave of a powerful ocean current, fully divested of the philosophy of the fleece. By AD 15 and the Third Seal, the Classical World was officially done, celestially speaking.

Unlike the Buddha at the beginning of the Age, if Jesus is a prince, it is of a kingdom that is not of this world. This is the influence of having left the Arian era fully behind. The classical myths and heroes are about princes and princesses, many of whom go on to become kings and queens.

The wise men were said to have seen the star of Jesus rising in the east. Indeed, they saw a new "Eastern Star" getting ready to align with the Vernal Equinox and knew it to be big news: part of what Revelation would later term "*a great sign.*" The Third Seal aligned with the East Point in AD 15. Any spiritual messenger would have to be born on or ahead of this date to be an effective navigator of its waters. A young carpenter would have been 23 years old if born in 7 BC, certainly old enough to be in the midst of his apprenticeship.

So that is the problem at the beginning of the Pisces timeline. What about the problem at the end?

The Second Problem with the Timetable

If Pisces ends with (as Revelation suggests) *Omega Piscium*, what about the other Fish? One of the two Fish of Pisces has not yet aligned with the Vernal Equinox. The first seven stars of the "Scroll" asterism were the Ribbon, the Rope, and the Fishing Line that bound the southern Fish to the Cord. The Eighth Seal, *Omega Piscium*, begins the new asterism, the western Fish of the constellation. Since the Vernal Equinox is coming in from "behind" the image, this would be the "Tail"

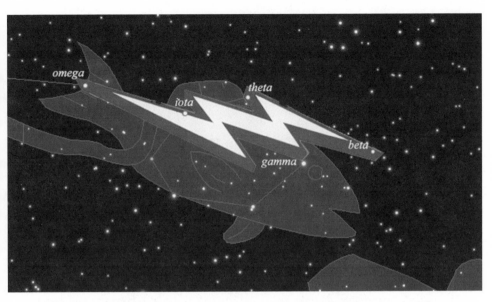

Both Chinese and western asterism begin and end with the same stars. The western "Fish" of Pisces includes lambda and kappa, the two stars in the belly.

of the Fish. *Beta Piscium*, the second brightest star in the constellation, lies at the other end and is generally depicted as the "mouth."

In precessional terms, we have about a thousand years until we get there. Five of the seven stars of this "Fish" constitute the Chinese asterism, *"Lightning." Omega Piscium* aligns with the Vernal Equinox in 2013. *Beta Piscium* does not align with the Vernal Equinox until the year 3097, 1084 years later!

So, we have two mythic patterns, two new heavenly "themes" that begin anew with these stars. Still, it's a constellation of two Fish. Why leave one of the two Fish of Pisces out of our calculations?

Here is why. Pisces is a constellation that is forty-five degrees in length. If you accept the premise that each of the twelve signs of the zodiac is entitled to equal portions of 360 degrees (30 degrees), Pisces is too big by half. It must give something up of its "territory."

While the observational system—based on stone markers, temples, maypoles, and the like—focused on certain stellar boundaries, with time, the advantages of evenly spaced, thirty degree measures between constellations became more apparent. So what *is* the distance between *Alpha* and *Omega Piscium* along the celestial sphere? Thirty-one degrees as measured by the parallels of declination. Very close indeed to the precise segment we would like one of the twelve to occupy. Why not find stars 30 degrees apart? Because there aren't any. At least, not along the ecliptic, nor of this magnitude.

In 1992, I gave a presentation to approximately fifty astronomers and physicists in Northfield, Massachusetts that included some of the notions offered here. (My focus in the talk was more astronomical and less Biblical.) In the crowd, one astute astronomer countered that my theory on *Alpha* and *Omega* couldn't be correct. He argued that the system of using the Greek alphabet (marking the brightest star in the constellation as *alpha*, the second brightest as *beta* and so on) could not have occurred before Johann Bayer introduced the system with his revolutionary *Uranometria* (Measuring the Sky). Bayer's collection of 51 star charts, published in 1603, provided greater detail than anything produced until that time. His series of stellar engravings became the new standard—not only by identifying more stars, but also by introducing twelve new constellations from the southern hemisphere unknown to Ptolemy, the previous astronomical standard-bearer. Our Northfield astronomer's point was that this system was unknown when Revelation was written.

While the *Uranometria* may indeed have raised the bar for astronomical standards, it was not necessarily the originator of the letter-designation system. The following analysis presents an alternative perspective.

> In the succeeding year appeared the "Uranometria" of Johann Bayer, the great Protestant lawyer of Augsburg ... This contained spirited drawings, after Durer, of the ancient forty-eight figures, with a list of 1709 stars and twelve new asterisms. These last were its noticeable feature, with the fact that the plates of the ancient constellations for the first time formally appeared Greek and Roman letters to indicate the individual stars, and so conveniently taking the place of the cumbersome descriptions till then in vogue.

Although this lettering did not come into general use until the succeeding century, Bayer had been anticipated in it fifty years before by Piccolomini of Siena, and even the Persians and Hebrews are said to have had something similar. Dr Robert White, of London, in his "Uranoskopia" of 1681, wrote of this last people:

"Aben Ezra tells that they first divided the Stars into Constellations, and expressed them all by the Hebrew Letters, which when they had gone through, they added a second Letter to express the shape, and oft-times a third to set forth the Nature of the Constellation."[4]

If, indeed, the Hebrews and the Persians had an ancient lettering system for the distant fires of heaven, why not the Greeks? They were certainly no strangers to either the Persians, the Hebrews, or the stars. The Persians used to come and visit regularly. The Hebrews they joined in writing Revelation. And the stars watched over them all.

The Prophets and Scroll

When viewed with an eye to the boundaries, the significance of the Scroll becomes even more apparent. If *Alpha* begins and *Omega* ends the series, there are only eight stars impacting the entire Age. The Scroll thus represents 7/8ths of the picture. If, on top of this, *"the eighth and one of the seven"* includes *Omega* then we have them all, from start to finish.

But this is not the only time the Scroll has been referenced in the Bible, and it leads us down a very interesting path, one that had been walked centuries earlier. Allusions to the Scroll occur in several places in the Good Book. The "seals" are part of the picture and we are warned of a time when the power of visionaries would be compromised.

For on you has Yahweh infused you a spirit of lethargy, he has closed your eyes (the prophets), he has veiled your heads (seers). / For you every

---

4 *Star Names, Their Lore and Meaning,* Richard Hinckley Allen, p. 13.

vision has become like the words of a sealed book. You give it to someone able to read and say, "Read that." He replies, "I cannot, because the book is sealed." / Or else you then give the book to someone who cannot read, and say, "Read that." He replies, "I cannot read."[5]

For one reason or another people are no longer able to read the sign posts of heaven. Isaiah wrote in the 8th century BC. He foresaw the upcoming celestial picture and the difficulties it would entail for Judaism. He also understood that through this period, people would no longer know how to interpret the Will of Heaven, the Will of God. During the *"Kingdom of the world,"* the Lord made us deaf and blind to the spiritual seasons of heaven. This was so that faith might be the cornerstone of the Age of Pisces.

Why am I able to read these maps? Because the period described by Isaiah is over. The veil is lifted. There are many things spoken of here that we will come to see. This is our time.

There are many threads we can follow on this trail through the books of the Bible. The Scroll, the sealed book and the seals are three. But we should also look for references to the "Time of the End" or the "Day of Yahweh." We find one of these clues in Daniel.

When the time comes for the End ...[6]

And he adds further clarity.

But you, Daniel, must keep these words secret and keep the book sealed until the End of Time.[7]

We are glimpsing the "Book of Seals" here, but little more. Daniel must wait until the end of the Epoch of Aries (168 BC), the end of the Age of Aries to reveal anything about the Seven Seals, or, as it's called by him, the book of seals. However, Daniel does tell us more than just

5 Isaiah 29:10–12.
6 Daniel 11:40.
7 Daniel 12:4.

that if we look a little deeper. In fact, it involves and solves one of the great mysteries of Daniel.

Time of the End vs. End Times

The End Times are generally based on divisions of what has come to be called "The Great Year." This is a reference to the amount of time it takes for the precession of the equinoxes to move one full circuit, currently thought to be about 25,765 years. Some cultures have divided this period of time into four, such as the Hopi; some have divided it into five, such as the Mayan, Aztec and Toltec; some have divided it into eight, such as the Etruscans, Celts and their megalithic predecessors; and some have divided it into twelve, such as the Hindus, Chinese and our own culture. We call this cycle the Twelve Ages.

Many of these traditions provide clues that lead us to think they are talking about the current end times, the end of the Age of Pisces. But the Book of Daniel gives us a glimpse of another "end time," the end of the Age preceding Pisces, the end of the stars of the constellation Aries. As each Age comes to a conclusion, there is the end of a period of cultural continuity, of social cohesion, that gives way to a new manner of being.

Writing at the beginning of the 6th century BC, Daniel was looking ahead to the end of his own era. He foresaw this coming in the 2nd century BC, four centuries in the future. After interpreting the dreams and enigmas of the king, Daniel had a dream of his own. He envisioned four beasts rising from out of the Sea. We have seen this imagery before. The Sea is the Cosmic Ocean that is the sky and all that is in it. From out of these four beasts will emerge four kingdoms: that of the Chaldeans, the Medes (the one under which he was presently serving), the Persians, and finally the Greeks. The prophesy took shape as portions of two dreams as he gazed into the "visions of the night." The angel Gabriel set the stage for Daniel as he said,

"Son of man, understand this; the vision shows the time of the end."[8]

---

8 Daniel 8: 17.

The angel continued,

"Come," he said, "I will tell you what is going to happen when the wrath comes to an end; this concerns the appointed End."[9]

The *"appointed End"* recorded by Daniel is the "end" of the Age of Aries. It is the *"end"* ordained by and seen coming on the clouds of heaven.

In his second vision, beginning with Chapter 8, Daniel's dream focused on the latter two of these four kingdoms, the most powerful of the four. The Persians are imagined as a Ram with two horns, one of which was taller than the other. The Persians consisted of a kingdom that was really a joint kingdom, shared by the Medes and Persians. The Persians (the taller horn), rose to power after the Medes, conquered them, and absorbed them into their ruling hierarchy.

The final kingdom is that of Alexander the Great, pictured as a *"he-goat that came from the west."* Greece indeed lies to the west of Persia and the Levant. This Goat had one majestic horn, which was Alexander. This Goat advanced on and charged the Ram, knocking it down and breaking both its horns. The Greeks smashed the Persian Empire in a devastating blow and advancing as far as India.

Then the he-goat grew more powerful than ever, but at the height of its strength the great horn snapped, and in its place sprouted four majestic horns, pointing to the four winds of heaven.[10]

At the height of his power Alexander died, leaving no heirs. His superlative kingdom was divided into four lesser ones amongst his generals. The Hellenistic Kingdoms were originally split up between Macedonia in the west (under Cassander), Egypt in the south (Ptolemy), Asia Minor in the north (Lysimachos) and Persia in the east (Seleucus).

Historians and Biblical researchers often attempt to graft onto this lineage the Roman Empire, which was to eventually absorb the Helle-

9 Daniel 8: 19.
10 Daniel 8:8.

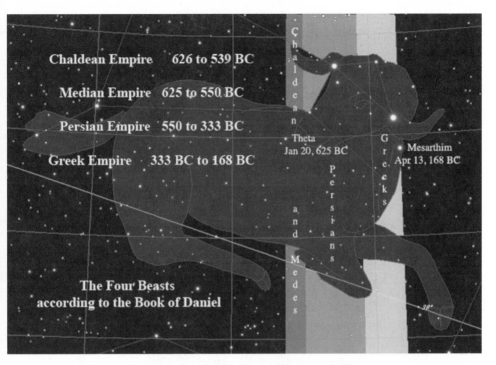

Arian stars herald the future; Theta in 625 bc,
19 Aries in 550 bc and Mesarthin in 168 bc

nistic Kingdoms. What they fail to understand is that this was the start of a new era. The benchmark in time, the End Times or the appointed End, had already passed. In the post-Alexandrian world it was the Seleucid King *Antiochus IV Epiphanes*, who defiled the Hebrew Temple and its most sacred shrine, finally closing the door on the Age of Aries.

> *Forces of his will come and profane the sanctuary citadel; they will abolish the perpetual sacrifice and install the disastrous abomination there.*[11]

In Daniel, chapters 11 and 12, these appointed "End Times" are again specifically referenced (11:35; 11:40; 12:4), with a fuller picture given of the dislocations to come.

---

11 Daniel 11:31.

In Daniel's *"visions in the night"* (Daniel 7:13), he was looking to heaven to determine the time line laid out there. As the Vernal Equinox aligned with *Theta Aries* in 625 BC, the Chaldean (626 BC) and Medes Empires, (625 BC) were getting their starts, fulfilling the requirements of his dream. At the end of this series, the Vernal Equinox aligned with *Gamma Arietes* (Mesarthim) in 168 BC, the last of the four stars in the Horns of the Ram, and the last major precessional star in the constellation of the Ram.

Aries was over, together with all that it represented. This was the appointed end, foreseen in dreams and visions in the night of which Daniel spoke.

The Romans were part of a new chapter that laid the groundwork for the Christian Church to move in and establish itself. The Roman *Republic* had been part of the Age of Aries. The Roman *Empire* was born of the Age of Pisces. The personalities of each of these civilizations were fundamentally different from each other.

With this celestial benchmark in 168 BC the world did not end, but classical civilization came to a grinding halt.

There is going to be a time of great distress, unparalleled since nations first came into existence.[12]

The Book of 2 Maccabees (5:11–14) describes in detail the suffering brought by the Seleucid king Antiochus IV at this time. Believing Judea was in revolt, he took Jerusalem by storm, massacring young and old, women and children. Forty thousand people were slain and another forty thousand sold into slavery.

The Book of Daniel was written for the Judaic people. To have their holiest shrine desecrated, to have their capital city decimated, was indeed an unparalleled blow. As we see, there are two "Times of the End" discussed in the Bible.

The first "Time of the End" is the end of the Vernal Equinox's

12 Daniel 12:1.

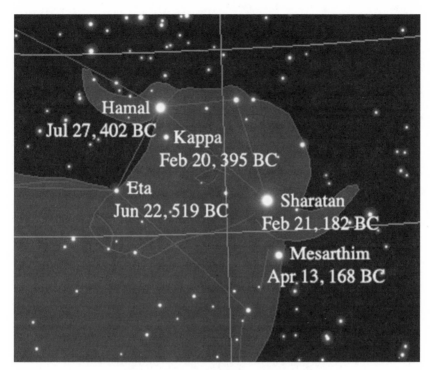

The four stars representing the Horns of the Ram

passage through the constellation Aries (168 BC). The second "Time of the End" is the end of the Vernal Equinox's passage through the constellation Pisces (AD 2013). They are separated by more than two thousand years. Jesus never refers to the "Time of the End" of Aries, because it has already gone by. He is only looking forward to the "Time of the End" of his Age, the Age of which He is the harbinger in the West, the end of Pisces.

We know Daniel was one of the prophets of the period of captivity. Just as Moses gained his star knowledge by being raised as a prince in the land of Egypt, Daniel was trained in the court of the king of Babylon as a youth. His education included methods of divination. He was an exile, a man who had lost his country. The Book of Daniel tells us Daniel was a good student with a natural talent and the favor of God.

The main historical problem with the Book of Daniel is that it covers too long a period to have been written by a single individual. The majority of the book was written from the vantage point of a slave in the king's court during the 6th century BC. Yet it is evident from the end of this book that much of it was composed between 168 and 164 BC or shortly thereafter. The events described, especially in relation to Antiochus IV Epiphanes, suggest a reflection on history rather than the predictions of a prophet. It is far too rich in intricate and accurate detail to be passed as prophecy. Daniel would have been too old to write it himself (at minimum, over three hundred years old!).

Those who "filled in" these lines from history after the fact were doing no more than the spirit (or Daniel) had asked them to do. The last star in the constellation of the Ram to align with the Vernal Equinox was Mesarthim, *Gamma Arietis*, in 168 BC. This was the end of the Age of the Ram. Daniel's successor prophets kept the words secret until the "Time of the End." Once the time of the prophecies had passed and become history, the priests were free to relate what Scripture was talking about. Time had turned on its tumblers and unlocked the mystery for us. Events revealed what was once the future. The time for mystery was over.

The implications of this realization are far reaching. It is a testament to how seriously "celestial foreknowledge" was taken. It was passed down through the generations and understood well enough to fill in the answers at the appropriate time.

Daniel originally wrote most of the work attributed to him when it occurred. Those who followed were part of his prophetic school or lineage. They obeyed their instructions. End of Time, 168 BC. The Book of Daniel backdated, 168 to 164 BC. They honored Daniel's request. The events described are how "Heaven"s Will" unfolded.

In Ezekiel the future of the House of Israel is being passed from "spirit" to the prophet, just as it is in Revelation.

The Son of Man Eats the Scroll

"But you, Son of man, are to listen to what I say to you; do not be a rebel like that rebellious tribe. Open your mouth and eat what I am about to give you."'

When I looked, there was a hand stretching out to me, holding a scroll. He unrolled it in front of me; it was written on, front and back; on it was written "Lamentations, dirges and cries of grief."

He then said, "Son-of-man, eat what you see; eat this scroll, then go and speak to the House of Israel."[13]

The reason Ezekiel had to eat the Scroll—as in Revelation—is that he needed to study and digest the information that was contained therein. Having done that, he can make predictions about what is to come and present the information to the people.

The term *"Son of man"* mystifies contemporary scholars, but it is symbolic imagery for Aquarius which can be applied in different ways. Here, it is being used to describe Ezekiel the prophet. Later Jesus becomes associated with the name, as well as with his return in the future. Aquarians work with science and the stars, both astronomy and astrology. They are the information gatherers. These are the waters they distribute from the celestial Urn. The term "Son of man" can be represented as part of the personality of the individual, as it seems to be in Ezekiel, or it can represent the stellar constellation, towards which the future (the Vernal Equinox in the 1st century AD) was headed.

"Sons of men"could either be Aquarians (those having their Sun in Aquarius), or those having Aquarius strong in their charts. For the record, I have Aquarius rising. I work with the stars. I've been chewing on this Scroll for over thirty years.

And what must the *"Son of man"* do? Yahweh addresses Ezekiel and explains he has appointed him "watchman for the House of Israel."[14]

Ezekiel is to be watching the stars and the regional developments

---

13 Ezekiel 2:8–3:1.
14 Ezekiel 3:17.

and how they will impact Israel. But he is asked *not* to be a rebel. This makes sense as Aquarians *are* the natural rebels, the revolutionaries of the zodiac. They are eccentric and march to the beat of a different drummer. Spirit is asking Ezekiel not to rebel, not to follow his maverick nature, but to get in line and work with God (for it is part of our Free Will to choose).

In Daniel, the term "*Son of man*" is used as something down the road, yet to come. It still lies in the future but is anticipated by the prophets.

> "*I was gazing into the visions of the night,*
> *when I saw, coming on the clouds of heaven,*
> *as it were a son of man.*[15]

If we look to the lines from Ezekiel (2:10), our Scroll is being handed to us, together with it's writing front and back. Stars have come, stars have gone. This time we are being given an encapsulated translation of the influence of the seven stars of the Scroll in Ezekiel. Collectively, they represent "*lamentations, dirges and cries of grief.*"

Isn't this exactly what history has shown? Is that not in fact what we have found as we look back on these dates armed with all the advantages of hindsight? When Ezekiel was being written in the 6th century BC, the Scroll still lay in the future, but it could be seen approaching in the "*visions of the night,*" like the Son of man "*coming on the clouds of heaven.*"

Even Jesus used the term to describe the coming Age.

> "*... the coming of the Son of man will be like lightning striking in the east and flashing far into the west...*[16]

Jesus repeated the term again.

---

15 Daniel 7:13.
16 Matthew 24:27.

"... then the sign of the Son of Man will appear in heaven ... "[17]

This is the *sign* of the Son of Man, one of the twelve *signs* of the zodiac. And it does what? It is striking in the East! In other words, it is aligning with the Vernal Equinox and becoming a new Eastern Star. This is exactly what we have been looking for.

It will appear in heaven because the Vernal Equinox will activate it, will give it life. It's always been there, but now the "power" will pass to Aquarius. God is directing it *"with power and great glory,"* and all that implies.

These lines suggest Aquarius will begin with a bang, possibly a huge natural event, such as the shifting of the Earth's core, coupled with an off-the-scales earthquake whose impact will create a social realignment culminating in a great battle between opposing forces.

Matthew and Revelation seem to suggest both, first one and then the other. It is the precise sequence that we are attempting to unravel here. Obviously, Jesus is lifting these lines of scripture from Daniel because he feels they are important. But he is giving us additional clues about what it will mean. Both Daniel and Jesus see the time of the *"Son of man"* coming; as do other prophets, but the events described will not transpire until after the time of the Great Persecution. *Omega* is the end, but it is also the beginning—the beginning of the labor pains.

> *You will hear of wars and rumors of wars, do not be alarmed, for this is something that must happen, but the end will not be yet. For nation will fight against nation, and kingdom against kingdom. There will be famines and earthquakes here and there. All this is only the beginning of the birth pangs.*[18]

In biblical terms this is the end of the period known to the Christians as the "Kingdom of the world" and the beginning of that known as the "Kingdom of our Lord" (Rev. 11: 15). We are simply moving

---

17 Matthew 24:30.
18 Matthew 24: 6-8.

from one astronomical image to the next in precessional sequence, from Pisces to Aquarius.

The power and focus is the Vernal Equinox. As the cataclysmic pages of history have shown, their manifestation is an impressive feat, demonstrating great power and glory.

Daniel, Matthew and Jesus are making it abundantly clear in these lines, supplying us with additional clues because the Time (in stellar terms) is here. We are much closer to these events in the New Testament than we were in Daniel. For the angel sent by Jesus in Revelation (unlike Daniel), the themes regarding the Scroll are not to be kept a secret. He provides us with added information.

Zechariah and the Flying Scroll

Once one begins to unravel Revelation, following its various threads throughout the Bible, a common story line begins to appear. In Zechariah we find an additional piece to the puzzle. This prophet makes it clear in the first line what year and month it is—the eighth month of 520 BC. In Zechariah we find ourselves again face to face with the Scroll, this time depicted as a *"flying scroll,"* one that wings its way through the sky. All celestial figures fly through the sky. Because of this many of them are adorned with wings.

> *Again raising my eyes, I had a vision. There was a flying scroll. The angel who was talking to me said, "What do you see?" I replied, "I see a flying scroll; it is twenty cubits long and ten cubits wide." He then said to me, "This is God's curse sweeping across the face of the whole country …"*[19]

First of all, note the refrain. After raising his eyes he had a vision. He's not rolling his eyes back into his head while in trance; he's looking up to the skies, up to the stars of heaven. He was understanding pictures and their meaning, "having a vision" in the same manner that we are seeing the thread and interpreting the story line now.

---

19 Zechariah 5:1-3.

The clues continue to point in the same direction, complementing one another. The Vernal Equinox was approaching the Scroll and they could see it coming in the same manner that we can look to the sky on a clear night now (if you know where to look—most people don't). You can see where the Vernal Equinox has now passed the Scroll and has aligned with the Eighth Seal, *Omega*.

The dimensions of the Scroll make it far too big to be a conventional parchment scroll. This is an appropriate way of saying that it was bigger than normal, which makes sense since it occupies more than half of the constellation. This style of mythic metaphor was used when a huge Scorpion killed Orion. Apollo sent an enormous scorpion, bigger than an elephant, to attack the broad-shouldered hunter. Of course, they're referring to the constellation Scorpio, which rises in the east as Orion sets in the west. In mythological terms, the Scorpion wins. He hangs around (rises) after Orion has passed out-of-sight below the horizon. In the stellar myths of the Egyptians, one rises, one sets; one lives, one dies.

There is agreement between Zechariah and Ezekiel about the "quality" of this grouping of stars. They are saying the same thing using different words. And what might that be? *Das ist nicht gut!* Zechariah calls it *"God's curse."* Ezekiel says *"lamentations, dirges and cries of grief."* But there is another indicator that suggests we're on the right track. Prior to describing his vision of the Scroll, Zechariah, like any good timekeeper, carefully dates it for us, providing both astronomical and historical evidence.

On the 24th day of the eleventh month (the month of Shebat), in the second year of Darius, the word of Yahweh was addressed to the prophet Zechariah (son of Berechiah), son of Iddo, as follows, "I had a vision during the night. There was a man riding a red horse standing among deep-rooted myrtles; behind him were other horses—red, chestnut and white." I said, "What are these, my lord?" And the angel who was talking said, "I will show you what they are." The man standing among the myrtles then replied, "Those are they who Yahweh has sent to patrol the world." They reported to the angel of Yahweh as he stood among the myrtles, "We have been patrolling the world, and indeed the whole world is at peace."[20]

This is the sort of thing an astrologer would be very careful to note—the time. (There's an old joke that runs around astrological social circles. How do you tell the astrologers at a party when the rock comes flying through the window? They're the ones looking at their watches.)

In Zechariah 1:1, he establishes the date as during the eighth month of *the second year of Darius.* That would have been during October–November in 520 BC. Six lines later he gives a second date, January–February of 519 BC. Another of the prophets, Haggai, is also very careful to flag this specific year. He opens his book with what he feels to be very important temporal information, *the second year of King Darius.* King Cyrus had issued his decree in 538. This is 520/519. That's 18 years later. Why the delay? What's happening here?

We're stepping into Jewish history at the beginning of their return from the exile. Daniel and Ezekiel lived during the period of captivity in Babylon (586–538 BC). Zechariah and Haggai date to the time of the return.

In 538 BC, when Cyrus the Persian overthrew his Babylonian predecessors and came to the throne, he issued an edict allowing formerly conquered peoples to return to their native lands. This was the time during which Ezra and Nehemiah were written, the return and rebuilding of their Temple and culture. There was considerable sadness, crying and wailing, recognizing all the kingdom of Judah once had, contrasted by all they had lost. Compared to Israel, Judah had been a humble kingdom, but they had kept their freedom. Now they were to be policed by the Persians. Both Haggai and Zechariah urgently attempted to encourage the people to rebuild the Temple so that once God was properly housed, honored and provided for, their homes, crops, and lives might be blessed, and prosperity could return.

The Temple was rebuilt in three years, beginning in December 520 BC, in the second year of King Darius. If the Jews, as the Romans did, waited for the first sliver of a crescent to appear in the east immediately

---

20 Zechariah 1:7–11.

after sundown and then begin their month, the date could be a day or two after the astronomical New Moon. Roman priests used to wait on hilltops and call out when they first spotted the young Goddess making Her premier appearance just before She sets in the west. Muslims do it to this day.

While the month and day are important to look at a chart for the construction of the rebuilt Temple, it is the year that we are most interested in here, the last month of 520 BC. The Temple construction was being inaugurated precisely as the Vernal Equinox crossed over a new eastern star, *Eta Arietis*, the seventh brightest star in the constellation of the Ram. If I am correct, Haggai and Zechariah were agitating to get the Temple built in order that they might better honor Yahweh by this celestially auspicious date. It had been eighteen years since the decree of Cyrus, yet they were now racing to make the finish line.

Looked at in this light, some of the lines of Scripture begin to make better sense. And Revelation is consistent.

I had a vision during the night.[21]

That is when the stars come out.

There was a man riding a red horse standing among deep-rooted myrtles.[22]

This was where they stood in astronomical time. The Vernal Equinox aligning with the star is symbolized by the man riding the red horse. He was standing among deep-rooted myrtles. The three stars "behind him" *(behind him were other horses—red, chestnut and white)* could either be the three stars in the rear of the Ram already passed, or, and more probably, they refer to the three stars in the Head and Horns of the Ram. These were just getting ready (in precessional terms) to cross.

The myrtle was a plant associated with Aphrodite (Venus) by the

---

21 Zechariah 1:8.
22 Zechariah 1:8.

Greeks. At the Veneralia, celebrated among the Romans on April 1, women removed the jewelry from the statue of Venus, washed her and adorned her with flowers. At the same time they bathed themselves in the public baths wearing myrtle wreaths on their heads. In both Greek and Hebrew customs, the myrtle was associated with love and marriage. Traditionally myrtle branches were given to the bridegroom as he entered the nuptial chambers after being married.

Venus is the goddess of peace, her bird the dove. The world is at peace. The red horse (war) is standing among deep-rooted myrtles, a period of deeply rooted peace. The Persians are the military muscle currently at work helping to secure a politically tranquil classical world.

Let's look at a star map.

Not all stars have names. Some are simply designated by their Greek letter prefix.

The rededication of the Temple was taking place just as *Eta Arietis* becomes the new eastern star, heralding a new epoch for civilization, a new stellar reorientation. It is my humble opinion that both Haggai and Zechariah were agitating for a new Temple not only because they were returning from exile, but also because they wanted to honor Yahweh *as* the alignment occured. This would have brought good favor at the start of a new epoch of history, a new "season" (Zero hours, minutes and seconds of Right Ascension, East Point, Spring) under heaven. Missing a Holy Day, especially of this magnitude, would not have been a good thing. They needed to do specific rituals in order to prepare for the way of the Lord.

But the prophets were looking ahead and making their predictions for another reason. The three brightest stars in the constellation of the Ram are found in the head. They are generally depicted as the horns of the Ram. In precessional terms their alignment, and the predictions as to what might transpire when they were triggered, are in order. The time, their future, was getting very close.

In Zechariah's second vision, in a familiar pattern, we are told more:

Then, raising my eyes, I had a vision. It was this: There were four horns. I said to the angel who was talking to me, "What are these horns, my Lord?" He said to me, "These are the horns which have so scattered Israel

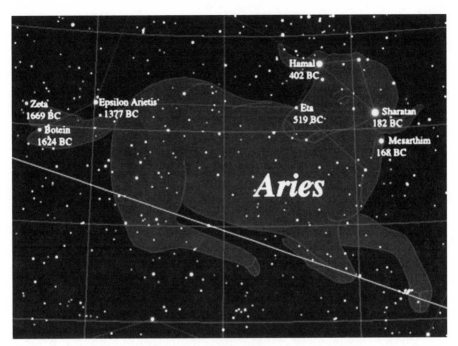

The seven brightest stars in the constellation Aries
[Hamal (Alpha), Sharatan (Beta), Mesarthim (Gamma),
Botein (Delta), Epsilon, Zeta, Eta]

and Jerusalem." Yahweh then showed me four smiths. And I said, "What
are these coming to do?" He said to me, "Those are the horns which have
so scattered Judah that no one has dared to raise his head; but to strike
down the horns of the nations who lifted their hands against the land of
Judah, in order to scatter it." [23]

These are the Horns of the Ram, which lay, in 520 BC, in the immediate future. They were next in (ecliptic, precessional) line. It is what we
would expect the prophets to be focusing their attention on *if* the stars
of heaven were important to them. There's little doubt as to what three
of the four stars were—the brightest three, *Alpha, Beta,* and *Gamma
Arietis.* The fourth was either *Kappa Arietis* or *Eta Arietis* itself, providing a visual symmetry to our four stars of the horns.

---

23 Zechariah 2:18–21.

The Vernal Equinox aligned with *Alpha Arietis*, Hamal, in 402 BC as the Roman war with Veii was in the midst of its ten-year-long conflict. It ended with *Kappa* in 395 BC as the war concluded. *Alpha* and either *Eta* or *Kappa* are the left horn as seen from Earth. The right horn is *Beta* and *Gamma Arietis*. Aries is ruled by Mars, the God of War. The horns of the Ram are the fighting, battling, confrontive portion of the constellation. The expectation was that they would bring war and conflict, scattering the House of Israel. Yet each of the conquerors that swept over the Promised Land were in turn extinguished. There was destruction (horns) and construction (smiths).

Time was moving through a period of history that was overseen by the stars in the constellation of the Ram. These are martial stars, providing an environment wherein tempers and testosterone are in saturated abundance. "Fear God or else" was the modality of the time. Heaped upon that, the stars of the Horns of the Ram are the most belligerent period of the entire constellation, providing a canvas for machismo, honor, glory and the strong right arm of God. But while these civilizations lived by the sword, they also died by the sword. Where are the Assyrian, Babylonian, Persian, or Greek overlords now? What happened to Alexander or Antiochus IV Epiphanes? In the final judgement, how long-lasting a role did they play?

While the Temple was rebuilt with *Eta*, it was later desecrated with *Gamma Arietis*, the final star of both the horns and constellation. The last of the four stars of the Horns to be triggered by the Vernal Equinox was *Mesarthim* in 168 BC.

In 168 BC, the inhabitants of Jerusalem were massacred while the Temple was plundered by Antiochus IV Epiphanes. A figure of Zeus was placed on the altar and possession of Jewish scriptures was made a capital offense. Jewish sacrifice was forbidden. Sabbaths and feasts were banned and circumcision outlawed. Altars to Greek gods were set up and animals prohibited to Jews (such as swine) were sacrificed. Priests were forced to eat pork on pain of death. Syrian soldiers took charge.

Further north, 168 BC was also the year of the Battle of Pydna, part of the Third Macedonian War. In historical terms, it was fought between Rome and the Antigonid (Hellenistic) dynasty. It marked the

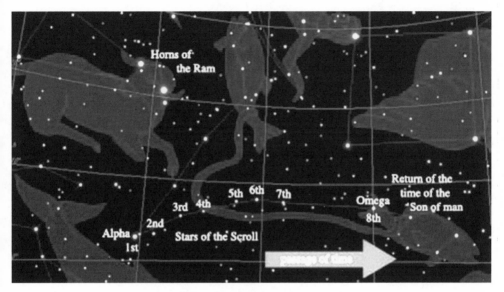

Three asterisms in a row:
Horns of the Ram, Stars of the Scroll and Son of man.

start of Roman ascendancy in the Hellenic world and the end of the Antigonid line of kings.

Let me translate that for you. It marked the end of Greece and the beginning of Rome as the principle political power of the Mediterranean. While this new ascendancy was not finalized with that particular battle, it marked a tipping point for both the Greek and Judaic cultures around a single year.

The last horn of the altar made its mark. Mesarthim was a beginning and an end. Say goodbye to Aries and the Hebrew and Hellenic cultures of the Classical World.

So what we have here are the Horns of the Ram, stars of the Scroll and coming of the Son of man on the clouds of heaven in correct celestial sequence. In Matthew, Jesus warned us about the "Time of the End," when the sign of the "Son of man" approaches and false prophets would arise to deceive even the elect.[24]

We are speaking of a point in heaven, a position in space. You're not

---

24 See Matthew 24:23–25.

going to find a person physically walking the Earth. The return of the Son of man speaks of a time, not an individual. Jesus and Ezekiel may have been Aquarians (or had Aquarius strong in their charts), and were therefore called "Son of man" as a nickname. There will be those who reflect the spirit of Jesus in what they do, as we all learn to pull together willingly in common cause and cooperation. Still, this is God's will. All is in order according to His "Master Plan."

There's another reference to the Four Horns, this time from Revelation itself.

The sixth angel blew his trumpet, and I heard a voice come out of the four horns of the golden altar in front of God. It spoke to the sixth angel with the trumpet, and said, "Release the four angels that are chained up at the great river Euphrates."[25]

The voice is from the Four Horns in front of the golden altar (the Vernal Equinox). The "spirit of war" (Aries, Mars, Ares) from an earlier epoch, was telling the angel that it was time to release the angels chained in the Mideast. War was to be unleashed. As we have already seen, the sixth angel was blowing his trumpet. The angel with the sixth bowl (one a reflection of the other) represents one of the more cataclysmic events of Revelation.

As the Temple was being rebuilt after the period of Babylonian captivity, *Eta Arietis* stood at the Star Gate. Although closer to the horns, *Eta* lies between two groups of three—the three brightest stars in the head and the next three brightest in the tail. In 520 BC it was a thousand years since a previous bright star in Aries aligned with the Vernal Equinox. It would be only 118 years until it aligned with *Alpha Arietis*, the brightest star of the constellation. In stellar timekeeping, that's not much. So the seventh star in brightness in the constellation Aries, *Eta*, anticipated the coming of the stars of the Horns. If, indeed, these stargazers of ancient civilizations were watching (and there is every indication that they were), then the picture on this stellar tapestry was beginning to become clear.

---

25 Rev. 9:13–14.

After waiting so long for a new spiritual "season" in 520 BC, these prophets were ready. The Temple (think of it as a celestial observatory) was the tool needed to help observe heaven to more carefully gauge precessional passage. This was one of the main functions of the ancient temples. One has only to look to the Egyptian shrines to realize this, or the ziggurats of Babylon, or the megalithic constructions of ancient Europe and the Americas. Even churches under the Masonic eye opened their doors and let the sunlight stream onto the altar on the feast day of the saint. Until modern times, temples have traditionally been used to help us connect with the will of heaven. Building the Temple after the alignment had passed would be unthinkable—not only in technical terms, but also for the underlying moral and spiritual implications.

However, the prophets could not do it by themselves. They must convince the congregation to supply the time, labor and materials to construct the Temple. The best they could do was to implore the people with their wisdom to get moving and pray it would be ready in time. And this was exactly what Zechariah and Haggai did in their two books.

We know from myth that Athena wove tapestries about the stories of gods and man, her fingers flying across the threads. Here we see the Judaic prophets doing the same—binding a weave of stars across stellar spindles of time, waiting and watching by their imaginative (and yet divine) looms in concerned anticipation of the results.

Thunderclaps

Having seen the pattern in Ezekiel and Zechariah, and how the story line changed with Jesus in Matthew and John in Revelation, another piece now began to drop into place. While interpreting the upcoming star patterns, the prophets in both cases discussed what was about to happen. But in each of these two examples, they were reluctant to go much further and interpret star patterns beyond their own time. This could in part be due to the dour nature of the upcoming archetype. With the Scroll following hard on the heels of the Horns, it might seem to be an extended period of doom and gloom.

As they stood at *Eta Arietis* and the time following the return
from exile, the focus of the prophets was on the power of the Horns,
the grouping coming up next, which was therefore of great social
interest. The Scroll, the next asterism in precessional line, was briefly
mentioned, but not much was said about it. The interpretation was
minimal.

With Revelation, details were given about each of the Seven Stars
of the Seals—the grouping they were in the middle of—with *"writing
on it back and front."*

The following star pattern was not much referenced. This was our
aforementioned Problem Two, the second fish of Pisces. *Omega* begins
the new star group as it ends the old. In the Chinese system, there are
only five stars in the asterism, beginning with *Omega* and ending with
Beta. As we visually inspect this asterism in a star map, however, there
seem to be seven stars in this "Fish."

Isn't it curious that we have yet one more reference to the number
seven? There were seven letters, seven churches, seven Spirits before the
throne of God, seven Seals, seven Trumpets, seven Thunderclaps and
seven Bowls. That is seven sevens. Among the asterisms of this constellation, the "Scroll" has seven stars and the "western Fish" has seven
stars. Being able to differentiate between them is one of the trickier
components to solving the puzzle. To better understand this latest connection once again we must return to the Asian constellational image,
"Lightning."

If *"Lightning"* is the "visual" for this collection of stars, what then is
the "voice" of lightning? The answer is simple. It is Thunder.

These are the mysterious Thunderclaps of Revelation 10. It was
curious to observe as we went through Revelation that the author conjured their image, only to immediately keep their meaning secret. He
wants us to know that they were there, but he doesn't want us to know
anything yet about what the "voice" of this series of stars has to say.

*Keep the words of the seven thunderclaps secret and do not write them
down.*[26]

---

26 Rev. 10:4.

This is the same thing the prophets did in the Hebrew Bible. They spoke in some detail of the upcoming celestial design, but only briefly mentioned the ones to follow. They consistently did not go into detail about it until its time was almost upon us.

In Daniel 12:4, he was again closely scrutinizing the stars in the Horns of the Ram, but spoke little of the Scroll. He was told to keep the words secret and the book sealed until the End of Time.

In Revelation John was also told to keep the Thunderclaps of Lightning a secret. The author of Revelation was most interested in the Scroll. For it defined their immediate future from the 1st century BC. This mirrors Daniel's instructions as noted.

Looking to the end of Lightning, if I don't miss my guess, it will be as the Vernal Equinox aligns with *Beta Piscium* that the "dragon" will be released, after *"the thousand years had passed..."* *"but only for a short time."*

> *He threw him into the Abyss, and shut the entrance and sealed it over him, to make sure he would not deceive the nations again until the thousand years had passed. At the end of that time he must be released, but only for a short while.*[27]

We won't be fooled again. At least not for a thousand years.

This outlines the next asterism, together with its reference to the Dragon, this reign of a thousand years. It begins 1084 years after *Omega, Beta Piscium* aligns, and it's done. Deception and greed return briefly at the end of a thousand years, are exposed, and Aquarius begins again, experiencing a second birth.

Although Revelation doesn't interpret the Thunderclaps, it has become obvious to me that we are looking at the days of *our* future. *Omega* is the end of the Scroll, but it is also the beginning of both Lightning and the Age of Aquarius.

There are two entry points into the new time, just as there was an overlap between Aries and Pisces. *Omega* is the start of the mathematically defined thirty-degree segment of the tropical zodiac (even if it is

---

27 Rev. 20:2.

a thirty-one degree segment). *Beta* is the end of entire constellation of the Fish. They both work, and each will have an impact. Revelation is attempting to interpret that impact.

Fortunately, the period in-between these two will be one of peace—at least once we have finished that for which *Omega* opens the gates. The "Eighth Seal" cuts both ways. It is still one of the Seven. Its opening is similar to theirs and is not yet finished.

What John seems to be saying is that the Son of man will marry the Bride and become aligned with the new epoch. There will then be one final blowout of a natural or politically-related event similar to the themes of the Seven Seals of the Scroll before we enter the thousand years of grace. This theme is repeated over and over again from Chapters 8 to 19. These pages describe how bad conditions become at the end of our time. Crime, corruption and greed run the show.

She is Queen on her throne, "*I am no widow and shall never be in mourning.*" If I am interpreting this correctly, and if the spirit speaking through John is correct, a natural event will come along that knocks the train off the tracks. As a result the playing field will be realigned. The advantages that helped to keep the old guard in place will be overwhelmed.

War will erupt from out of the Euphrates.

This is what is recorded by both the Sixth Trumpet and Sixth Bowl; the Trumpets *herald* the event. The Bowls *are* the event. There will be one final battle. It will not be popular with the majority of the people on the Earth. It will produce a new martial lord, one who begins a reign of a thousand years, the same length of time during which the Dragon is sealed in the abyss.

> *... and reigned with Christ for a thousand years. This is the first res-urrection; the rest of the dead did not come to life until the thousand years were over. Happy and blessed are those who share in the first resurrection ...*[28]

---

28 Rev. 20:4–6.

These were the souls under the alter of the Fifth Seal, who asked how much longer they had to wait. *Omega Piscium* is the time of their release. There will be a thousand years of peace. Then, as *Beta Piscium* completes the *constellation* of Pisces and its asterisms, there will be a time for a second battle and a "second death," with which those who have gone through the "first death" do not need to concern themselves. As we have already mentioned, there is a period of a second judgment which picks up with Rev. 20:6,

> ...*the second death cannot affect them but they will be priests of God and of Christ and reign with him for a thousand years.*

Each Age produces a different line of "kings and priests" to deal with the lessons of that Age. During the Age of Taurus, it was an agricultural line of kings and priests that we see in Sumerian, Egyptian, and Harappan cultures. During Aries, there were martial overlords. Pisces produced kings and priests molded by the Church.

> *When the thousand years are over, Satan will be released from his prison and will come out to deceive all the nations in the four quarters of the earth, Gog and Magog, and mobilize them for war. His armies will be as many as the sands of the sea; / they will come swarming over the entire country and besiege the camp of the saints, which is the city that God loves. But fire will come down on them from heaven and consume them. / Then the devil, who misled them, will be thrown into the lake of fire and sulphur, where the beast and the false prophet are, and their torture will not stop, day or night, for ever and ever.*[29]

Solution? Work on things that are honorable through your lifetime. Be good to people. Help them in any of a number of ways that makes life easier, and pick the avenue that best works for you. Treat as you would be treated, honor as you would be honored, love as you would be loved. Good advice then, good advice now.

---

29 Rev 20:7–10.

Trumpets and Bowls

Among the many instances of the number seven, two, in particular, seem to be mirror images of each other. A number of the images in Revelation seem to be repetitions of the timing of the entry into the New Age, with alternative scenarios of what will happen under each one. None of these are necessarily mutually exclusive events.

The sevens that we will be examining under this heading are those of the Trumpets and Bowls. As we've already seen, the Trumpets are linked to the seven flaming lamps, the seven Spirits of God in front of the throne. The Trumpets are in the presence of God. These are the seven visible planets that serve *whoever* sits on the throne, *whenever* they sit there. They are defined as the "eyes" of God, who watch over the whole world, rather than parts of various asterisms.

The references to the seven Trumpets are distributed from Chapters 8 to 11. Let's compare these to the seven Bowls found in Chapter 16 one by one.

Not only do these two series parallel each other, the Trumpets bear a striking similarity amongst themselves. It seems the same event is happening over and over again, with some foreign object coming out of the skies—whether natural or manmade—which strikes the Earth with enough force to to substantially change the course of events here on the Earth.

Personally, I don't believe these are a series where a third of the Earth is impacted, and then another third, and then another, etc. My impression is that we are looking at a singular event that may impact a third of the Earth, period. It's being observed from different vantage points, in how it impacts the sky, the Earth, oceans, rivers and streams, etc. Certainly, the first five Trumpets sound very similar in nature. The Sixth Trumpet seems to bring on war as a result of this devastation. The Seventh completes the process, marked by the start of the Age (again), with lightning, thunder, hail and an earthquake as Mother's Nature's fanfare to the beginning of Aquarius. Once again, our asterism is called "Lightning."

Not only do the first five Trumpets seem to be heralding the same

Table of the Seven Trumpets and Seven Bowls

1st Trumpet: hail and fire, fell onto the earth earth burned up.	1st Bowl: emptied bowl over earth disgusting and virulent sores.
2nd Trumpet: a great mountain, all on fire, dropped into the sea.	2nd Bowl: emptied bowl over sea turned to blood killing creatures of the sea.
3rd Trumpet: a huge star from the sky, burning like a ball of fire, fell on rivers and springs.	3rd Bowl: emptied his bowl into rivers and water springs they turned to blood.
4th Trumpet: a third of the Sun, a third of the Moon, and a third of the Stars.	4th Bowl: emptied his bowl over the Sun scorch people with flames.
5th Trumpet: a star that had fallen from heaven onto Earth out of the smoke dropped locusts.	5th Bowl: emptied his bowl over throne of Beast darkness, pains and sores.
6th Trumpet: voice from the four horns release the four angels chained by the Euphrates.	6th Bowl: emptied his bowl over great river Euphrates Armageddon.
7th Trumpet: Kingdom of the World becomes the Kingdom of our Lord, beginning of the reign lightning, thunder, earthquake and hail.	7th Bowl: emptied his bowl The end has come. lightning and peals of thunder most violent earthquake ever.

event, but there's another angel introduced together with the angels of the Trumpets in Rev. 8: 3. He is doing the same thing.

> *Another angel, who had a golden censer* (a small shovel used to carry live coals)... *who filled it with fire from the altar, which he then threw down on to the earth; immediately there came peals of thunder and flashes of lightning, and the earth shook.*

This a synopsis of what we are reading under the Trumpets and the Bowls. Fire from above resulting in an earthquake at the end. The repetitions may simply be a way of underscoring the importance of what is attempting to be communicated here in symbolic form. By combining the themes announced by the Trumpets together with those brought on by the Bowls, we are doubling the number of "clues" that we are being given about each event.

The Day of Yahweh

Revelation is nothing if not a book of imagery. One of the more powerful images that comes to the surface in this tale is "the day of God." One of the earliest references to it is in the book of the prophet Amos. It speaks of foreboding with dark days on the horizon.

> *Will not the Day of Yahweh be darkness, not light,*
> *totally dark, without ray of light?*[30]

Several prophets repeat this theme in various ways. Throughout the Bible, it appears as the day of Yahweh, day of God, or even the day of Jesus Christ.

> *… so you will understand fully that you can be as proud of us as we shall*
> *be of you when the Day of our Lord Jesus comes.*[31]

Zephaniah begins his lament with these words.

> *The great day of Yahweh is near,*
> *near, and coming with all speed.*
> *How bitter the sound of the day of Yahweh,*
> *the day when the warrior shouts his cry of war.*[32]

---

30 Amos 5:20
31 2 Cor 1:14
32 Zephaniah 1:14

Revelation dips its quill into the same archetypal inkwell. We see a modified "Great Day" of ill boding.

They said to the mountains and the rocks, Fall on us and hide us away from the One who sits on the throne and from the retribution of the Lamb. For the Great Day of his retribution has come, and who can face it?[33]

We interpreted this earlier as the coming of the Vikings. Ten books later, the "Great Day" of retribution is referenced again.

"...to call them together for the war of the Great Day of God the Almighty..."[34]

Such images follow from other Old Testament progenitors.

Human pride will lower its eyes,
human arrogance will be humbled,
and Yahweh alone will be exalted, on that day.[35]

Amos, Isaiah, Zephaniah and John all wrote during different times, with different political landscapes. What is Isaiah referring to here? Why will human arrogance be brought low?

In the case of Isaiah, it is clear that he foresaw the wrath that would be unleashed on Israel by Assyria, venting God's anger on his chosen ones for their defiance.

What will you do on the day of punishment,
when disaster comes from far away?
To whom will you run for help
and where will you leave your riches,

33　Rev. 6:16–17.
34　Rev. 16:14.
35　Isaiah 2:9.

to avoid squatting among the captives
or falling among the slain?[36]

Isaiah elaborated on his his promise of the devastation Israel had called on itself.

Look, the Day of Yahweh is coming,
merciless, with wrath and burning anger,
to reduce the country to a desert
and root out the sinners from it.[37]

What is happening? Some believe Isaiah and the other prophets foresee different disasters about to unfold on Israel, among which were the following:

The first is in **722** BC when Northern Israel was defeated by Sargon and the **Assyrians**. The silver and gold religious artifacts were taken from the Temple, the ten tribes deported and lost to the pages of history. The prophets who focussed on and warned of this up-coming calamity were Amos, Hosea, Micah and Isaiah.

Then, in **598, 597 and 587** BC, Judah, the more southerly kingdom (representing the two remaining tribes) was defeated, its citizens deported after successive battles. According to Jeremiah a total of four thousand six hundred persons, presumably counting just the males, were forced to uproot their homes and leave with their conquerors. This time they were defeated by Nebuchadnezzer and the **Babylonians**. Daniel, Ezekiel, Zephaniah, Naham and Habakkuk were the prophets concerned with this period of Jewish history.

In **168** BC the inhabitants of Jerusalem were massacred and the Temple desecrated and plundered by Antiochus IV Epiphanes and the **Syrians**, one of the four resulting kingdoms left behind in

---

36 Isaiah 10:3.
37 Isaiah 13:9.

the wake of Alexander's conquests. Daniel referenced this period in considerable detail, which makes his text one of the many enigmas of the Bible. Following the "time of the end" (of the Age of Aries), the "scribes of Daniel" were freed from the constraint of not being able to explain what happened. They filled in the historical blanks after the fact.

Finally, in **ad 70** the Emperor Titus defeated the Hebrews and destroyed the temple in Jerusalem, leaving only the west (Wailing) wall. These were the **Romans**, and the Temple has not yet been rebuilt. This is the same time period for the writing of the Book of Revelation by John, somewhere between AD 65 and 90.

Given the waves of destruction just referenced, this presents an awful picture of suffering. The early prophets saw darkness on the horizon. Jerusalem and the children of Israel would be attacked, savaged, massacred, starved, and plagued in various waves. Their people killed, humiliated and deported, the majority lost to history. *These* were the trepidations foreseen by these early prophets and ignored by their contemporary congregations. Knowing the storms that lay on the horizon, the prophets lamented that people only wanted pleasant predictions and refused to mend their ways. But for the days ahead, pleasant predictions were not to be had. The Bible made it clear that the choice was up to the people. The Book of Jonah is an example. If they correct their ways and relinquish deceit—treating each other with integrity and respect—all would be well. The answer was so simple. The prophets tried to tell the people to no avail. Their frustration and exasperation over the consequences must have been enormous. You can hear it in the scripture they left behind.

Associations to the "Day of the Lord" make their appearances across the centuries, in both Old Testament and New. If we consider that under the themes of the Ram's horns and the Cord of the Fish, each of these Star Gates is one of a series of difficulties, the literature begins to make more sense. History has shown that each of these stars is similar in that they invoke terrible consequences, yet each historical event is distinctive in and of itself. This is why they were grouped together mythologically. They are part of an ongoing theme.

The prophets focussed on the series of stars in the Horns of the Ram. The writer(s) of Revelation focussed upon the stars of the Cord (Scroll).

Many of the "Day of the Lord" images draw upon clouds, darkness and thunder (Joel 2:11, 3:16) to describe the epiphany of the Lord on His day, remembering the "Lord of the storm" (Ps. 29), and the "one who rides on a cloud" (Ps. 68:4). Even earthquakes become part of the story. There's seismic activity with a giant earthquake prophesied as the end of the calamities and the true beginning of the thousand-year reign.

Returning to the Hebrew Bible, here is a page from history depicting the Assyrians attacking the southern kingdom of Judah recorded in 2 Kings.

In the fourteenth year of King Hezekiah, Sennacherib king of Assyria advanced on all the fortified towns of Judah and captured them. Then Hezekiah king of Judah sent this message to the king of Assyria at Lachish, 'I have been at fault. Call off the attack, and I will submit to whatever you impose on me.' The king of Assyria exacted three hundred talents of silver and thirty talents of gold from Heszekiah king of Judah, and Hezekiah gave him all the silver in the Temple of Yahweh and in the palace treasure. At which time, Hezekiah stripped the facing from the leaves and jambs of the doors of the Temple of Yahweh, which king of Judah had put on, and gave it to the king of Assyria.[38]

The nation of Israel, the northern kingdom, was destroyed, its people killed or deported. This begins the loss of the ten tribes of Israel. Even if separate elements of the tribes did later gather under the loose southern skirts of Judah, they never re-emerged on the pages of history as distinct ethnic elements.

This is what the prophets saw coming and about which they were

---

38 2 Kings 18:13–16.

desperate to warn their people. But they were frustrated by the people's lack of concern.

Pharaoh's Vision

Before we submit our test of the hypothesis that the stars of the constellations were a major source of the prophecies for the Book of Revelation and the prophets of the Hebrew Bible, let's take a large step back in time to examine another legend. While the seven layers of each of the planetary planes were said to have their own sphere of influence as the soul descended at birth and re-ascended at death, it was the 8th layer that held the realm of the fixed stars, a realm whose path we have been examining here.

We've relied on myth, legend and metaphor while composing this work, but it has also been framed by astronomy and history—pinpointing specific dates that had huge consequences for Rome, the Christian Church, and the Jewish people. Not only did the prophets look to the stars, but so did the Egyptians—where the Hebrews spent an extended period of captivity—look to the heavens to determine the future. The astronomy of Egypt began before the building of the pyramids, approximately 2000 or more years earlier.

For those monitoring the cardinal points of the compass, precession's slow evolution allowed them to look down the ecliptic path into the future. While the Vernal Equinox was passing along the Neck of the Bull, it was not difficult to see the upcoming stars of the Ram and Fish in a single night's sky and to feel concern about the centuries to come. These constellations of Fire and Water had ominous implications for the days ahead.

Lacking solid history, the Arabs of the Middle East proliferated legend. The most ancient tradition about the Great Pyramid is that it was erected to memorialize a tremendous cataclysm in the planetary system which affected the globe with fire and flooding.

Arab authors recount that the pyramids were built before the deluge by a king who had a vision that the world would be turned upside down, and that the stars would fall from the sky. According to

The Neck of the Bull

these Arab sources, the king placed in the pyramids accounts of all he had learnt from the wisest men of the times, including the secrets of astronomy, complete with tables of the stars, geometry, and physics, treatises on precious stones, and certain machines, including celestial spheres and terrestrial globes. They also speak of "Malleable glass."[39]

According to this account, the pyramids were built before the Great Flood, before the globe was impacted by fire and flood. They were built before the Age of Aries Fire Constellation, bringing Indo-European invasions and militant self-destruction. The Water Constellation Pisces swept away wisdom and learning in its ecumenical undertow. The stars did fall from the sky. Astrology, astronomy and even science itself were lost as disciplines. The world was literally turned upside down. Today we use Sun signs to identify the month during which we were born. The Egyptians marked each month by the Full Moon, the designation exactly opposite the system we use today.

The Book of Revelation was being used as an informative primer for various traditions, to highlight their value as tools of wisdom, a time capsule preserving human knowledge for future generations. We've seen this list before. The New Jerusalem coming down from heaven, its walls rising up to the same height, three gates on each side. The celestial stream flows from the throne through the middle of the

---

39 *Secrets of the Great Pyramid,* Peter Tompkins, Harper and Row, p. 217. .

city. Herbology, gemology, numerology, astronomy, astrology, exaltations, and fixed star observation are to be found in a single revelatory package. The mainstays of the occult tradition, practiced by healers, wizards, and witches through the generations are here being venerated as disciplines to be preserved and protected—a dramatic reversal of the centuries-long Church dogmas that would follow.

At the end of Revelation, the spirit speaking through John returns to images from Isaiah, and so shall we. The New Jerusalem comes from out of Heaven. The mountain is the path the stars, planets and constellations all follow as they ascend and descend daily through the sky. Each has its voice, and collectively they speak the Word of God.

> *"In the days to come*
> *the mountain of the Temple of Yahweh*
> *shall tower above the mountains*
> *and be lifted higher than the hills.*
> *All the nations will stream to it,*
> *Peoples without number will come to it; and they will say:*
> *"Come, let us go up to the mountain of Yahweh,*
> *to the Temple of the God of Jacob*
> *that he may teach us his ways*
> *so that we may walk his paths;*
> *since the Law will go out from Zion,*
> *and the oracle of Yahweh from Jerusalem."*
> *"He will wield authority over the nations*
> *and adjudicate between many peoples;*
> *these will hammer their swords into plowshares,*
> *their spears into sickles.*
> *Nation will not lift sword against nation,*
> *There will be no more training for war.*[40]

---

40 Isaiah 2:2–4.

How Great His Signs

After *"chewing on the scroll"* for some time we've become more familiar with the general picture and its mechanism. We have seen the Stream and a few of its tributaries. They all lead to the sea, marking a period of time we think of as our history.

Let's pause for a quick review. In a few short pages we have covered a lot of territory. Let's homogenize a few of these themes. We've been looking at many archetypes attempting to interpret their various weaves.

> *How great his signs,*
> *how mighty his wonders!*
> *His kingdom is an everlasting kingdom,*
> *his empire endures age after age.*[1]

For literally decades I have watched the heavens, studying both scripture and historical records in an attempt to understand what it was that we were being told. I have followed where the path has led. Piece by piece the picture has slowly revealed a few of its secrets.

We stand on the threshold of a New Age and a new vibration. We are seeing the elements of this puzzle come into focus together with its warnings. Now it is time to reveal the results of our test of the hypothesis.

The following extract is a column I posted in February of 2013 on my Internet newsletter, *Athena's Web*. It was part of my regular series, a review of what we had gone over in detail in several earlier issues. You have seen these clues before.

---

1 Daniel 3:33.

The Star of Bethlehem

Star in the East

After Jesus had been born at Bethlehem in Judaea during the reign of King Herod, some wise men came to Jerusalem from the east. "Where is the infant king of the Jews?" they asked. "We saw his star in the east and have come to do him homage." When King Herod heard this he was perturbed, and so was the whole of Jerusalem. He called together all the chief priests and the scribes of the people, and inquired of them where the Christ was to be born. "At Bethlehem in Judaea," they told him, "for this is what the prophet wrote:

> *And you, Bethlehem, in the land of Judah,*
> *you are by no means least*
> *among the leaders of Judah,*
> *for out of you will come a leader*
> *who will shepherd my people Israel."*

Then Herod summoned the wise men to see him privately. He asked them the exact date on which the star had appeared, and sent them on to Bethlehem. "Go and find out all about the child," he said, "and when you have found him, let me know, so that I too may go and do him homage." Having listened to what the king had to say, they set out. And there in front of them was the star they had seen rising: it went forward and halted over the place where the child was. The sight of the star filled them with delight, and going into the house they saw the child with his mother Mary, and falling to their knees they did him homage.[1]

This passage from the second chapter of the Book of Matthew is one of the most stunning, and often quoted, endorsements of astrology in the entire Bible. Its general sense is that a star in the East spoke

---

1 Matthew 2:1–11

to the astrologers, alerting and guiding them to the birthplace of the new king. Based upon this information, they traveled many miles to a distant land to pay homage to the child.

In our sequence on the "End Times," outlined in the discussion of the Book of Daniel, it naturally follows that after the end there should be a new beginning. Astrologically speaking, after the end of the Age of Aries, the Age of Pisces began in earnest. With this new heavenly testament came a Messiah, bringing the gospel of heaven's new celestial outline. Although the historical records have long been combed for some unusual stellar event in trying to find the Star of Bethlehem—whether supernova, comet, or other occurrence—it seems that none save the astrologers took note of this portent. This implies that this was no more than a natural, nightly configuration involving the planets and heavens we all know and with which we are familiar.

If Matthew had recorded the exact date which was given Herod by the wise men, we would not now have the confusion which has risen around the timing of the messianic birth. Throughout this book, we have discussed the larger framework of the "Ages," the transitioning of different epochs, the interplay of celestial and terrestrial phenomena. We know that with the beginning of the first millennium, the epoch of the Sign of the Fish had arrived. But some inner trigger was needed to set off the larger mechanism. This is the series of events described in the opening work of the New Testament.

An Alternate Point of View

We must pause for a moment to first acknowledge the dark underside, the flip side of the coin that we will soon be examing in some detail. It is our contention that the birth of the Messiah was foretold by wondrous, but natural, signs in the heavens that were recognized by the wise men of old.

However, this line of interpretation stands in stark contrast to the views of some others who have also studied this phenomenon and have drawn far different conclusions about the role of the Ancient Wisdom in the story of the Christ child. Here then is a more sinister view of the role of astrology in the Bible story. I obviously reject this vision, but present it here to offer the reader some balance before we continue.

> The "astrologers from eastern parts," hence from the neighborhood of Babylon, whose visit to King Herod after the birth of Jesus resulted in the slaughter of all the male infants in Bethlehem, were obviously not servants or worshipers of the true God. As to the "star" seen by them, many suggestions have been given as to its having been a comet, a meteor, a supernova, or, more popularly, a conjunction of planets. None of such bodies could logically have "come to a stop above where the young child was," thereby identifying the one house in the village of Bethlehem where the child was found. It is also notable that only these pagan astrologers "saw" the star. Their condemned practice of astrology and the adverse results of their visit, placing in danger the life of the future Messiah, certainly allow for, and even make advisable, the consideration of their having been directed by a source adverse to God's purposes as relating to the promised Messiah.[2]

With that necessary bit of "full disclosure" housekeeping accomplished, let us proceed to a more upbeat and, I believe, more accurate presentation of the role of astrology and astronomy in helping to unveil the deeper mysteries of the Bible.

Synoptic Vision

There are many astronomical contenders for the claim of the original "Star of Bethlehem." The most obvious phenomena, as mentioned in the *Watch Tower Bible* quote above, are shooting stars, comets, and novae, or possibly a conjunction of planets. History records several of these celestial observations around the time in question.

There was a particularly bright comet that appeared in 44 BC, shortly after the death of Caesar. Shakespeare makes a reference to it in one of his plays. In 17 BC, there was another comet that was visible for

2 *Watch Tower Bible*, p. 1033.

an evening throughout the Mediterranean; and another appeared in AD 66, shortly before Nero committed suicide. In the Orient, the Chinese give a lengthy description of Halley's Comet in 12 BC, although there is no Mediterranean mention of it. As far as Novae are concerned, there are only two listed around this period of time—in 134 BC and AD 173. The problem with any of these phenomena, though, is that none of them are capable of coming to a halt.

> *And there in front of them was the star they had seen rising:*
> *it went forward and halted over the place where the child was.*[3]

On December 17th, 1603, Johannes Kepler was watching an alignment in the heavens—an approaching Jupiter Saturn conjunction in the sign Pisces. While later looking through his notes, Kepler remembered something he had read by the rabbinic writer Abarbanel, referring to an unusual influence which Jewish astrologers were said to have ascribed to this alignment. They stated that the Messiah would appear when there was a conjunction of Saturn and Jupiter in Pisces. Kepler wondered if, in fact, this could have been the original Star of Bethlehem. He determined the positions of these two planets around the time of the birth of Christ. Since Herod died in 4 BC, the Messiah must have been born before this date. Kepler calculated that the triple conjunction of Jupiter and Saturn (they aligned three times in the course of a year) occurred in 6 BC. (It was, in fact, 7 BC.) Kepler felt this might have been the original "star" signaling the birth of the Christ child; but which one of the three alignments? Because Kepler was both an astronomer and astrologer, some of his ideas were a little too radical for contemporary society. His musings were forgotten until the 19th century. His idea is now, however, one of the most popular contenders for the fabled "Star of Bethlehem."

Unbeknownst to our *Watch Tower Bible* commentator, it's obvious to any astrologer that a star "moving forward and then halting" is retrograde motion; when planets as seen from the Earth from the geocentric

---

3 Matthew 2:10.

perspective, appear to station and reverse direction. This motion is lost in heliocentric astronomy where planets always move "forward" around the Sun. Computers now ascertain planetary motion with considerable mathematical accuracy. After the first Jupiter Saturn conjunction in 7 BC, Saturn went on to pivot within a degree of the Midheaven (due South or highest point in the sky for transiting planets) over Bethlehem. That is within four minutes of 24 hours of being exactly overhead at the birthplace at the time of the pivot—precisely as the text says! As a fraction, that would be the equivalent of one chance out of 360.

Why should it be an astrologer, rather than an astronomer, who makes this fairly simple connection? The answer is easy. Like our for-bearers of old, we look at heaven with the same eye—seeing it in the same way, from a geocentric point of view. And besides ...

Astrologers were the first to realize its implications.

The Birth of the Messiah

The precision of Saturn's pivot over Bethlehem has a multitude of implications. First, it defines the initial Jupiter Saturn conjunction as the "star" referenced in the Book of Matthew. Second, it marks the year and season (but not necessarily the day) in which Jesus was born. (It is possible the Messiah was born under the exact Jupiter Saturn conjunction, but this is not specifically stated in the Bible.) Third, it provides the precise day the Magi left Jerusalem and set out for Bethlehem, having just talked with King Herod. And fourth, it hints at the predictive accuracy of ancient astronomy.

Saturn's pivot actually occurred just prior to sunrise, as the skies were beginning to lighten, precisely the time of day that people might set out for day journeys before the hot summer sun is high in the sky over the Levant,[4] where they could see this "star" pivoting.

---

4 Levant |ləˈvantləˈvänt| archaic: the eastern part of the Mediterranean with its islands and neighboring countries. ORIGIN: late 15th century, from French, literally "rising," present participle of lever "to lift," used as a noun in the sense "point of sunrise, east."

Putting Things in Perspective

Looking at the Star of Bethlehem, examining its secrets, if we can ascertain the date of any portion of this alignment, it would provide a wonderful tool in helping to understand the framework of Matthew and the New Testament.

Saturn and Jupiter are the two outermost visible planets. They are furthest from the Sun. They were used as one of many "hour hands" to mark the passage of extended periods of time by those who observed heavenly motion.

In the Bible, the Saturn Jupiter conjunction of 7 BC was first observed by astrologers, the Wise Men.

Saturn and Jupiter form conjunctions every 20 years. For an extended period of time, they fall in signs of the same element. In one 200-year period, from 225 to 7 BC, this conjunction occurred in water signs (Cancer, Scorpio or Pisces) for ten out of twelve alignments. This is the sort of thing that catches astrologers' attention, as did this one.

There were several Saturn Jupiter conjunctions in the constellation Pisces, the sign of the (then) upcoming Astrological Age. Such Piscean conjunctions occurred in 126, 66, and 7 BC, as well as AD 54. The prophets had much to speculate about how this combination might manifest itself. The rabbinic writer Abarbanel felt a new king (Saturn is the planet of worldly rulership) would appear for the Jews, a people ruled by Pisces.

Saturn Jupiter conjunctions in Pisces were all the rage at the time. People were pondering both it and the New Age—just as we now ponder what Aquarius will bring. Obviously, it caught the attention of the three Magi. But does it follow that astrologers might have had a special interest in, and noted the position of, a planet's station (the planet going retrograde, i.e. "stopping" and changing direction)?

A little more than one hundred years after the events of 7 BC, the first surviving comprehensive work on astronomy, astrology, and geography was written by Claudius Ptolemy. His astronomical observations were made between AD 125 and 140. For the next thousand years and beyond, the works of this author were to set the industry standard for both excellence and science. In a chapter on prediction, taken from a former work by Hipparchus (190–126 BC), Ptolemy claims that eclipses are the most auspicious:

> ... the strongest and principal cause... exists in the ecliptical conjunctions of the Sun and Moon ...[5]

Ptolemy then goes on to say,

> "One part of the observations, required in forming predictions in cases of this nature, relates to the locality of the event, and *points out the cities* of countries liable to be influenced by particular eclipses, or by *occasional continued stations of certain planets*, which at times remain for a certain period in one situation. These planets are *Saturn*, Jupiter, and Mars; and *they furnish portentous indications, when they are stationary.*" (empasis added)[6]

Ptolemy was here describing established Chaldean and Egyptian doctrine, outlining precise instructions of what to watch for as determined by ancient astrologers.

The Saturn station (pivot) occurring over Bethlehem in 7 BC as recorded by Matthew, was a text book case of what Ptolemy described. Both astronomical and historical evidence suggest that the Saturn pivot of 7 BC is the one mentioned at the outset of the New Testament. Can we now locate the date of that event more precisely than just the year?

The Child in the Manger

> *"Where is he that is born King of the Jews? For we have seen his star in the east, and are come to worship him ..."* When Herod the king had heard these things, he was troubled, and all Jerusalem with him.[7]

For these Eastern astronomers, the identity of the newborn King

---

5 Ptolemy, *Tetrabiblos* Chapter V, p. 53.
6 Ptolemy, *Tetrabiblos* Chapter V, p. 53.
7 Matthew 2:2–3

of the Jews must have been the first and obvious question. They may have been surprised to find that it aroused nothing but startled concern in Jerusalem. (The Jews of the Holy City were either unaware of the ancient schools of astrology or those who were chosen to keep their knowledge secret from Herod and the masses for some reason.[8])

> Herod, the hated tyrant, was alarmed. The announcement of a new-born king brought his sovereignty into question. The people on the other hand were pleasurably startled, as appears from other historical sources. About a year after this conjunction of planets which has just been described, a strong Messianic movement came into being. Flavius Josephus, the Jewish historian, records that about this time a rumour went around that God had decided to bring the rule of the Roman foreigners to an end and that a sign from heaven had announced the coming of a Jewish king. Herod, who had been appointed by the Romans, was in fact not a Jew but an Idumaean.[9]

The rumor was correct, although the end of Roman rule would take centuries to accomplish and the Jewish king would come to rule over a more spiritual realm.

"We saw his star rising ..."

Astrologers today basically study the same principles that were at work two thousand years ago when Ptolemy's *Tetrabiblos* was written. What would astrologers have looked for as they gazed heavenward?

---

8 It seems obvious that some Jews were familiar with astrology. During their period of captivity and since the time of Nebuchadnezzar, many thousands had lived in Babylon. Some had even studied at the School of Astrology in Sippar. For an extended period, these two cultures had coexisted and were familiar with each other's wisdom. With time and location interweaving the two traditions, it makes sense that the Chaldeans (the astrologers or magi) might have been familiar with Jewish writings and prophecies.
9 Werner Keller, *The Bible as History*, p. 330

First, they knew a New Age was dawning. The vernal equinox was shifting out of the constellation Aries into Pisces. Rumors reported that the Saturn Jupiter conjunction in Pisces foretold the birth of a new Jewish king. Saturn, according to several older sources, was the planet associated with the Jews. Tacitus went so far as to equate Saturn with the god of the Jews. According to an old Jewish tradition, Saturn protected Israel.

And when one considers Saturn literally went forward and halted over the place where the Messiah was born, this is a simple astronomical observation. However, its importance was not generally noted by any except astrologers.

... for we have seen his star in the East ...

The helical rising of a star is seen when it first appears out of the glare of the rising morning Sun, only to quickly disappear in the growing daylight. The next morning, it is visible a little longer, and so on until it slowly ascends in the early morning/night sky. A planet must be between 7 and 15 degrees ahead of the Sun to rise helically. Jupiter's helical rising in 7 BC occurred during the first week of March. Saturn made its helical appearance in the middle of the same month. March represented the start of their observational cycle—when the Magi would have seen the "star in the East" from Babylon at sunrise.

Every astronomer/priest knew that Jupiter is faster and brighter than Saturn, and was about to catch and conjunct it. The first alignment between these two in 7 BC occurred at the end of May. Since this was the celestial signal which had alerted the magi, it's probable that the Messiah was actually born on, or within a few days of May 29, 7 BC, however, the Bible does not stipulate this. After the conjunction, Saturn and Jupiter moved "forward" in the heavens until the end of the first week in July, when Saturn pivoted over Bethlehem beginning its retrograde motion. Ptolemy states that the pivots of Saturn, Jupiter, and Mars were auspicious—with the cities over which they pivot being most strongly affected.

The one date in this series that we can ascertain with a fair degree of confidence—if we believe the story the Bible records for us—is the pivot over Bethlehem. This was the day the magi left Jerusalem to witness the star's "coming to a halt" over the place where the child was born. It suggests that the Christ Child had already been born. This would have been July 7th, 7 BC in the Julian calendar. The timing makes it improbable that the legendary late December "Christmas birth" of the child was, in fact, the true birth date—if our seasonal timetable is correct.

Christmas Day

Christendom celebrates Christmas from December 24th–25th. Astronomers and historians, secular and ecclesiastical, are unanimous that December 25th of the year one was not the authentic date of the birth of Christ, neither as regards the year nor the day. The responsibility for this error lies at the door of the Scythian monk Dionysius Exiguus, who lived in Rome and made several mistakes and miscalculations. In the year AD 533, he was instructed to fix the beginning of the new era by working backwards. But he forgot to count the year zero which should have been inserted between 1 BC and AD 1. He also overlooked the four years when the Roman emperor Augustus had reigned under his own name Octavian.

... when Jesus was born ... in the days of Herod the king ...

In 40 BC Herod was designated king of Judaea by the Romans. His reign ended with his death in 4 BC. Jesus must therefore have been born before 4 BC.[10]

The Mystique of the Star

No star has captured the attention of more people, provoked more debate, or inspired more wonder than the Star of Bethlehem. Prophecy

---

10 Werner Keller, *The Bible as History*, p. 331.

stated that it signaled the birth of a new king; one that, as it turned out, was to rule Western civilization for the next two thousand years.

We have been examining the theory that the Saturn station—following the first Jupiter Saturn conjunction of 7 BC—was in fact the star heralding the birth of the Messiah and the one which the Wise Men followed.

The literary evidence comes from the Book of Matthew, the first work of the New Testament. One common misconception people have is the image of a sudden brilliant light, or a powerful radiance in the sky associated with the Star of Bethlehem. Quite simply, this is not what Matthew says and is nowhere mentioned in the Bible. It seems that this brilliance has been grafted retroactively onto the Star. It is not documented by scripture. A Saturn Jupiter conjunction, even if exact, is not much more visually dynamic than Jupiter by itself. Saturn is often mistaken for one of the "fixed" stars of heaven if measured in terms of brilliance alone. It is because it is a "wanderer" that it is distinctive. It moves against the backdrop of the constellations, but is not that "big" as seen from Earth's sky. None but the magi seem to have noticed this Star.

We examined historical evidence that Saturn was thought to be linked to the Jews, such as Tacitus' claim that it was it their "God." Astrological textbooks of the time taught students to look for the precise stations of the planets, noting the specific cities over which they pivoted. We even have evidence that the Eastern astrological schools paid particular attention to the Jupiter Saturn conjunction of 7 BC.

In 1925, a German scholar by the name of P. Schnabel deciphered a number of Neo-Babylonian cuneiform "papers" from a famous institution of the ancient world; the School of Astrology at Sippar in Babylonia.

> Among endless series of prosaic dates of observations he (Schnabel) came across a note about the position of the planets in the constellation of Pisces. Jupiter and Saturn are carefully marked in over a period of five months. Reckoned in our calendar, the year was 7 BC.[11]

---

11 Werner Keller, *The Bible as History*, p. 328.

This represents intriguing historical evidence within astrological circles in the East. We have documented interest in this conjunction, and have asserted that at least three of the magi thought enough of heaven's signs to make the trip to the Jewish promised land to witness and pay homage to the new born king.

In the series of three conjunctions between Saturn and Jupiter in 7 BC, there is only one time that a planet could have moved forward and then halted. This is the initial retrograde pivot. Both Saturn and Jupiter pivoted after their first conjunction, but only Saturn's pivot occurred over Israel/Palestine.

Is it not curious that the celestial indicator which marked the inception of the Age of Pisces and the Christian Epoch should be rediscovered as the new millennium beagn to open? This is good news, and bodes well for the future.

Somebody should tell the Pope.

Eastern Star

"We have seen his star in the east"[12] said the Wise Men, according to the Authorized Version. The translation is however incorrect. The words "in the east" are, in the original, "En té anatolé"—the Greek singular. But elsewhere, "the east" is represented by "anatolaí"—the Greek plural. The singular form "anatolé" has, it is maintained, quite a special astronomical significance. It implies the observation of the early rising of the star, the so-called heliacal rising. The translators of the Authorized Version could not have known this.

When "en té anatolé" is translated properly, Matt 2:2 reads as follows:

We have seen his star appear in the first rays of the dawn.

That would have corresponded exactly with the astronomical facts, if the constellation under discussion, and this, of course, is the big

---

12 Matthew 2:2.

question, was the Star of the Wise Men, the Star of Bethlehem, the Christmas Star.[13]

Away in a Manger

Now at this time Caesar Augustus issued a decree for a census of the whole world to be taken. This census, the first, took place while Quirinius was governor of Syria, and everyone went to his own town to be registered. So Joseph set out from the town of Nazareth in Galilee and traveled up to Judea, to the town of David called Bethlehem, since he was of David's house and line, in order to be registered together with Mary, his betrothed, who was with child. While they were there the time came for her to have her child, and she gave birth to her child, her first born. She wrapped him in swaddling clothes, and laid him in a manger because there was no room for him at the inn.[14]

As our astronomical evidence presented above has indicated, Jesus was probably born between the helical rising of Jupiter and Saturn in early March of 7 BC and July 7, 7 BC, when Saturn "pivoted," or began its retrograde motion over Bethlehem. Matthew initially indicated the heliacal rising in these words:

... we saw his star as it rose ...[15]

Matthew continues and identifies this as the sign by which the astronomers were led to discover the birth of the Messiah:

And there in front of them was the star they had seen rising; it went forward and halted over the place where the child was.[16]

The historical data for the birth of the Messiah at this time coordinates as follows: Augustus Caesar ruled from 30 BC to AD 14, which

---

13 Werner Keller, *The Bible as History*, p. 331
14 Luke 2:1–7
15 Matthew 2:2
16 Matthew 2:9

provides a general framework. We know that Herod died in 4 BC. If he indeed ordered the slaughter of innocents after the Messiah was born, it must have been prior to 4 BC. The first census took place while Quirinius was governor of Syria. So this narrows the window of the Messiah's birth to between 8 and 6 BC.

The details arguing that the Saturn Jupiter conjunction was the probable Star of Bethlehem have been discussed. And we have surmised that if this alignment did indeed mark the birth of the Christ child, it was probably fairly close to May 29th, 7 BC, near the first exact conjunction (there were three that year) of Jupiter and Saturn.

Matthew and Luke tell us quite a bit about the birth of the Christ child. But I have often wondered if there wasn't more in the allegory of the birth; if scripture didn't hold some additional clues in the telling of the tale. The image which stands out to me is that of the Christ child's birth in the manger.

There is, in fact, a star grouping known as the "Manger." It is located in the constellation Cancer, and together with its two closest companions—Asellus Borealis and Asellus Australus or the Northern and Southern Donkeys—it is a manger between two asses.

The question is: were there any significant conjunctions to this stellar grouping between March and July of 7 BC which might reflect the story of the birth?

We know that the Moon makes a full circuit of the zodiac every month, and would have aligned with this cluster four times during this four-and-a-half month period. Astrologically speaking, it would make sense for the Moon to step into this role—as it could be celestially interpreted as the birth (Moon) of the child in the Manger (conjunct Praesaepe, the star known as the manger); but since the Moon makes an entire circuit of the zodiac once every month, this alone would seem doubtful as a sole indicator.

Were there any other more significant alignments during the spring of 7 BC which might better be considered to fulfill the announcement of the birth of the Messiah by the heavens?

On May 30th, Venus conjuncted Praesaepe—also known as the Beehive Cluster or Manger. On the following evening the Moon con-

juncted both Venus and this stellar grouping within 48 hours of Saturn
and Jupiter's alignment to form our Star of Bethlehem.

Among the traditional astrological interpretations for these three
Cancerian groupings are these: stabs, wounds, and the danger of a
violent death.

> *While they were there the time came for her to have her child, and she*
> *gave birth to her child, her first born. She wrapped him in swaddling*
> *clothes, and laid him in a manger because there was no room for him at*
> *the inn.* "[17]

Matthew and Luke tell us about the birth of the Christ child. But
is it possible that the "story" is a heavenly reflection, a "mythological"
recreation of events taking place not only on Earth, but in Heaven as
well? If so, our chief celestial clue may be the image of the birth in the
manger.

We have discussed the star grouping known as the "Manger,"
located in the constellation Cancer, together with its two close companions, Asellus Borealis and Australus (Northern and Southern
Donkeys). The question is, where there any significant conjunctions
to this stellar grouping between March (when Saturn and Jupiter
emerged out of the rays of the Sun in the "East"), and July, 7 BC, when
the "astronomers" of the time saw Saturn "halting" (retrograding) over
the place of the Messiah's birth?

On May 30th, 7 BC, Venus conjuncted this position, the only visible
planet to do so during this window of time. On the following evening,
May 31st, 7 BC, the Moon joined the alignment and conjuncted both
Venus and the Manger, just as Saturn and Jupiter aligned to form our
now famous Star of Bethlehem. If this mythological application is
correct, we have narrowed the astronomical margin to within a period
of about 48 hours of the birth of the Christ Child simply using some
of the imagery supplied by the Good Book.

---

17 Luke 2:1–7

Athena's Web: It Is Written

In each age the lives and manners of men are different and God has established for each age a definite span of time which is determined by the circuit of the Great Year. Whenever this circuit comes to an end and another begins some marvelous sign appears either on earth or in heaven so that it becomes at once clear to those who have made a thorough study of the subject that men of a different character and way of life have now come into the world and the gods will be either more or less concerned with this new race than they were with their predecessors. All sorts of changes occur, they say, as one age succeeds another and in particular with regard to the art of divination one can observe that there are times when it rises in prestige and its predictions are accurate because clear and unmistakable signs are sent from heaven; and then again in another age it is not held in much honor, since for the most part its practitioners are relying on mere guesswork and are trying to grasp the future with senses that have become blunt and dim. This, at all events, was the story told by the wisest men among the Etruscans who were thought to know more than most about such things.[1]

The die is cast. *Omega* has come and gone. Did you catch it?

---

1 *Athena's Web*, February 15, 2013.

APPENDIX THREE

Moon Mail: 2013

For years now, *Athena's Web* has been alluding to the *Alpha* and the *Omega*; in columns, during presentations, and in independent publications. A recent *Moon Mail* essay, which went out with the New Moon on February 10, 2013 talked about it. Here is that long column verbatim:

Moon Mail (2013) on the New Moon

"I am the Alpha and the Omega,
the First and the Last
The Beginning and the End ... "[1]

... of Pisces, the constellation and sign of the Fish. Of the two Fish of Pisces, the ecliptic, (annual path of the Sun), runs closer to the Western Fish; the one that both rises and sets before its celestial northern twin. But this Fish, together with its cord, was described somewhat differently by the Chinese. This "ribbon," "cord," or "fishing line" was marked by the seven stars we have come to know as the "Seven Seals." As the Vernal Equinox "rolled over" each of these points, their influences were "released" and bathed the Earth much like the mythic "arrows" of Apollo, Artemis or Cupid found their mark.

But the Chinese saw these stars as a different set of images. The Seven Seals were thought to be *Wae Ping*, a "Rolled Screen." It consisted of the stars $\alpha, \xi, \nu, \mu, \zeta, \varepsilon$, and δ (alpha, xi, nu, mu, zeta, epsilon and delta), all of which are considered to be part of the "cord" in the West, while the balance of the stars are those comprising what we see as the "Fish."

---

1 Rev. 22:13.

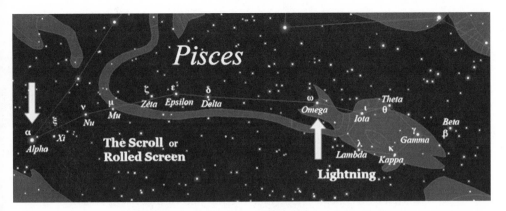

*The Seven Seals, marking Alpha, together with
the Eighth Seal, marking Omega*

B (beta), a four and a half magnitude star, is given by *Al Achsasi* as *Fum al Samakah*, the Fish's Mouth, descriptive of its position near that feature in the western-most of the two. With γ, θ, ι and ω (gamma, theta, iota and omega) it was the Chinese *Peih Leth*, Lightning.

Omega Piscium stands as a boundary stone in the corner of a celestial field. It marks where one's property ends and another begins, or in this case, where one vibration ends and another begins.

For WebHeads who have been following the column for years, this is what we've been talking about. From March into June, 1995 the Web explored precisely this treatise in detail.

The day is past, the symbolism is in.

Ask any astronomer.

When did *Omega Pisces* reach zero hours, zero minutes and zero seconds of Right Ascension? Right Ascension is the measuring stick astronomers used to track the stars.

We now have a new eastern star.

It's that easy.

Starting on March 17th, 1995 and running for fourteen consecutive weeks through June 16th (1995) we went over the implications, in detail, Seal by Seal and finished by determining the date when this theory would be tested.

At that time we said 2013 was when *Omega* would be triggered.

Alpha Piscium marked the start of the new vibration, a New Age for those living a little over two thousand years ago. As far as *Revelation* is concerned the mythic "Finger of God" seems to point to the Romans. The theater is certainly set on a Roman stage. We can date these "Seals" astronomically, and did. If these dates are accurate and historical events unfolded under each Seal, when was the next date in the future? When was the test of the hypothesis?

The *First of the Seven Seals* occurred when the Vernal Equinox aligned with *Alpha Piscium*, marking the start of the new epoch, the then New Age. This was when Rome began its period of political ascendancy. The other six seals also triggered major events in Rome's and later the Church's history which we more fully covered in 1995. The *Second Seal* was the War with Hannibal, the *Third Seal* was Tiberius coming to power, the *Fourth Seal* an extended period of time historically described as the "nadir" of Roman civilization. The *Fifth Seal* was the Lombards, *the Sixth* the Vikings, and *the Seventh* was the secular schism of the Church into Roman Catholic and Greek Orthodox.

The formula is simple. You use the astronomy to determine the date historically. Then you start your research. It has been my experience that there is a turnover, the beginning of a new dynasty that occurs as a "new guiding star" orients us to a particular focus. *Omega* (ω) *Piscium* is thus both the End of the "*Scroll*" (referred to once in Revelation as "the Eighth Seal"), and the beginning of "*Lightning*," just as it is the end of the cord and beginning of the western Fish (the tail constellationally). You might be interested to learn that the prophets of the Hebrew Bible called the Scroll, "*God's Curse*."

From Moon Mail 1995

The following essay is from a column I published in *Moon Mail* in June of 1995. I offer it verbatim,. This was the end of our series on Revelation for that year.[2]

---

2 *Moon Mail,* June 16th, 1995.

The Last Word

But the final clue we will leave with you is from the Book of Matthew, where Jesus is being questioned about the end of time.

"Tell us, when is this going to happen, and what will be the sign of your coming and of the end of the world?"[3]

And after several other clues, he states…

"… because the coming of the Son of Man (Aquarius) will be like lightning striking in the east and flashing far into the west."[4]

The Vernal Equinox in heaven marks East, both astronomically and astrologically. According to the Chinese, *Omega Piscium* is the star that marks the beginning of the sub-set *Peih Leih*- Lightning.

"When lightning strikes in 2013; the New Age dawns."[5]

That was back in 1995. In 1992, I had offered the presentation to the fifty astronomers and physicists in Northfield, Mass when I was challenged on the letter-dating of the stars. In 2003, we talked about this issue in a two-hour video presentation on the Ages for Greenfield Community Television. This is not a recent development.

Here's a quote from an independent publisher for whom I had written an article in 2012 for her annual 2013 publication.

"According to Cerow's research and calculations, the shift of the Great Ages will be in full force when the Vernal Point reaches Omega Piscium on February 11, 2013, some 8 weeks after the Winter Solstice of 2012."

— *Janet's Planets, 2013*—The Age of Aquarius, p. 88.

---

3 Matthew 24:3.
4 Matthew 24:27.
5 *Athena's Web*, June 16, 1995.

Pope Benedict XVI

When "Lightning strikes in the East" is a moment in TIME. That time—spoken of in 1992, 1995, 2003, 2013, and on many other occasions within the strands of the Web—has pinpointed the mark.

Just as the *New York Times* said in their opening sentence,

February 11, 2013: VATICAN CITY — The decision, delivered in Latin and in unemotional tones by Pope Benedict XVI to a gathering of cardinals on Monday, came *"like a bolt out of the blue,"* one of the participants said, and it soon ricocheted around the world."[6]

The Pope quit. *Alpha* started the Age, *Omega* ends it. [end *Moon Mail* quote]

—*Moon Mail*, February 10, 2013

---

6 *New York Times,* February 11, 2013.

Lightning striking the Vatican on the same day the Pope quit.

The Age of Aquarius[1]

by Don Cerow, NCGR IV

Welcome to the Age of Aquarius.[2]

We are a generation that is perched on the dawn of a new epoch, a new vibration. The world is changing. Everything from politics to industry to our mortgages turns on a new pivot, and we are lucky enough to be able to witness the unfolding.

There are those who feel as though the Age has already begun. Others believe that the Age is not yet here, and the called for changes have not yet fully unfolded. Both are correct.

As we look around us, electricity fills the air. Lights, power, technology, refrigeration, computers, smart phones, microchips, and science are all manifestations of the New Age at work, of a brave new world already (up and running).

But the use of fossil fuels, oil, coal, and natural gas, the inability of Congress to get things done due to party allegiances, the growing intensity of storms and the general weather patterns, are all indications

---

1–This article originally appeared in *Janet's Plan-its*™ *2013 Celestial Planner Easy-to-Use Astrology Calendar,* © 2012 Janet Booth (AstrologyBooth.com).

2–The Great Ages are stages of cultural development that are part of a very long cycle known as the Great Year. Each Age is associated with a zodiac constellation and fosters associated activities. (Writing and improved means of transportation were developed during the Age of Gemini. Great monuments were built during the bull-worshipping Age of Taurus. Metallurgy and weaponry advanced during the warlike Age of Aries. The Age of Pisces has been dominated by the Christian religion, symbolized by the fish.) The timing for an Age is shown by the position of the Sun each year at the start of spring (the vernal equinox). This point shifts backwards relative to the zodiac constellations at a rate of about one degree every 72 years. Each year's position precedes the prior year's slightly; thus the phenomenon is known as the Precession of the Equinoxes.

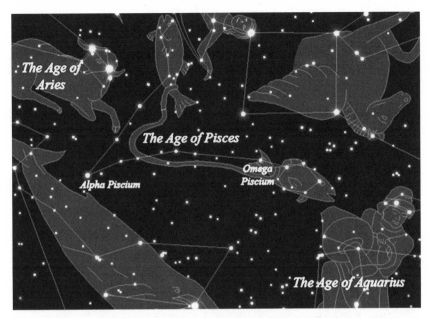

Alpha Piscium and Omega Piscium are the stars that observationally "benchmark" the Age of Pisces.

Revelation 22:13 says, "I am the Alpha and the Omega, the First and the Last, the Beginning and the End." When Revelation was written in the first century AD, the "New Age" (Pisces) stretched out before them, describing what the future would hold.

According to the author's research and calculations, the shift of the Great Ages will be in full force when the Vernal Point reaches Omega Piscium on February 11, 2013, some 8 weeks after the Winter Solstice of 2012. (Watch the Vernal Equinox and its Full Moon of 2013 (on March 27) for dramatic triggers to these celestial mandates.)

that the Age of Pisces is not yet over. We are building to a crescendo with the warming of the planet being the substantial catalyst that inaugurates these changes.

According to the Bible, the new Age will be special, where we foster a renewed connection with the Divine, where we see God in each other and treat the planet with respect, nurturing both her and her resources in such a way that they sustain us, both for now and for the children of the future.

Toren van Babel (Tower of Babel), 1565 • by Pieter Breugel de Oude
    Genesis 11 refers to a world-wide city that was under construction but
beginning to wind down at the end of its epoch. The pillars of civilization
were crumbling at the end of the Age of Gemini, an AIR sign. Gemini is
communication. These are the tower of Babel references where everyone
speaks a single language, and that language is the symbolic language of
the sky, stars and planets, astrology.

Here is the Book of Revelation's look at the coming Age, and what it
will mean for humanity. It marks the passing of the old Age, Pisces, here
referred to as the "sea" and "sadness." Pisces is a water sign that is said to
rule the oceans.

21:1 *Then I saw a new heaven and a new earth; the first heaven had*
disappeared now, and there was no longer any sea. I saw the holy city,
and the new Jerusalem, coming down from God out of heaven, as beau-
tiful as a bride all dressed for her husband. Then I heard a loud voice call

*The New Jerusalem,
1897 • by Gustave Doré
We are entering
Aquarius, another
AIR sign, and we will
return to building a
world-wide community
once again, referred to in
Revelation as the New
City, the New Jerusalem.
God broke apart the
world wide community
that was being built at
the end of the Age of
Gemini (read* The View
Over Atlantis), *and we
will start rebuilding it
again once we move the
oil dynasty and all its
many support industries
to the back burners.*

*from the throne, "You see this city? Here God lives among men. He will
make his home among them; they shall be his people, and he will be their
God; his name is God-with-them. He will wipe away all tears from
their eyes; there will be no more death, and no mourning or sadness. The
world of the past is gone."*

Aquarius is the new heaven as the Vernal Equinox moves into the
territory of that constellation. Different people have different opinions,
but it is generally felt that the precessional cycle lasts anywhere from
24,000 to 26,000 years. Since there are twelve signs to the zodiac, each
"Age" lasts from about 2,000 to 2,200 years apiece. In the West, the Vernal
Equinox (also known as the East Point or Spring) is used as the 'marker'

to determine where we are. For the last two thousand years, this marker has been moving through the constellation Pisces, and is currently in the process of entering the celestial territory of Aquarius. Precessional motion moves in reverse order (Aries, Pisces, Aquarius) compared to the more familiar seasonal order (Aries, Taurus, Gemini). In India, the Autumnal Equinox is used in lieu of the Vernal Equinox as the hour hand of heaven. Either is appropriate. Except for the gender slur (our Biblical quote should read, "Here God lives among his people" rather than "Here God lives among men"), the astrological sentiment holds up well, as Aquarius is often held aloft as a sign of communal peace. The heavenly mandate will generate a new vibration on earth. The vibration of Pisces is passing, and the Earth it engendered will pass away with it. The old ways are coming to a conclusion.

The New Jerusalem is not a city located in Israel, but the new cosmopolitan community that will be found everywhere on the Earth. It is a new consciousness, a new way of understanding, a new way of being. The marriage of heaven and earth is an ancient association, as the new Earth, like a new season, is born of heaven's authorship. It is a new beginning.

Like the birth of the United States of America, which reflects a Moon in Aquarius, it may be an Age born of revolution. As has often been the case, this revolution may be violent, but then again, it may be peaceful. In the twentieth century, we have been given examples of how a peaceful revolution can be possible. It will be our choice, and our contribution to the coming epoch, if we chose peace over fear.

A Final Word (for now)

On the date, *Athena's Web* called for it, decades in advance. Frances is a pope who brings a different understanding, of a *"New and Improved"* Testament.

Lightning literally struck Saint Peter's basilica when Pope Benedict quit during a thunderstorm on the evening of February 11th, 2013. Four days later, a meteor struck Russia with devastating force, injuring over 950 people. Like the Pope and the Church, was this a sign of things to come?

These are our clues. It will be like lightning striking in the East.

> *"Happy the man who reads this prophecy,*
> *and happy those that listen to him,*
> *if they treasure all it says,*
> *because the Time is close..."*[1]

I am the Alpha and the Omega, the First and the Last, the Beginning and the End.[2]

Time has touched *Omega*. The Lamb has opened the Eighth Seal. Windstorms are shifting, growing more powerful with each year. Aquarius is an Air sign. This is the essential essence of the archetype *"Lightning."* We must still deal with the themes of this passage (they are happening on the world stage all around us for those who have eyes to see). These are the beginnings of the labor pains of the New Age.

But they herald the era of people treating each other, not as enemy but as friend, not as divisions but unified. The time of duality, of the two Fish, is over, but there is still a final card to play, one that will end in a devastating earthquake.

---

1 Rev. 1:1-3.
2 Rev. 20:18.

So let us not be blind to our differences, but let us also direct attention to our common interests and the means by which those differences can be resolved. And if we cannot end now our differences, at least we can help make the world safe for diversity. For, in the final analysis, our most basic common link is that we all inhabit this small planet. We all breathe the same air. We all cherish our children's futures. And we are all mortal.[3]

If correct, the upcoming events will give us a chance to help each other under adverse conditions. How will we treat each other when the chips are down?

That remains to be seen.

Blessing to All, and good luck.

---

3 John F. Kennedy, *American University speech*, June 10, 1963.

Index